Enlightenment and the Creation of German Catholicism

This book tells the story of how eighteenth-century German Catholics rethought the Church. Educated German Catholics envisioned a Church that would solidify the link between religion, civilization, and morality. As the first account of the German Catholic Enlightenment, this book explores the ways in which eighteenth-century Germans reconceived the relationship between religion, society, and the state. Seeking a balance between Germany and Rome, Catholic reformers desired a national Church that would enjoy a large measure of autonomy but would still be in communion with the universal Church. In trying to reform the Church, educated Catholics in the Holy Roman Empire questioned not only what it meant to be Catholic, but also what it meant to be German. In the process, they created German Catholicism. Arguing that German confessional identities were recast in the eighteenth century, this book forces a revision of our understanding of the German Enlightenment and its place in modern German history.

Michael Printy is currently a visiting scholar in history at Wesleyan University. He earned his Ph.D. from the University of California, Berkeley, and his B.A. from Yale University. He has published articles in *German History* and *Catholic Historical Review*, and he is the co-editor of *Politics and Reformations*, a two-volume Festschrift for Thomas A. Brady, Jr. (2007). He was awarded a Fulbright Fellowship for study in Germany in 1994 and a DAAD Fellowship in 1999.

D1722351

Enlightenment and the Creation of German Catholicism

MICHAEL PRINTY

Wesleyan University, Connecticut

CAMBRIDGE
UNIVERSITY PRESS

CAMBRIDGE UNIVERSITY PRESS
Cambridge, New York, Melbourne, Madrid, Cape Town, Singapore,
São Paulo, Delhi, Dubai, Tokyo, Mexico City

Cambridge University Press
32 Avenue of the Americas, New York, NY 10013-2473, USA

www.cambridge.org
Information on this title: www.cambridge.org/9780521181518

First published 2009
First paperback edition 2010

A catalog record for this publication is available from the British Library

Library of Congress Cataloging in Publication data

Printy, Michael O'Neill.
Enlightenment and the creation of German Catholicism / Michael Printy.
p.   cm.
Includes bibliographical references and index.
ISBN 978-0-521-47839-7 (hardback)
1. Catholic Church–Germany–History–18th century.   2. Germany–Church
history–18th century.   3. Enlightenment–Germany.   4. Germany–
Intellectual life–18th century.   I. Title.
BX1534.P75 2009
282′.4309033–dc22
2008044141

ISBN 978-0-521-47839-7 Hardback
ISBN 978-0-521-18151-8 Paperback

Contents

Acknowledgments

This book is based on my doctoral dissertation in the history department at the University of California at Berkeley. Materially, this study has been supported by a Fulbright grant, a scholarship from the German Academic Exchange Service (DAAD), and several grants sponsored or administered by the University of California, Berkeley, and the department of history, including grants from the Mellon Foundation and the Center for German and European Studies, as well as a research stipend from the Robbins Collection.

I am grateful to the staff of the Bavarian State Library in Munich, the Bibliothèque National de France in Paris, the University of California library system, and the Wesleyan University Library. Luminita Florea and the staff of the Robbins Collection at Berkeley provided essential advice for a neophyte in canon law. Clare Rogan, curator of the Davidson Art Center at Wesleyan, helped me find the print by Franz Anton Maulbertsch reproduced on the cover. I am grateful to the Davidson Art Center for the permission to reproduce it. I would also like to thank the staff and faculty at Wesleyan's Humanities Center, History Department, and College of Letters, for assistance and intellectual companionship. I am especially grateful to Jill Morawski for providing me with a genial place to work at the Humanities Center and to Ethan Kleinberg for looking out for me.

Portions of the book have been read and commented on by Margaret Anderson, Helmut Walser Smith, David Hamlin, Christopher Ocker, Ulrich Lehner, Carla Hesse, Magda Teter, and Ethan Kleinberg. I am particularly grateful for the efforts of Richard Schaeffer, James Sheehan, Marc Forster (who also shared the manuscript of his book *Catholic Germany from the Reformation to the Enlightenment* before publication),

Thomas A. Brady, Jr., and two anonymous readers for their insightful comments on the whole manuscript. Eric Crahan at Cambridge has been very helpful in moving this book along.

Tom Brady has been a model advisor and mentor. His close readings and detailed comments on numerous drafts and iterations of this project have shaped my approach to scholarship. His careful advice reflects his genuine concern for my development as a scholar. His confidence encouraged me to maintain a broad perspective when the details of my project seemed overwhelming. I consider it a great fortune to have been – and to continue to be – his student. Kathy Brady deserves special mention for all her efforts and attention over the years.

On the personal front, my wife Katherine Kuenzli has, among other things, put up with dozens of oddly named, long-dead German monks. More importantly, she read early drafts of the entire dissertation as well as the final book, patiently listening to my confused ideas before they found their way to paper. I cannot imagine a better intellectual and personal companion. Our children Oliver and Nora keep things interesting and are a true source of joy. Ruedi and Cecile Kuenzli have provided essential material and moral support, not to mention the baby-sitting.

Finally, my parents, Joan and O'Neill Printy, have been unfailing in their understanding and encouragement. Their unquestioning confidence in me is a vital source of strength. To them I dedicate this book.

Chapter 9 incorporates significant portions of my article "From Barbarism to Religion: Church History and the Enlightened Narrative in Germany," *German History* vol. 23, no. 2 (2005). I am grateful to the editors for permission to reprint this material.

I

Introduction

Enlightenment and the Creation of German Catholicism tells the story of how eighteenth-century German Catholics rethought the church. They imagined a church independent of, though still in communion with, Rome. Led by educated, "Enlightened" German Catholics in partnership with the state, the church they envisioned would solidify the link between religion, civilization, and morality. The reform program of this cohort of educated bourgeois Catholics represented the culmination of several generations of pious renewal and religious reform. As such, it was part of a broader Catholic Enlightenment throughout Europe. But reform Catholicism in Germany had its own dynamic and set of problems that distinguished it from other such programs in the Catholic world. The most important of these were the political fragmentation of the Holy Roman Empire, the vitality of popular Baroque Catholicism, and the biconfessional nature of German society. Educated German Catholics sensed that the church needed to be strengthened against a series of interrelated threats. Religion's "cultured despisers" (in Schleiermacher's terms) were increasingly vocal in their attacks on revealed religion. The political structure of the Holy Roman Empire – which provided the institutional guarantee for the Catholic church in Germany – was menaced by the rise of Prussia. Protestants were constructing a powerful narrative that emplotted German nationalism as a rejection of Roman Catholicism. Finally, educated German Catholics felt that the expressive forms of devotion and traditional piety of the baroque church had become outmoded, and they worried

I

about the persistence of "superstition" among the common people.[1] German Catholic intellectuals rethought the church and its devotions in the idiom of their age, and in so doing sought to create a new form of religiosity that they saw as both appropriate to modern times and faithful to the traditions and doctrines of the church.

German Catholic thinkers sought to forge a unified German church that was at once national and universal. They did not want to cut all ties to the Roman church, but instead to assert the rights of the German church within the larger communion. In their bid for autonomy, Enlightened Catholics asserted the "liberties" of the German Catholic church against Roman encroachments. Educated German Catholics' claim of intellectual and moral supremacy in the church entailed a rejection of many of the practices and attitudes of baroque Catholicism. As was true for much of Europe in the eighteenth century, bourgeois Catholics were forced to confront their growing sense of alienation from the beliefs and practices of a large segment of the population. German Catholics did not abandon the church, but instead sought to remake it in their own image. German Catholicism was thereby recast by its Enlightenment in a manner similar to the creation of a national German literary culture by a relatively restricted circle of writers and the reading public in the age of Goethe and Schiller.

This book's subject is German Catholicism's rethinking of itself and the world in the eighteenth century, but its argument forces a larger revision of our understanding of the German Enlightenment and its place in modern German history. Looking back on a century that had only recently concluded, Karl Friedrich Stäudlin, a professor of theology at Göttingen, noted in 1804 that

The Germans are still on the whole a very religious nation [*Nation*], and true religious formation [*Bildung*] and Enlightenment have attained a higher level among them than among any other nation. Just as it was among the Germans that the Reformation had its beginnings, so too among them in the eighteenth century there began a new revolution in religious knowledge and in the theological sciences, only this time without disturbance, violence, and war.[2]

---

[1] Rudolf Schlögl, *Glaube und Religion in der Säkularisierung: Die Katholische Stadt – Köln, Aachen, Münster – 1700–1840* (Munich: Oldenbourg, 1995), 237–8 and Wolfgang Altgeld, *Katholizismus, Protestantismus, Judentum: über religiös begründete Gegensätze und nationalreligiöse Ideen in der Geschichte des deutschen Nationalismus* (Mainz: Mathias-Grünewald Verlag, 1992).

[2] K. F. Stäudlin, *Kirchliche Geographie und Statistik*, 2 vols. (Tübingen: 1804), 324.

Stäudlin's observation is significant not only because it expresses a typical Enlightenment conviction of the essentially moral character of religion, but also because of his further comment that his statement applies to a "very significant portion of clergy and laity of all religious parties in Germany, and can be put forth as a general characteristic of the nation."[3] Catholics, as well as Protestants, were active participants in this religious revolution, as Stäudlin recognized, and this book will rectify an imbalance in the historical literature by shifting our view of eighteenth-century Germany to a new perspective.

Defining the nation has long been a central problem in German history, and by emphasizing that religious innovation stood out as a marked feature of the German character, Stäudlin pointed to the central place of theological controversy and religious division in postmedieval German history. At the same time, Stäudlin's observation also emphasized that, for all their divisions, Germans possessed a shared history. To Stäudlin, Christianity was the glue that held German society together – a somewhat surprising observation when one reflects on the fact that the division of Christendom into competing confessions served as the motor for German history in the early modern period and played a prominent role in German politics, culture, and society at least until 1945. "To us alone among nations," the Catholic historian Ignaz von Döllinger remarked in 1863, "has fate ensured that the sharp blade of ecclesiastical division would continually cut through us. We are carved into almost equal parts, but can neither separate from one another, nor really live properly together."[4]

In providing the first full account of the German Catholic Enlightenment, *Enlightenment and the Creation of German Catholicism* gets to the heart of this long-standing German problem by looking at the ways in which eighteenth-century Germans rethought the relationship between religion, society, and the state.[5] The book argues that confessional identities in the late eighteenth and nineteenth centuries grew out of the religious establishments of Old Regime Germany and that, more importantly, these identities survived the collapse of the legal and institutional underpinnings

[3] Ibid., 325.
[4] Quoted in Georg Schwaiger, ed., *Zwischen Polemik und Irenik. Untersuchungen zum Verhältniß der Konfessionen im späten 18. und frühen 19. Jahrhundert* (Göttingen: Vandenhoeck & Ruprecht, 1977), 5.
[5] To date, the most comprehensive attempt to outline the contours of the Catholic Enlightenment in Germany is the series of essays edited by Harm Klueting et al., *Katholische Aufklärung: Aufklärung im katholischen Deutschland*, Studien zum achtzehnten Jahrhundert, vol. 15 (Hamburg: Meiner, 1993).

that had been worked out in the Reformation settlements of the sixteenth century. Moreover, the book demonstrates how the Enlightenment was the agent of this transformation: in rethinking the relationship of Christianity to the state, to civil society, to notions of progress and human nature, and to history, Germany's religious Enlightenment enabled the transition from the "Holy Roman Empire of the two churches" to the modern dilemma of competing Protestant and Catholic ideas of what it meant to be German.[6] The result was the creation of overlapping ideas of the nation that would play off one another for the next 150 years.

Much of the previous paragraph will sound unusual even (or perhaps especially) to readers familiar with the historiography of early modern and modern Germany. German history – and with it the German Enlightenment and ideas of German national identity – have for so long been written as if Protestants were the only historical actors of any significance that the ways in which German Catholics rethought their church in the eighteenth century has been almost entirely ignored. Moreover, the very notion of a Catholic Enlightenment will strike many as oxymoronic, given the ways in which Western modernity has so often been predicated on a putative rejection of Catholicism.[7] This book seeks to overturn these views.

The underlying assumption of the book is that the Protestant and Catholic Enlightenments in Germany proceeded along parallel paths and

---

[6] The phrase is from Christopher Ocker, *Church Robbers and Reformers in Germany, 1525–1547: Confiscation and Religious Purpose in the Holy Roman Empire* (Leiden and Boston: Brill, 2006). Protestants had their own divisions among themselves as well, not only between Lutherans and Calvinists, but within these confessions.

[7] For an overview of recent attempts to bring religion back to the Enlightenment, see Jonathan Sheehan, "Enlightenment, Religion, and the Enigma of Secularization: A Review Essay," *American Historical Review* 108, no. 4 (2003). Also important on this topic is David Sorkin, *The Berlin Haskalah and German Religious Thought: Orphans of Knowledge* (London: Vallentine Mitchell, 2000). The most recent intervention on behalf of a thoroughly secular understanding of the Enlightenment has been Jonathan Irvine Israel, *Radical Enlightenment: Philosophy and the Making of Modernity, 1650–1750* (New York: Oxford University Press, 2001). Against Israel's strongly argued view that a "radical Enlightenment" – inspired by Spinoza's demolition of received justifications for religious power and authority – motivated the response of a moderate (or religious) Enlightenment across Europe, this book argues that the German Catholic rethinking of the church was rooted in a deep legal and theological tradition with little reference to a unitary philosophical or radical opposition. Jonathan Sheehan's *The Enlightenment Bible: Translation, Scholarship, Culture* (Princeton: Princeton University Press, 2005), on the contrary, has demonstrated how attention to practices and institutions in the eighteenth century can show us how religion was transformed by an Enlightenment that was not, as the older literature would have it, always opposed to revealed religion. The implications of these different approaches is nicely summed up by Ritchie Robertson, "Religion and the Enlightenment: A Review Essay," *German History* 25, no. 3 (2007).

not – as the literature usually suggests – that Catholics in Germany weakly aped Protestant developments. This book seeks to rectify an imbalance in the scholarly literature. Only once we have a complete picture of the transformations of German Catholicism in this period will we be able to begin the process of reassessing the Protestant Enlightenment as well. This book shows how German Catholicism was recast by its Enlightenment even as the institutional framework of the *Reichskirche* and the Holy Roman Empire became unglued. This book proposes alternative genealogies for the nineteenth-century Catholic revival in Germany and thereby attacks one of the most unyielding conundrums of nineteenth-century German history. Although much has been written on the enormous Catholic revival in the nineteenth century, we know almost nothing about what preceded it. If the received view of eighteenth-century German Catholicism as backward, unchanging, and somnolent is correct, such a church cannot be the progenitor of the confident, popular, and politically adaptable German Catholicism of the nineteenth century. On the contrary, this book shows how German Catholicism was created out of its own resources.[8]

The argument of this book therefore implies a larger revision of the Protestant Enlightenment, although this subject will not be pursued in detail here.[9] With the rise of the absolutist state and its secular

---

[8] Scholarship on nineteenth century German Catholicism has, with some justice, mainly focused on the vigorous, ultramontane revival. For example, Christoph Weber's *Aufklärung und Orthodoxie am Mittelrhein, 1829–1859* (Munich, Paderborn and Vienna: Ferdinand Schöningh, 1973) demonstrated how "Enlightened" priests and theologians were pushed aside by orthodox bishops and their lay supporters. David Blackbourn's *Marpingen: Apparitions of the Virgin Mary in Bismarckian Germany* (New York: Oxford University Press, 1993) showed how Catholics could defy the Prussian state and ecclesiastical authorities. Michael Gross's *The War against Catholicism: Liberal Identity and the Anti-Catholic Imagination in Nineteenth-Century Germany* (Ann Arbor: University of Michigan Press, 2004) argued that anxiety over the vigorous Catholic revival lay at the heart of German liberalism. I am not suggesting that the church envisioned by Enlightened reformers was the church German Catholics wound up with in the nineteenth century. As I discuss in the "Conclusion," the destruction of the *Reichskirche* by Napoleon shifted the debate over the German church to new terrain. By rethinking the church in the eighteenth century, however, German Catholics provided the conceptual tools with which a German Catholic church could be allayed against the dominant narrative of Germany as a Protestant nation. Catholics were split, however, over the direction the church should go in accommodating modern developments. Educated, bourgeois German Catholics were progressively sidelined in this discussion as the nineteenth century progressed.

[9] Two recent interventions in the literature on the German Enlightenment have drawn our attention to its religious context. Thomas Ahnert's *Religion and the Origins of the German Enlightenment: Faith and the Reform of Learning in the Thought of Christian Thomasius* (Rochester: University of Rochester Press, 2006) puts Thomasius' religious

justifications for power, the eclipse of orthodox establishments, the political weakness of the papacy, and the diminishing fear of forceful re-Catholicization, Protestants as well were forced to rethink their Churches. As the dramatist and amateur theologian Gotthold Ephraim Lessing (1729–1781) noted, religious movements are like "barrels of cider fermenting in the basement . . . one sets the other in motion; *one* does not move by itself."[10] The project is directed at understanding one of the central peculiarities of German history, namely the persistence of two major confessions in a single polity. Whereas in much of Old Regime Europe relatively cohesive national cultures emerged within religious and political structures that had been reshaped by the settlements at the end of the Reformation and Wars of Religion, Germany remained biconfessional, with two major confessions enjoying legal status under Imperial law.[11] This book engages the renewed scholarly interest in the ways not only in which religion and ecclesiastical institutions shaped national culture, but also in which those cultures were recast in the eighteenth century. By focusing attention on the Holy Roman Empire – and by insisting that both confessions (Protestant and Catholic) were remade – the book reconnects one of modern Germany's central cultural conflicts back to the eighteenth century.

Olaf Blaschke has suggested that the renewed intensity with which confessional identities were contested in the nineteenth century constituted a "second confessional age."[12] Questioning the tendency among social historians to assert that the nineteenth century was predominantly a "bourgeois" century or an age of "secularization," Blaschke noted that religious conflict and, more significantly, the hardening of confessional

commitments at the core of his philosophy, whereas Ian Hunter, in *Rival Enlightenments: Civil and Metaphysical Philosophy in Early Modern Germany* (Cambridge: Cambridge University Press, 2001), outlines the ways in which the post-Westphalian religious settlements could be undermined by a revival of metaphysics. Neither book, however, looks at Catholic Germany.

[10] Gotthold Ephraim Lessing, *Werke*, vol. 7, *Theologiekritische Schriften I und II* (Munich: Carl Hanser Verlag, 1970–), 715.

[11] At the heart of this refashioning lay a new fusion between church and state. While this union was constituted in very different ways in accordance with local conditions, one can nevertheless still discern similarities among the successes of the Gallican church in France after the Fronde (1648–1653), the church of England after the Restoration (1660), and the primacy of Reformed (Calvinist) churches in the Dutch Republic. In each of these – and other establishments – stable states and societies formed (with varying degrees of toleration for religious minorities) under the supervision of a fusion of church and state.

[12] Olaf Blaschke, "Das 19. Jahrhundert: Ein Zweites Konfessionelles Zeitalter?," *Geschichte und Gesellschaft* 26 (2000).

identities were the hallmark of the age. This book therefore serves as a contribution to the debate over the relationship between the "first" confessional age of the sixteenth century and, to adopt Blaschke's term, the second confessional age of the nineteenth century.[13]

Differing confessional definitions of the nation, scholars have shown, were exacerbated by social and political conflict in nineteenth-century Germany.[14] Moreover, it is clear that the dominant Protestant definition of the German nation was resisted by Catholics not because they felt no loyalty to the state or did not have a sense of being German, but because they did not buy into the "integrative" nationalism that reached its apex with the *Kulturkampf*.[15] Catholics, in Wolfgang Altgeld's words, did not oppose the idea of a nation. "What they did oppose was the equation of the national idea with religion!"[16] While this book will not pursue these questions too far into the nineteenth century, it does show how a concept of German Catholicism was articulated contemporaneously with its more prominent Protestant counterpart. It also will show why this Catholic idea became so problematic in the nineteenth century by highlighting the ways in which the national idea was formulated by a distinct group of educated Catholics as part of a two-front struggle. On one side, German Catholics laid claim to the nation against similar attempts of their Protestant counterparts. On the other side, they sought to assert their vision of social, moral, and religious reform as part of a broader *Aufklärung*. As Rudolf Schlögl has suggested, Reform Catholicism in Germany was a response to a shift in lay piety, a piety that drew educated Catholics closer to their Protestant counterparts.[17] But as the nineteenth century progressed, ultramontane ecclesiology and populist practice gained the upper hand in German Catholicism, leading many bourgeois Catholics into a "sort of internal exile."[18] Schlögl and others have drawn our attention to

[13] For an overview suggesting the continuities from the sixteenth to the nineteenth centuries, see Joel F. Harrington and Helmut Walser Smith, "Confessionalization, Community, and State Building in Germany, 1555–1870," *The Journal of Modern History* 69, no. 1 (1997).

[14] See Helmut Walser Smith, *German Nationalism and Religious Conflict: Culture, Ideology, Politics, 1870–1914* (Princeton: Princeton University Press, 1995) and Altgeld, *Katholizismus, Protestantismus, Judentum.*

[15] Smith, *German Nationalism and Religious Conflict*, 237–8.

[16] Wolfgang Altgeld, "Religion, Denomination and Nationalism in Germany," in Helmut Walser Smith, ed., *Protestants, Catholics and Jews in Germany, 1800–1914* (Oxford and New York: Berg, 2001), 56.

[17] Schlögl, *Glaube und Religion in der Säkularisierung.*

[18] Lucian Hölscher, "The Religious Divide: Piety in Nineteenth-Century Germany," in Smith, ed., *Protestants, Catholics and Jews in Germany, 1800–1914 (2001)*, 46. See also

the social context of shifting Catholic belief. For all the important contributions of social historians, however, we do not yet have a synthetic
account of the reform vision of educated Catholics in the eighteenth
century. This book, therefore, is an intellectual history that will delineate
not only how these educated Catholics rethought the church, but also
how the subsequent tensions *within* German Catholicism originated in an
unresolved conflict at the heart of their project.

RETHINKING THE CHURCH: CATHOLIC ENLIGHTENMENT AND REFORM CATHOLICISM

"The church," declared the fathers at the Second Vatican Council

> has always had the duty of scrutinizing the signs of the times and of interpreting
> them in the light of the Gospel. Thus, in language intelligible to each generation,
> she can respond to the perennial questions which men ask about this present life
> and the life to come, and about the relationship of the one to the other.[19]

Balancing between a return to the sources (*ressourcement*) and modern-
ization (*aggiornamento*), the "council yearns to explain to everyone how
it conceives of the presence and activity of the Church in the world of
today."[20] Half a millennium earlier, Nicholas of Cusa wrote that "the
matters being debated by this holy Council of Basel" called for elaboration and justification. In order to dispel worries about the Council's
"novelty," Cusa would "make known some of the learning of the ancient
authors" and "demonstrate the superior qualities of our enlightened
forebears."[21] Rooted in the language of the past, yet directed toward
contemporaries, Cusa's *Catholic Concordance* was at once a program for
reform and reconciliation – of church and Empire. Though widely differing from the documents of Vatican II, Cusa's *Catholic Concordance*
also sought to reaffirm the place of the church in "language intelligible to
[his] generation." In these two conciliar ages – the early fifteenth century
and the later twentieth – church thinkers made the case for a restatement
of universal norms and values, couching their innovation in a rhetoric of

---

Thomas Mergel, *Zwischen Klasse und Konfession. Katholisches Bürgertum im Rheinland 1794–1814. Göttingen* (Göttingen: Vandenhoek & Ruprecht, 1994).

[19] Second Vatican Council, Pastoral Constitution on the Church in the Modern World,
Gaudium et Spes (1965), §4.

[20] *Gaudium et Spes*, §2.

[21] Nicholas of Cusa, *The Catholic Concordance*, trans. Paul Sigmund (Cambridge: Cambridge University Press, 1991), 3.

continuity, but understanding the need to speak to their contemporaries in new ways.[22]

While not a conciliar age, the latter third of the eighteenth century witnessed a vigorous and ambitious reform program for the German church. German Catholics' efforts were made possible by a confluence of crisis and opportunity. The rise of Protestant Prussia threatened the balance of power in the Empire, and, while there was a growing sense of Germany as a nation, its literary and philosophical culture was overwhelmingly associated with Protestantism. Catholics remained tied to a culture and religion that was Latin and universal. In order to strengthen the church, Catholics sought to adapt it to new times. They took advantage of the political weakness of the papacy in the eighteenth century and the economic recovery from the Thirty Years' War.

German Catholics found themselves between two great historical movements: the final stage of Roman centralization of the church, and the emergence of the secular absolutist state. The church they imagined was caught between the Roman universal church and German particularism. German Catholics partook of an Enlightenment idiom of public debate, applying a habit of criticism to the church.[23] They were part of a growing class of educated readers and writers who increasingly found themselves in the service of the state. Whereas in Protestant Germany the state and the church continued a partnership cemented by the Reformation, in Catholic Germany the Counter-Reformation alliance of church and state began to unravel in the eighteenth century. In the ensuing vacuum, German Catholic thinkers sought to forge a unified German church that was at once national and universal. The assertion of intellectual and moral supremacy in the church on the part of educated German Catholics entailed a rejection of many of the practices and attitudes of Baroque Catholicism. As was true for much of Europe in the eighteenth century, bourgeois Catholics were forced to confront their growing sense of alienation from the beliefs and practices of a large segment of the population. In Germany they did not abandon the church, but instead sought to remake it in their own image.

The reform program of educated German Catholics falls under the rubric of the two overlapping, yet at times disjunctive, notions of reform

---

[22] On the rhetoric of Vatican II, see John O'Malley, "Vatican II: Did Anything Happen," in David Schultenover, ed., *Vatican II: Did Anything Happen?* (New York: Continuum, 2007).

[23] The phrase "habit of criticism" is from Peter Gay, *The Enlightenment: An Interpretation*, vol. 1, *The Rise of Modern Paganism* (New York: Norton, 1966), 121.

Catholicism and Catholic Enlightenment. The former, more narrowly directed, deals with practical efforts, such as those to change the liturgy, religious practices, administration of church property, or the education of priests and laypeople. Reform Catholicism is usually understood in national context, though this is not necessarily so. The second term, Catholic Enlightenment, is broader and more ambitious in scope. At its heart is the central problematic of the relationship of Catholicism to the emergence of the modern world. This term would seem to entail a rejection of much received wisdom about the antireligious nature of the Enlightenment – although that older view is slowly receding – and has been variously construed. For the purposes of this book, I see a fundamental feature of the Catholic Enlightenment (by its very nature international) to be a rejection of the hitherto reigning moral pessimism and Augustinian rigorism at the heart of much of early modern Christianity.[24] While, for conceptual clarity, we may distinguish between these two movements, they were of course intimately connected. This book deals especially with reform Catholicism in Germany – by which I mean the territories of the Holy Roman Empire – as a concrete program, but I will also make the case that this program was part of a larger Enlightenment throughout the Catholic world in the eighteenth century.[25]

As the product of educated, largely urban Catholic *Bürger*, the reform program did not entail a rejection of the Catholic church, but rather an effort to adapt it to new times. The Catholic Enlightenment in Germany was not merely the result of the importation of certain set of anticlerical and antireligious ideas that Catholics simply tried to rearticulate in a language appropriate to their own situation. Instead, it was the culmination of several generations of pious renewal and revival. As Rudolf Schlögl has argued, the Catholic Enlightenment should be understood as an attempt to

---

[24] Recent work (most prominently by Dale van Kley) suggests that Jansenist-inspired neo-Augustinian piety was allied with a gallican and conciliar ecclesiology to offer a two-pronged assault on papal authority and baroque religion. By shifting the focus from France and the Low Countries to the Holy Roman Empire, my book presents significant exceptions to the prevailing view of the Catholic Enlightenment. While important strains of Jansenist thought did lie behind the movement for reform in Catholic Germany, my book complicates this picture of the Catholic Enlightenment as a failed Jansenist insurgency. The Jansenist attack on baroque Catholicism must be weighed against the latters' vitality and its eighteenth-century transformation. For further discussion see Michael Printy, "The Intellectual Origins of Popular Catholicism: Catholic Moral Theology in the Age of Enlightenment," *Catholic Historical Review* 91, no. 3 (2005).

[25] Although we differ in some matters of interpretation, I would like to acknowledge a conversation with Dale van Kley for helping me formulate this distinction.

adapt to a "massively changed lay piety" among urban Catholics.[26] A distinctively German lay piety resulted from the efforts of lay and clerical Catholic authorities to bolster the religion in response to the Protestant Reformation. This included especially the intensive missionary work of the Jesuits in the cities, where the Fathers fostered lay sodalities that served as anchors of piety.[27] In the wake of the Thirty Years' War, however, a widening rift emerged within German Catholicism mostly along social lines even as the religion as a whole experienced a revival.[28] German Catholicism was marked by an especially strong and persistent baroque style that was firmly grounded in the countryside. Germany's political decentralization and the relative strength and autonomy of cities, abbeys, and smaller territories fostered a long-standing commitment to local religion, the most tangible manifestation of which was in a culture of pilgrimages and shrines. This continued vitality of popular and rural Catholicism would give the Catholic Enlightenment and its reform program in Germany a particular edge, as educated Catholics sought to reform (which in many cases meant to suppress) practices and institutions that were not only dear to their co-religionists, but were themselves practices that had featured prominently in the historical evolution of the German Catholic *Bürgertum*. This dynamic emerged over the course of the recovery from the Thirty Years' War, and was indeed a sign of the confidence of German Catholicism now firmly grounded in the Westphalian treaties.

Like the rest of Germany, the Catholic church had been laid low by the devastation of the war. Churches, monasteries, and other ecclesiastical foundations were left in ruins. The initial thrust of Tridentine reforms ground to a halt as grand plans of education and renewal were supplanted by more pressing needs to rebuild. Moreover, a Catholicism that drew its energy from vigorous resistance to Protestant advances and was most aptly represented by the Jesuits lost its force in the wake of a war that was seen by many as a result of such confessional fervor.[29] Toward the end of the seventeenth century, signs of renewal were apparent, evidence of

---

[26] Schlögl, 333.

[27] Louis Châtellier, *The Europe of the Devout: the Catholic Reformation and the Formation of a New Society*, trans. Jean Birrell (New York: Cambridge University Press, 1989). For the role of other orders, such as the Capuchins, see Marc Forster, *Catholic Revival in the Age of the Baroque: Religious Identity in Southwest Germany, 1550–1750* (New York: Cambridge University Press, 2001).

[28] This and much of what follows are indebted especially to Marc Forster, *Catholic Germany from the Reformation to the Enlightenment* (Palgrave Macmillan, 2008).

[29] Forster, *Catholic Revival in the Age of the Baroque*. On the role of the Jesuits in the war – which was not as uniform or monolithic as sometimes portrayed – see Robert

which is perhaps most readily seen in the profusion of churches and monasteries rebuilt in a distinctive baroque style that dot the south German landscape.[30] The German Catholic church, it seemed, had well recovered from the depredations of the Thirty Years' War and the ensuing economic depression. The flourishing of baroque abbeys and pilgrimage churches in southern Germany testified that German Catholicism was on the rise. Yet that rise coincided with papal withdrawal from the normal political process of the Empire in 1648. If the eighteenth century signaled the fulfillment of a long-standing process of religious renewal, the war – and more precisely, the Peace – shifted the center of energy away from Rome-directed renewal back onto the German church itself.

The political and diplomatic consequences of the war were fundamental for the refashioning of German Catholicism in the Old Regime. Even as the energy of Catholic renewal driven by international confessional politics lost steam, local churches flourished. This is not to say that the Catholic church in Germany became insular, given that religious orders such as the Capuchins were carrying out important missions.[31] Yet the return to the local after 1648 reminds us in some ways just how innovative the Rome-led Catholic offensive had been in the wake of the Council of Trent. The century and a half between Westphalia and the dissolving of the Empire in 1806 presents a significant break in the progression from the Tridentine Counter-Reformation to the Ultramontane Catholicism of the nineteenth century. The defeat of the universalistic

---

Bireley, *The Jesuits and the Thirty Years War: Kings, Courts, and Confessors* (New York: Cambridge University Press, 2003).

[30] The casual observer of the early eighteenth century would note the flourishing of magnificent and stately baroque abbey, churches, and palaces – monuments which still draw religious and touristic pilgrims. Artists and craftsmen such as Cosmas Damian Asam who had first applied their trade in Italy were now wandering north to accept commissions in Southern Germany. Just as secular princes often aped the courtly practices of Versailles, it seemed that German prelates were taking their cue from the triumphant Roman baroque. See in particular the discussion on monasteries in the German lands in Derek Beales, *Prosperity and Plunder: European Catholic Monasteries in the Age of Revolution, 1650–1815* (Cambridge: Cambridge University Press, 2003). See also Thomas DaCosta Kaufmann, *Court, Cloister, and City: The Art and Culture of Central Europe, 1450–1800* (Chicago: University of Chicago Press, 1995), 367f. Kaufmann notes that in Southern Germany,

> it has been estimated that at least two hundred churches of some artistic significance were erected between 1700 and 1780: many of them were constructed in the period 1710–1760, mainly in the Catholic areas of Bavaria, Franconia and Swabia.

[31] Marc R. Forster, *The Counter-Reformation in the Villages: Religion and Reform in the Bishopric of Speyer, 1560–1720* (Ithaca: Cornell University Press, 1992).

vision of a re-invigorated Catholic Empire in 1648 returned the German Catholic church back to its roots. This shift in political fortunes for the church meant that German Catholicism in the Old Regime once again relied on the power of the nobility and the ecclesiastical states.[32] It would build on that recovery well into the eighteenth century.

The present book is motivated by the conviction that what is most needed is a synthesis of intellectual issues to highlight the long-term significance of political and institutional developments. But these concepts were articulated against the background of real and desired reforms. These reforms occurred in a series of fits and starts throughout the eighteenth century, and at differing paces befitting the fragmented nature of the Holy Roman Empire. Over the course of the century, the general pattern was one of consensus giving way to conflict. church–state relations in eighteenth-century Catholic Germany defy easy characterization because these very concepts were themselves undergoing a process of differentiation and redefinition. Nevertheless, several watershed moments can be laid out to underscore the general thrust of developments.[33]

The Seven Years' War, concluded in 1763, was in many ways a shock to the Empire and marked a gradual shift away from commitment to imperial institutions by the major and mid-level states. Related to this was a tendency of Habsburg policy to distinguish its hereditary territories from the Reich, and to recognize that dynastic interests were increasingly at odds with the role of the Emperor as protector of the Reich. As rulers and their ministers sought to come to terms with the need for more robust

---

[32] The ecclesiastical states made up the most distinctive element of the *Reichskirche*. With the exception of the papal state, they were the last remnants of a medieval system of governance in which temporal authority was in the hands of an ecclesiastic. The medieval emperors sought support in the church, which prayed for the ruling dynasty and supported it financially and militarily. In return, the church was rewarded with endowments and the temporal rights that eventually became the basis for the ecclesiastical states. Like the free imperial cities (*Reischstädte*), these states were *reichsunmittelbar* – fully independent polities subject only to the emperor and Diet. While the most influential of these were the three Archbishoprics of Mainz, Cologne, and Trier (confirmed as electors by the Golden Bull of 1356) the other ecclesiastical foundations (*Stifte*) played an important role in imperial politics. Bishops were elected by the cathedral chapters, which had the right to select bishops to be later confirmed by Rome. Lawrence G. Duggan, "The Church as an Institution of the Reich," in *The Old Reich. Essays on German Political Institutions 1495–1806*, James A. Vann and Steven Rowan, eds. (Brussels: 1974), 151.

[33] The most comprehensive account, from which the following survey is largely drawn, is Karl Otmar von Aretin, *Das Alte Reich, 1648–1806. Band 3, Das Reich und der österreichisch-preussische Dualismus (1745–1806)* (Stuttgart: Klett Cotta, 1997), 226–92.

administration and finance, they also came to see that the patchwork structure of the Catholic Church in their territories hindered the forging of a unified state. Moves toward *Staatskirchentum* (state church), as opponents of this policy considered it, were most dramatic in Bavaria and the Habsburg monarchy.

In the 1760s and 1770s, the Bavarian electors attempted to limit the wealth and independence of the richly endowed monastic foundations in Bavaria with laws that curtailed donations to monasteries (amortization laws) and limited their tax privileges. Even more dramatic was the erection of a Munich Nunciature in 1784 by Pius VI in conjunction with the wishes of the Elector, which unleashed a widespread controversy throughout the Empire. A long-standing wish of the Bavarian rulers was the creation of some sort of unified diocese or province for all their territories. Many different bishops had spiritual authority in Bavaria, but nowhere did diocesan boundaries entirely coincide with secular ones. The nuncio, as direct representative of the pope, would have authority over all Wittelsbach territory (including the Palatinate), thereby undercutting the rights of the local bishops.[34] In this case, the Curia worked with the temporal authority, much to the consternation of the German episcopate as a whole.

The drive toward a state church was even more pronounced in the Habsburg monarchy. Again, reforms were not always undertaken in direct opposition to the papacy, such as the early suppression of some monastic houses with papal permission. After all, the Jesuits were suppressed by papal bull in 1773, albeit under the intense pressure of the Catholic powers. After his accession to sole rule in 1780, Joseph II continued and intensified the policies of his mother (and her chief minister Kaunitz). These policies caused enough worry that Pius VI traveled to Vienna to see him, although the pope failed to win any significant concessions.[35] Joseph proceeded brashly against the diocese of Passau 1783, where he sought to incorporate portions of the diocese that lay within Austrian territory into the newly created bishoprics of Linz and St. Pölten.[36] Significant, too, was the suppression of some 600 monasteries in the Habsburg

---

[34] The Munich nuncio was to have spiritual authority – the power to grant dispensations and absolution, and to re-organize diocesan boundaries – that surpassed those of the permanent nuncios in Cologne, Vienna, and Lucerne.

[35] Elisabeth Kovács, *Der Pabst in Teutschland: die Reise Pius VI. im Jahre 1782* (Vienna: Verlag für Geschichte und Politik, 1983).

[36] Aretin, *Das Alte Reich, 1648–1806. Band 3, Das Reich und der österreichisch-preussische Dualismus (1745–1806)*, 230f.

Monarchy.[37] His other major reforms relating to the church were the Edict of Toleration (1781, extended in 1782) granting limited toleration to Protestants and, subsequently, Jews, and a marriage law of 1783 that emphasized the nature of marriage as a civil contract, thereby placing it under the purview of the state. Joseph died in 1790, and many of his policies were put on hold or reversed, though the Josephine system of state supervision over the church remained largely intact until 1848. These programs and their development form an important element in the events and ideas recounted in this book and will be sketched in as needed, but they are not the main focus. Instead, these particular conflicts between elements in the state and elements in the church are the institutional background to the ideological thrust of Catholic reform thinking – but a thinking that was, like the various interests and approaches – never uniform.

From the outside, then, reform ideas and programs can seem rather contradictory. Many bishops, for example, looked to secular princes and the Emperor as an ally against the pope. But, as the erection of the Munich Nuntiature in 1784 showed, princes were quite happy to work with the pope and to weaken the bishops when their states stood to benefit. It will not be necessary here, however, to unravel the dizzying array of interests inherent in Old Regime politics. Important for this book is the recognition that these political and institutional struggles fostered a heated and public discussion about the constitution of the *Reichskirche*, and that this public discussion provided the intellectual conditions for rethinking the church.

In 1763, a canon-law treatise *On the State of the Church and the Legitimate Power of the Roman Pontiff* by the suffragan bishop of Trier Niklaus von Hontheim galvanized a cohort of German Catholics and laid the groundwork for the flowering of reform ideas and programs.[38] Hontheim, writing under the pseudonym Febronius, argued that the pope should be granted only honorary primacy among bishops, and that the papacy had falsely accrued jurisdictional primacy over the church through centuries of mistaken legal assumptions and even forgery. Hontheim's work fell on fertile ground because Catholic education and scholarship had prepared a generation to engage in reform and revitalization of the church. Much of this early work was done by monks and other clergy who – with

---

[37] Derek Beales argues, however, that this had the long-term effect of strengthening monasticism in Austria, given that monastic suppressions in other parts of Europe after the French Revolution were much more sudden and thorough. He cautions against seeing Joseph's policies as irreligious or cynical. See Beales, *Prosperity and Plunder*, 179–228.

[38] Hontheim's work is the subject of the next chapter.

varying degrees of self-consciousness – sought to counteract the influence of the Jesuits and the Rome-centered Catholicism they championed. This effort coincided with the political and economic revival of German Catholicism of the late seventeenth- and early eighteenth centuries.

Opposition to the Jesuits was a hallmark of the Catholic Enlightenment in Germany – and indeed in the rest of Catholic Europe as well.[39] This opposition, while not as dramatic as the expulsion of the members of the Society from Portugal and France, culminated in the worldwide suppression (though without effect in Prussia and White Russia) of the Jesuits by Clement XIV's bull *Dominus ac Redemptor* in 1773. In Germany, the main source of tension was in the sphere of education, over which the Society had effective control. The growing opposition to Jesuit education there came not from the type of anticlericalism that has typified the French Enlightenment, but from the "old orders," that is to say from monastic institutions that had been cultivating libraries and scholarship to rival some of the best work of the Society of Jesus.[40] In this, the reform program of educated German Catholics must be understood as the further development of, rather than opposition to, a century of pious renewal.

BETWEEN GERMANY AND ROME: ENLIGHTENMENT AND THE CREATION OF GERMAN CATHOLICISM

In rethinking the church, German Catholics sought a balance between a Rome-centered universal church and a long-desired national church

---

[39] Richard van Dülmen, "Antijesuitismus und katholische Aufklärung in Deutschland," *Historisches Jahrbuch* 89, no. 1 (1969); Dale K. Van Kley, "Catholic Conciliar Reform in an Age of Anti-Catholic Revolution. France, Italy, and the Netherlands, 1758–180," in *Religion and Politics in Enlightenment Europe*, James Bradley and Dale K. Van Kley, eds. (Notre Dame, IN: University of Notre Dame Press, 2001); Dale K. Van Kley, *The Jansenists and the Expulsion of the Jesuits from France, 1757–1765* (New Haven: Yale University Press, 1975). I discuss this "revolt against the fathers," at length in Chapter 6.

[40] Richard van Dülmen stresses the importance of the cloisters for the Catholic Enlightenment in Germany. He also notes that in the early decades of the century, the leading reformers and writers were monks. By the 1780s, however, many of the most prominent reformers were secular priests such as Michael Ignaz Schmidt or Anton Wittola. The early Catholic Enlightenment of the monks focused on scholarship and science, whereas the later Catholic Enlightenment shifted toward an emphasis on reform and education in conjunction with the state. See Richard Van Dülmen, *Propst Franziskus Töpsl (1711–1796) und das Augustiner-Chorherrenstift Polling* (Kallmünz: Michael Lassleben, 1967), 4–5. Despite the seemingly narrow title of the book, van Dülmen's account Töpsl and his participation in the German Catholic Enlightenment presents a broad view of the movement with great insight.

that, while still in communion with Rome, would enjoy a large measure of autonomy. Educated German Catholics thereby confronted the dilemma of the "double universalism"[41] of Christianity and of Enlightenment cosmopolitanism facing their Protestant counterparts, but with a further twist. For the effort to rethink and adapt the church to new times was carried out by the same people who were also confronting the question of what it meant to be German, and the lack of a firm resolution to this dilemma would tear at German Catholics for the century and a half following Napoleon's destruction of the Empire. Educated German Catholics not only needed to situate themselves within – and make claims on – an international and socially diverse Catholic community; they also confronted competing notions of "German" that had taken on particular sharpness with the rise of Prussia and the solidification of a vernacular literary culture increasingly associated with Protestantism. Defining the "nation" is one of those knotty problems with which German history is notoriously replete,[42] and its central problematic – the conflict between the universal and the particular – lay at the heart of the Catholic Enlightenment as well.[43]

"We are one people with one name, one language, and one common sovereign," wrote Friedrich Carl von Moser in 1766 in a celebrated treatise on the "German National Spirit":

We live under a single constitution that determines our respective rights and duties under the law. We are bound together in a common freedom and united by a national assembly directed toward this goal. In terms of inner power and strength, we are the first state [Reich] in Europe, many of whose royal crowns shine upon German heads. And yet, despite all this, we have for centuries been a

---

[41] For the phrase, see Michael Maurer, "Die konfessionelle Identität des Bürgertums um 1800," in *Die Säkularisation im Prozess der Säkularisierung Europas*, Peter Blickle and Rudolf Schlögl, eds. (Ependorf: Bibliotheca Academica, 2005), 410.

[42] See James J. Sheehan, "What is German History? Reflections on the Role of *Nation* in German History and Historiography," *Journal of Modern History* 53, no. 1 (1981).

[43] Despite – or perhaps because of – the decline of the prestige of the nation state, historians continue to evaluate its origins and evolution in ways that move beyond the sociological and anthropological approaches of Benedict Anderson and Ernst Gellner. David Avrom Bell has emphasized the importance of religion in the formation of nationalism. See David Avrom Bell, *The Cult of the Nation in France: Inventing Nationalism, 1680–1800* (Cambridge: Harvard University Press, 2001). See also P. Gorski, "The Mosaic Moment: An Early Modernist Critique of Modernist Theories of Nationalism," *American Journal of Sociology*, 105, no. 5 (2000) and Pasi Ihalainen, *Protestant Nations Redefined. Changing Perceptions of National Identity in the Rhetoric of the English, Dutch and Swedish Public Churches, 1685–1772* (Leiden: Brill, 2005).

political enigma. Preyed upon by neighbors, we are an object of their ridicule unique in the history of the world. Disunited among ourselves, our division renders us powerless. Strong enough to harm – yet unable to save – ourselves. We care nothing for the honor of our name and are indifferent to the law; we are jealous of our sovereign, mistrustful of one another, arbitrary in our principles and violent in their execution. We are a people at once great and despised. We have the possibility to be happy, but are in fact to be pitied.[44]

A nation great in potential, yet trod upon by neighbors – one of the persistent myths of German history – it was exaggerated and distorted, with disastrous consequences in the twentieth century. In the nineteenth century, however, Germany's "special path" to modernity was actually celebrated in some quarters: the country had achieved national unification and a modern economy under Bismarck without the horrors of the French revolution. But the Holy Roman Empire and the persistence of German Catholicism presented major stumbling blocks to a coherent historical narrative. German Catholicism was cast as an anomaly in a nation widely – if incorrectly – believed to be essentially Protestant in nature. The Catholics seemed out of place and puzzling in, when not downright disruptive of, the land of Luther, Ranke, and Bismarck. The Holy Roman Empire seemed to some to have been a regrettable hindrance to Germany's emergence as a nation-state. Later, the Empire was cast as a prime culprit in the pathology of a misdeveloped German modernity. The modernizing, secularizing narrative implied by these views has only recently begun to unravel. Not only is the nation-state's prestige dropping, but the veritable explosion of religion and religious questions both in the United States and in the global South has become too pressing to ignore.[45] The historiographical innovation of this book grows out of this change of perspective.

The problems of German nationhood Moser identified arose from the peculiarities of the Holy Roman Empire. Long derided as a weak, privilege-bound institution, the Empire has recently benefited from a more nuanced view of its role in the early modern European state system.[46] In particular, there is a newfound appreciation for the ways in which the

---

[44] Friedrich Carl von Moser, *Von dem Deutschen Nationalgeist* (1766; Reprint, Notos, 1976), 5.

[45] Philip Jenkins, *The Next Christendom: The Coming of Global Christianity* (New York: Oxford University Press, 2002).

[46] Karl Otmar von Aretin, *Das Reich: Friedensgarantie und europäisches Gleichgewicht, 1648–1806* (Stuttgart: Klett-Cotta, 1986); Peter H. Wilson, *From Reich to Revolution: German History, 1558–1806* (New York: Palgrave Macmillan, 2004); Peter Hartmann, *Kulturgeschichte des Heiligen Römischen Reiches 1648–1806* (Vienna: Böhlau, 2001);

Empire managed (more or less) to peacefully balance a plurality of religious, linguistic, and political entities. With Frederick the Great's seizure of Silesia in 1740 as the only major breach, the Empire preserved the religious and political constitution so arduously negotiated at Münster and Osnabrück in 1648.[47]

The Empire and Imperial institutions found their footing again in the decades after the Peace of Westphalia, but they were constantly challenged by the series of dynastic struggles that defined eighteenth-century war and diplomacy. Although the failure of Habsburg ambitions to form a strong central monarchy in the Empire had been decisively turned back in 1648, the smaller German territories were constantly on notice against Habsburg aggrandizement. The rise of Hohenzollern Prussia as a serious rival – indeed a threat – to Habsburg power at first seemed to indicate that the Empire's days were numbered, especially after the War of Austrian Succession. However, the smaller German territories – a "third Germany" wedged, as it were, between two contending great powers – still found the collective security of the Empire and its legal culture of use in preserving their "liberties." The second great German conflict of the eighteenth century, the Seven Years' War, again shook the Empire and its political culture. But it was really only the disruption brought from the outside 30 years later that exploded the tension and distrust that had grown over the preceding decades.[48] Even as the idea of the Empire was being praised in the later eighteenth century for its ability to preserve German liberties, its long-term viability was slowly being undermined by the emergence of strong secular states. The larger dynasties' commitment to the Empire – so vital to the smaller polities – was rendered fragile enough to crack completely under Napoleon.

Nevertheless, the period following the Seven Years' War witnessed a rapid growth in public discussion and debate over programs for reform of state and society. This assumption about the centrality of the state and other institutions to "Aufklärung" was a marked feature of the German Enlightenment. Germany shared this age of Enlightenment with its

and Karl Otmar von Aretin, *Das Alte Reich 1648–1806*, 4 vols. (Stuttgart: Klett-Cotta, 1993–2000).

[47] This is not to say that there was not great strain put upon the system, especially during the Seven Years' War, or during the expulsion of Protestants from Salzburg in the 1730s. But there was no large-scale foreign intervention for religious reasons as there had been in the Thirty Years' War.

[48] Much of this from Wilson, *From Reich to Revolution: German history, 1558–1806*, Chapter 8.

European neighbors, but it had neither a unified state nor a single established confession – two factors essential for understanding the nature of the German Enlightenment.[49] The Enlightenment in Germany was the product of a literate, educated class of readers and writers, who more and more found themselves in the service of the state or the church.[50] This universal class of bureaucrats and professionals – to use Hegel's terminology – was less bounded by locality than their city-dwelling ancestors, and is to be distinguished from the particular or traditional "estates" enshrined in German law and tradition.[51] This universal estate was therefore created by the church and the state. In order to understand the bourgeoisie's role in shaping the Enlightenment, this book will explore how those two institutions were being remade.[52]

In Protestant countries, religious affairs and the administration of the church had fallen under the authority of the prince at the time of the Reformation. In contrast, the hierarchy of the Catholic church in Germany had managed to maintain its independence to a much greater degree. As proponents of the "confessionalization" thesis have argued, Catholic and Protestant states demonstrated a certain similarity – despite their wide-ranging doctrinal differences – in the ways in which the elaboration and enforcement of confessional systems were key factors in the formation of the early modern state.[53] However, while the Protestant prince

[49] For an overview, see, most recently, Hartmann, *Kulturgescichte des Heiligen Römischen Reiches 1648–1806*.

[50] For recent treatments of the German Enlightenment, see James Schmidt, ed., *What is Enlightenment. Eighteenth-Century Answers and Twentieth-Century Questions* (Berkeley and Los Angeles: University of California Press, 1996) as well as the aforementioned works by Thomas Ahnert and Ian Hunter. For a recent exception to the general silence on the Catholic Enlightenment in Germany, see the brief treatment in H. C. Erick Midelfort, *Exorcism and Enlightenment. Johann Joseph Gassner and the Demons of Eighteenth-Century Germany* (New Haven: Yale University Press, 2005).

[51] G. F. W. Hegel, *Grundlinien der Philosophie des Rechts* (Leipzig: Meiner, 1911), 167, §205. Compare Mack Walker, *German Home Towns: Community, State, and General Estate, 1648–1871* (Ithaca: Cornell University Press, 1998).

[52] The classic account is Friedrich Meinecke, *Weltburgertum und Nationalstaat: Studien zur Genesis des deutschen Nationalstaates* (Munich: R. Oldenbourg, 1908). See as well the brief yet insightful discussion in Nicholas Boyle, *Goethe: The Poet and the Age. Vol. 1: The Poetry of Desire (1749–1790)* (Oxford: Oxford University Press, 1992), 6–24. According to Boyle, Goethe's independence from the "official tradition of German culture" – whether that of church, state, or university – set him off from the rest of his countrymen.

[53] One of the classic statements of the problem is Ernst Walter Zeeden, *Die Entstehung der Konfessionen: Grundlagen und Formen der Konfessionsbildung im Zeitalter der Glaubenskämpfe* (München: R. Oldenbourg, 1965). While the emphasis on the relationship of confession building and state formation by proponents of the

could be seen as the *summus episcopus*,[54] the Catholic sovereign saw himself as the advocate of the church (*advocatus ecclesiae*). This difference in political theology would be the source of great tension in the second half of the eighteenth century, as Catholic territorial lords wrestled with the ecclesiastical hierarchy over the wealth of the church and its jurisdictional boundaries. As the German states in the eighteenth century grew more similar in function and ethos, the churches proceeded on divergent paths.

Moser's tract *On the German National Spirit* chastised Germans for their disunity while exhorting them to place their hopes for the nation in the Empire.[55] While not without partisan implications, the tract encapsulates the way in which the nation was a category of thought into which eighteenth-century Germans could pour their aspirations for political and social change, even if ideas about the essence of the nation varied widely. For Catholics, the nation provided a template for rethinking the Church as well. In trying to reform the Church, educated Catholics in the Holy Roman Empire questioned not only what it meant to be Catholic, but also what it meant to be German, and in the process they created German Catholicism.

$$\star\star\star$$

The remainder of this book explores this process of rethinking in two parts, reflecting the dual directions of the Catholic Enlightenment reform program: toward securing legal and institutional autonomy from Rome in conjunction with the territorial state, and in asserting intellectual and moral authority over the broad Catholic population. The story told by this book is largely an intellectual history, in which ideas about the church are situated in a series of intellectual, political, and social

confessionalization thesis has been salutary, the argument that religious identities in the modern age were formed top-down by this process has not always held up under scrutiny. For a critique see Forster, *The Counter-Reformation in the Villages,* and *Catholic Revival in the Age of the Baroque.*

[54] This is not to say that the prominent role of the prince in reforming the church was part of the original program of the early Reformers. Rather, it was an idea that evolved from the practical necessities of the Reformation. The Lutheran concept of the "invisible church" made room for the secular authorities to reform the "visible" or institutional aspects of the church without profaning the Word. See Martin Heckel, *Staat und Kirche nach den Lehren der evangelischen Juristen Deutschlands in der ersten Hälfte des 17. Jahrhunderts*, vol. 6, Jus ecclesiasticum (Munich: Claudius-Verlag, 1968); Johannes Heckel, "Cura religionis, ius in sacra, ius circa sacra," in *Festschrift Ulrich Stutz, Kirchenrechtliche Abhandlungen 117/118* (Stuttgart: F. Enke, 1938).

[55] Moser soon after became a (not-so) secret propagandist for Joseph II. See Derek Beales, *Joseph II: In the Shadow of Maria Theresa, 1741–1780* (Cambridge: Cambridge University Press, 1987), 130.

contexts. Part One looks at rise of territorial absolutism and the mutual redefinition of Church and State in the eighteenth century. Chapter 2 discusses the bid of German canon lawyers to forge "Gallican" liberties for a German church autonomous from Rome. Chapter 3 examines the ways in which Catholic princes and ministers – especially in Bavaria and Joseph II's Austria – sought to curtail long-held taxation and legal privileges enjoyed by the church, while still considering the prince the "advocate of the church." Chapter 4 details the ways in which transformations of the nature and role of the modern state in the eighteenth century affected the ecclesiastical states *and* the ways in which the *Reichskirche* functioned as the backbone of the Empire. Finally, Chapter 5 returns once more to canon lawyers and their attempt to redraw the legal and ideological boundaries between church and state in a way that preserved the "liberty" of both.

Part Two moves beyond the institutional and legal context of the first part to examine more closely the reform program in light of those who would carry it out. Chapter 6 looks at the church envisioned by educated German Catholics and examines it as part of the broader Catholic Enlightenment. Chapter 7 explores the ways in which the church was rethought in the public sphere and surveys pragmatic reforms from educational policy to liturgical reforms and limits on monastic professions. Chapter 8 shows how the reform of the secular clergy was at the heart of the Enlightenment project not only to adapt the church to modern times, but also to propagate "Enlightened Catholicism" to the broader population. Chapter 9 discusses the ways in which German Catholics envisioned the church as a potential vehicle for national unity despite the division of Germany into rival confessions. The book concludes by pointing to the ways in which the Catholic project of the Enlightenment – seemingly rendered obsolete by Napoleon and a revived ultramontane church in the nineteenth century – in fact recast and redefined German Catholicism for the following century.

PART ONE

PERFECT SOCIETIES: RETHINKING THE CHURCH AND THE STATE

State and religion – civil and ecclesiastical constitution – secular and churchly authority – how to oppose these pillars of social life to one another so that they are in balance and do not, instead, become burden on social life, or weigh down its foundations more than they uphold it – this is one of the most difficult tasks of politics.

– Moses Mendelssohn, *Jerusalem*[1]

---

[1] Moses Mendelssohn, *Jerusalem: or, on Religious Power and Judaism*, trans. Allan Arkush (Waltham: Brandeis University Press, 1983), 33.

2

The Liberty of the German Church: Febronianism and the German Gallicans

THE ANCIENT CONSTITUTION OF THE GERMAN CHURCH

"Scholars," the Trier Auxiliary Bishop Nikolaus von Hontheim proclaimed in his 1763 legal broadside against the papacy, "ought to be considered the natural defenders of both the church and state."[1] This sentiment underpinned the German Catholic rethinking of the church and was in many ways its *leitmotif*. From the outset, the Catholic reform program of the eighteenth century combined pious concern for religious renewal with intellectual engagement. Educated German Catholics did not see religion and reason as opposed – instead they sought to strengthen the bonds between them by rethinking and adapting the church to new times. In this, we can see how a relatively small group of German Catholics laid claim to the mantle of Christian humanism (a claim made explicit by Michael Ignaz Schmidt toward the end of the century) to express their sense of responsibility for the church. Given the ways in which the Church was embedded in the Old Regime culture of rights, privileges, and liberties – of law, in short – the initial phase of the German Catholic rethinking occurred largely through jurisprudence.

The political universe of German Catholics in the eighteenth century was shaped by the consequences of the Peace of Westphalia. Indeed, the German commitment – Protestant and Catholic alike – to the "constitution" (*Verfassung*) of the Empire may to a large degree be traced the success of the

---

[1] Nikolaus von Hontheim, *Justini Febronii JCti de Statu Ecclesiae et Legitima Potestate Romani Pontificis Liber Singularis, ad Reuniendos Dissidentes in Religione Christianos Compositus* (Frankfurt: 1763), IX, §2, 2, 562. "Eruditi debebunt censeri *nati defensores Sacerdotii & Imperii*."

Westphalian treaties in preserving, more or less, confessional peace.[2] The confessional stability provided by the Peace emboldened Catholics to clamor for more independence from Rome. This sense of security enabled German Catholics to seriously consider the proposition that they did not need Roman help in preserving their religion against the Protestants. Against this background, it was German canon lawyers who first began to rethink the church. More than any other single event, the publication of Hontheim's treatise (under the pseudonym of Febronius) *On the State of the Church and the Legitimate Power of the Roman Pontiff* in 1763 brought historical canon-law scholarship into a very public debate in Germany over the nature of the Catholic church.[3]

Hontheim's treatise – published in the same year that the Seven Years' War came to an end – is often cited as the first salvo in the German Catholic Enlightenment, and was in many ways its most significant literary product. There was no *direct* connection between the program of the pseudonymous Febronius for episcopalian autonomy from Rome and the later, practical reform programs of the Catholic Enlightenment in the 1780s and 1790s in such areas as liturgical reform or restraints on popular practices. However, the underlying concepts of *de Statu Ecclesiae* – the liberties of the German church and the papacy as an obstacle to German religious reunification – formed the basis upon which the German Catholic reform program would build. *De Statu* was not a wholly original work, in the sense that its major premises could be easily traced to other works in canon law and church history.[4] Nevertheless, Hontheim's "single book" more than any other work galvanized a generation of educated German Catholics. In order to understand why this book on the history of canon law had such an effect, we will need, in what

---

[2] On the role of the Empire in political thought into the eighteenth century, see Wolfgang Burgdorf, *Reichskonstitution und Nation. Verfassungsreformprojekte für das Heilige Römische Reich Deutscher Nation im Politischen Schrifttum von 1648 bis 1806* (Mainz: Philipp von Zabern, 1998).

[3] Volker Pitzer, *Justinus Febronius. Das Ringen eines katholichen Irenikers um die Einheit der Kirche im Zeitalter der Aufklärung,* vol. 20, *Kirche und Konfession* (Göttingen: Vandenhoek & Ruprecht, 1976). The best short account in English is now Ulrich L. Lehner, "Johann Nikolaus von Hontheim's Febronius: A Censored Bishop and his Ecclesiology," *Church History and Religious Culture* 2 (2008), 93–121. For a version of Hontheim's text, see Johann Nikolaus von Hontheim, *Justinus Febronius abbreviatus et emendatus (1777),* Religionsgeschichte der frühen Neuzeit 5, Ulrich L. Lehner, ed. (Nordhausen: Bautz, 2008).

[4] This was indeed part of Hontheim's strategy: he tried to make his points by citing approved authors to avoid condemnation.

follows, to explore the growing historical interests of German Catholics, of which there were two major aspects.[5]

The first aspect of this historical interest may be categorized as a methodological interest in law and history that links the German Catholic Enlightenment to a broader association in the seventeenth and eighteenth centuries of legal scholarship and theories of political authority (which for much of the early modern period meant ecclesiastical authority as well). For France, this tradition is often characterized as "legal humanism," and for England, "ancient constitutionalism."[6] In both the French and English cases, humanists and lawyers foraged in the misty pasts for historical evidence of "liberties" against the encroachments of would-be absolute kings and popes. Similarly, German Catholic canonists in the eighteenth century sought to "restore" the liberties of the German church – in this case against the "encroachments" of the Roman Curia – by appealing to a putatively ancient church law and discipline. The second, related, aspect of the German canonists' interest in history has to do with the way in which they used the past as a normative program for the present. The rhetoric of the German canonists touched on those most significant epochs of German and universal church history: the Investiture Struggle, the Concordat of Worms, and the Conciliar era.

In their legal theories, the German canonists pursued a line of inquiry that emphasized that the law of the church was broader than the canons found in the classic papal collections.[7] They often stressed the early law of

---

[5] Raab, citing Ludwig Timotheus Spittler (1752–1810), frequently refers to the "irruption" of historicism into German canon law scholarship as the Catholic "intellectual revolution [*katholische Ideenrevolution*]." See Heribert Raab, *Die Concordata Nationis Germanicae in der kanonischen Diskussion des 17. bis 19. Jahrhunderts. Ein Beitrag zur Geschichte der episkopalischen Theorie in Deutschland* (Wiesbaden: Franz Steiner, 1956), 132.

[6] The seminal treatments are Donald Kelley, *Foundations of Modern Historical Scholarship: Language, Law, and History in the French Renaissance* (New York: Columbia University Press, 1970) and J. G. A. Pocock, *The Ancient Constitution and the Feudal Law. A Study of English Historical Thought in the Seventeenth Century. A Reissue with a Retrospect* (Cambridge: Cambridge University Press, 1987 [1957]). I owe the insight to David Lieberman.

[7] The main collection of church law, known as the *Corpus Iuris Canonici*, was considered valid law in the Catholic church until the promulgation of the Codex Iuris Canonici in 1917. The Corpus was composed of (1) The Decrees of Gratian (ca. 1140); (2) The Decretals of Gregory IX, divided into five books and promulgated in 1234; (3) The Liber Sextus Decretalium, promulgated by Boniface VIII in 1298; (4) The "Clementines," a set of canons compiled by Clement V but promulgated by John XXII in 1317; (5) The "Extravagantes" of John XXII, published in 1325 (so called because they had "wandered outside" the earlier decretals); and (6) The "Extravagantes Communes," collected

the church, and sought above all to relativize papal "innovations" by pointing out where papal practices differed from earlier usage. They claimed to want to restore the liberties of the German church, and drew much of their inspiration from Gallican theories. The German canonists based their claims to German particular rights on the public law of the German church. They sought to prove, for example, that the Acceptation of Mainz in 1439 laid out the fundamental rights of the German Imperial church, much along the lines of the Pragmatic Sanction of Bourges for the French church.[8] The German canonists did not try to codify canon law, but rather attempted to define a common canon law "accommodated to the German nation." Their work reflects the tensions inherent in their desire to describe a particular law within the universal church – a church between Germany and Rome. In practice, this meant a turn to historical scholarship that tried to prove the antiquity of their positions. The rest of this chapter will tell the story of the German episcopal movement as seen through the eyes of the German canonists. For it was first through jurisprudence that the German Catholic reformers made their claims on the church.

THE HISTORICAL SCHOOL OF CANON LAW

Central to the conviction that the papacy had infringed on the liberties of the German church was the historical thesis that much of what the popes claimed as their right was based on usurpation and, at best, pious fraud. This latter emphasis on the results of fraud arose largely from the controversy over the Pseudo-Isidorian Decretals. The veracity of these decretals had been doubted already at the time of their appearance.[9]

---

decrees of various popes (1261–1484). For brief accounts, see articles on "Corpus Iuris Canonici" and "Extravagantes," in *The Oxford Dictionary of the Christian Church*, F. L. Cross, ed. (third edition edited by E. A. Livingstone, Oxford: Oxford University Press, 1957 [1997]). See also Anders Winroth, *The Making of Gratian's Decretum* (New York: Cambridge University Press, 2000; Constant van de Wiel, *History of Canon Law*, *Louvain Theological and Pastoral Monographs*, 5 (Louvain: 1991); and James A. Brundage, *Medieval Canon Law* (New York: Longman, 1995).

[8] Raab, *Die Concordata Nationis Germanicae in der kanonischen Diskussion des 17. bis 19. Jahrhunderts*.

[9] The controversy over Pseudo-Isidore referred to the false decretals attributed to Isidore Mercator, a collection of canons forged around 850 and subsequently included (in part) in the Decretals issued by Gregory VII and later popes. For a time it was believed that the redactor of the collection was St. Isidore of Seville (d. 636). These forgeries purported to be letters from popes and councils from the first to the eighth centuries, and particularly aimed to defend bishops against their metropolitans by establishing the pope as the

Composed, as so many other medieval forgeries, as part of a process of defending local rights and privileges as the central authority of the Carolingian Empire unraveled, they eventually transcended their original context and were taken up into the law of the church.[10] In particular, the forgers (for this was most likely the work of a highly trained and educated group, not a sole individual) wanted to defend the rights of bishops against secular lords as well as against metropolitans. The false decretals made appeals to the pope easier (by claiming that earlier popes had already established this right) to prevent the deposing of bishops.[11] The Magdeburg Centurians took up the theme of the falsity of the Pseudo-Isidorian decretals to demonstrate the ways in which the illegitimate rule of the papacy was bent on establishing the reign of the anti-Christ.[12] Yet is was not until the French Reformed jurist David Blondel[13] presented a thorough analysis of Pseudo-Isidore's sources in 1628 that even most Catholic scholars had to accept the falsity of the decretals.[14] Baronius, author of the *Annales Ecclesiatici*, granted the point that the decrees were false, though he of course did not accept the conclusion the all subsequent accretion of papal authority was either wholly based on Pseudo-Isidorian

protector of their rights. A brief synopsis is Horst Fuhrmann, "The Pseudo-Isidorian Forgeries," in *Papal Letters in the Early Middle Ages*, Detlev Jasper and Horst Fuhrmann, eds., *History of Medieval Canon Law* (Washington, D.C.: Catholic University of America Press, 2001).

[10] The extent to which canon law was derived from forged materials is a subject of great dispute. The other prominent example of the use of forgery to legitimate the powers of the church is of course the Donation of Constantine, exposed by Lorenzo Valla in 1440. On the problem of forgery in the Middle Ages, consult the multivolume series, *Fälschungen im Mittelalter: internationaler Kongress der Monumenta Germaniae Historica, München, 16–19 September 1986*, 6 vols., Schriften der Monumenta Germaniae Historica, 33 (Hannover: Hahn, 1988–1990).

[11] Fuhrmann, "The Pseudo-Isidorian Forgeries," 140f.

[12] Horst Fuhrmann, *Einfluß und Verbreitung der pseudoisidorischen Fälschungen*, 3 vols., Schriften der Monumenta Germaniae Historica, vol. 24 (Stuttgart: Anton Hiersemann, 1972–1974). The *Mageburg Centuries* was one of the first great collaborative histories. Led by Flacius Illricus (1520–1575), the Centuriators sought to present the history of the church in light of Luther's Reformation. Presented by "century," the work sought to show how the true, invisible, church had survived, despite the continued assault by worldly matters.

[13] David Blondel, *Pseudoisidorus et Turrianus Vapúlantes* (Geneva: 1628).

[14] Already in the fifteenth century, however, Nicholas of Cusa had raised doubts about the decretals in *The Catholic Concordance*. See the translator's introduction to Nicholas of Cusa, *The Catholic Concordance*, trans. Paul Sigmund (Cambridge: Cambridge University Press, 1991), xxxi. Blondel's work had been directed against a Jesuit scholar's (Francisco Torres) attack on the *Centuries*. Francisco Torres, *Francisci Turriani Societatis Iesu Aduersus Magdeburgenses centuriatores pro Canonibus apostolorum: & epistolis decretalibus pontificum apostolicorum libri quinque* (Florence: 1572).

claims, or could not be proven independently.[15] It is hardly surprising, however, that in the polemical battles between Protestants and Catholics, the forgeries that supposedly underpinned papal claims to primacy would be pounced upon by Lutheran and Reformed historians alike. It was not until the development of Gallican theories of the independence of the French church from Rome that Catholics began to embrace the thesis (publicly, at least) of the forgeries as the basis for papal usurpation in such a way that idealized ancient church discipline – that is, in the years before the Gregorian revolution.[16]

Ideas alone, however, do not make history. What accounts for the intense interest in the Pseudo-Isidorian decrees and their legacy among German Catholics in the eighteenth century – that is, more than 100 years after Blondel's definitive exposure? The Catholic "discovery" of the forgery on its own does not explain its significance. Germans after 1648 were not just imitating their Gallican neighbors. Why, then, did they begin to propagate the thesis that not only were the decretals false, but also papal primacy and authority were likewise on shaky ground? How did jurisprudence lay the foundation for the German Catholic Enlightenment? The ancient constitutionalism of the German Gallicans, like all such political theories, emerged from the confluence of learning *and* political opportunity.

Intellectually, the German canonists were able to pull away from Rome by expanding their conception of the *sources* of church law. In effect, this meant expanding the notion of valid church law beyond the received boundaries of the *corpus juris canonici*. Gratian, the legendary (and possible mythical) "first canonist," initiated the discipline by seeking to "harmonize" the "discordant canons" of the church.[17] Gratian collected decrees of the popes and the councils. The classical body of canon law, the *corpus juris canonici*, was made up of these authorized

---

[15] Fuhrmann, *Einfluß und Verbreitung der pseudoisidorischen Fälschungen*. On Baronius, see Huburt Jedin, *Kardinal Caesar Baronius: der Anfang der katholischen Kirchengeschichtsschreibung im 16. Jahrhundert* (Münster: Aschendorff, 1978) and Cyriac K. Pullapilly, *Caesar Baronius, Counter-Reformation Historian* (Notre Dame: University of Notre Dame Press, 1975).

[16] Two key authors in this struggle were Edmund Richer (1559–1631) and Pierre de Marca (1564–1662). Richer's *De ecclesiastica et civili potestate* (Paris, 1611) laid out several positions that would be subsequently adopted by those in favor of limiting the powers of the popes and the temporal power of the church. De Marca's *De concordia sacerdotii et imperii: seu de libertatibus ecclesiae gallicanae libri octo* (Paris, 1663), written at the behest of Richelieu, laid out the legal case for the liberty of the Gallican church. De Marca's work was subsequently imitated by the Lutheran canonist Johann Schilter, *De Libertate Ecclesiarum Germaniae, libri septem* (Jena, 1683).

[17] On Gratian's identity and significance, see Winroth, *The Making of Gratian's Decretum*.

collections (from the Decrees of Gratian to the *Extravagantes* complied by John XXII in 1325).[18] The papacy took the lead in rationalizing and centralizing the rather diffuse law of the church as part of the great Reform (sometimes known as the Gregorian Revolution).[19] Consequently, those forces within the Catholic church that sought to emphasize their independence from Rome also needed to demonstrate the possibility for a different legal order.

One way in which this rather fundamental ecclesio-political struggle manifested itself was in the various attempts to present the law of the church in a unified fashion. Before 1917, when the Catholic church issued the Code of Canon Law (revised in 1983), the law of the church was based on the *corpus juris canonici* and subsequent collections (the most significant addition being the Tridentine decrees). Before the Code was promulgated, church law was still in some ways similar to a common law system in that ultimately the relevant tribunal would have to resolve differences between conflicting practices and decisions. A uniform code for the entire Catholic church could not be promulgated until it had been made clear as to who possessed authority do so. The ecclesio-political struggles between popes and councils needed first to be decided before an authoritative Code could be issued. The 1917 Code was therefore the culmination of a century of ultramontane centralization. In earlier eras, the lack of a singular authority meant that differing versions of canon law – as reflected in the profusion of books and interpretations of church law – could also flourish. This is why ecclesiastical jurisprudence was the discipline in which fundamental questions of church politics and authority were fought, and why canonists were at the forefront of these disputes in the early modern era.[20]

The introduction of a historical method into canon law provided a wedge to be used against the ultramontane canonists.[21] The most

---

[18] See Note 7 above.

[19] This is why the power of the papacy became so identified with canon law. After all, it was the body of canon law that Luther burned after receiving the Bull of excommunication – registering his fundamental objection to the "legalization" of the Church.

[20] According to Willibald Plöchel, the early attempt by Thomasso Campanella (1568–1639) to codify Church law is instructive. It required a totalitarian authority in which secular and spiritual authorities were united. Willibald M. Plöchel, *Geschichte des Kirchenrechts. Band V: Das katholische Kirchenrecht in der Neuzeit. Dritter Teil* (Munich and Vienna: Velag Herold, 1969), 253–72. See also Jean Gaudemet, *Les Sources du Droit Canonique, VIIIe–XXe siècle* (Paris: Cerf, 1993), 197.

[21] Ludwig. T Spittler, *Geschichte des kanonischen Rechts, bis auf die Zeiten des falschen Isidorus* (Halle: 1778), iii. Spittler considered this to constitute the beginning of the

wide-ranging and influential of these new approaches to the law of the church was by Zeger-Bernard van Espen (1646–1728).[22] His principle work, *Jus Ecclesiasticum Universum* (1700), broke new ground on several fronts. Van Espen's organization of the church law may rightly be seen as the confluence of two major strains of canon-law scholarship. While he follows Enricus Pirhing (1606–1679) in his bid for comprehensiveness, the real inspirational model is that of Giovanni Paolo Lancelotti's (1522–1590) thematically organized *Institutes*.[23] Of lasting

"revolution of ideas" for German Catholics. Raab, *Die Concordata Nationis Germanicae in der kanonischen Diskussion des 17. bis 19. Jahrhunderts*, 132.

[22] The Louvain canonist was very influential even after his principle work was placed in the Index. He had Gallican and Janenist sympathies, which eventually brought him afoul of the curia when he supported the election of the Vicar General of Utrecht who had himself consecrated without Roman approval. Soon after, Van Espen refused to support the formulary of Alexander VII (a tool aimed at rooting out Jansenist sympathizers in the church) and the constitution *Unigenitus*. Rather than recant he fled from the Austrian Netherlands to the Dutch Republic, and died soon after. For short overviews see the entries in *The New Catholic Encyclopedia* and *Lexikon für Theologie und Kirche*. See also F. Claeys Bouuaert, "Un canoniste d'ancien régime: Zeger Bernard van Espen," *Ephermerides theologicae Louvanienses* 38 (1962); G. Cooman, M. Van Stiphout, and B Wauters, eds., *Zeger-Bernard van Espen at the Crossroads of Canon Law, History, Theology, and Church–State Relations*, vol. 170, Bibliotheca Ephemeridum Theologicarum Lovaniensium (Leuven: Leuven University Press, 2003); Gustave Leclerc, *Zeger-Bernard van Espen (1646–1728) et l'autorité ecclésiastique. Contribution à l'histoire des théories gallicanes et du jansénisme*, Studia et Textus Iuris Canonici, 2 (Zurich: Pas Verlag, 1964); and M. Nuttinck, *La vie et l'oeuvre de Zeger-Bernard van Espen* (Louvain: Bureaux du Recueil, Bibliothèque de l'Université, 1969).

[23] The Dillingen Jesuit Enricus Pirhing's 1670 *Jus Canonicum* tried to treat the entirety of the canon law systematically but followed the order of the Decretals of Gregory IX, as well as the successor collections of Boniface VIII, the Clementines, and the Extravagantes. Pirhing's work aimed to provide a comprehensive view of canon law, yet he did not stray from its classical organization. His approach differed fundamentally from that of Giovanni Paolo Lancelotti, who suggested to Pope Paul IV (r. 1555–1559) that canon law needed to be taught following the model of the Institutes of Justinian. Lancelotti was called to Rome in 1557 to begin this work. When it became clear that it would not receive official approbation, Lancelotti published it privately in 1563 as *Institutiones iuris canonici, quibus ius Pontificum singulari methodo libris quattuor comprehenditur*. Although it did not have official sanction as the official method for teaching canon law, Paul V did allow it to be published along with the Corpus Iuris Canonici in 1605. Lancelotti's *Institutes* thus remained very influential, but since they fell short of being officially promulgated, they lacked binding authority and left room for other methods of organizing the canon law. The *Institutes* is divided into four books, treating persons, things (which in this context includes sacraments), judgments (meaning also trials), and finally crimes and punishments. It is not intended to give an exhaustive account of the canon law, but rather to serve as an introduction and guide. The innovation is in the novel method of summarizing valid law. The sources of the law for this text remain the decretals of the popes – Lancelotti's *Institutes* was therefore intended to serve as an introductory supplement and official guide to the received *Corpus Iuris Canonici*.

significance was the way in which van Espen opened up the question of the sources of church law.[24] Hence van Espen's model could as easily be adopted by Prospero Lambertini (who reigned as Pope Benedict XIV from 1740 to 1758) in his own works on church law.

In employing "*ius ecclesiasticum*" in his title, Van Espen indicated that legitimate authority in the church was broader than the hierarchy itself. By qualifying it with *universum*, he stated that he was treating the entirety of church law. Van Espen was not the first to use *ius ecclesiasticum*, but the title signaled that he would try to outline the law of the church without relying solely on the canons. Van Espen's organization offered a conceptualization of the totality of the church law. It also attempted to provide the material of the law needed by the student or practitioner. The important question was therefore one of the *sources* of the law; it was also a question about legitimacy of the law and the relationship between the church and civil society, and in a sense about the very definition of "church."[25]

According to van Espen, only the historical study of church discipline allowed one to understand contemporary practice, and to know where recent laws had modified or abolished ancient usage.[26] He acknowledged that the study of church law was related to theology, and that he could not avoid discussion of issues normally reserved to the theologians.[27] This is significant because one of van Espen's most contentious innovations was to broaden the notion of the sources of church law. Canonists, in van Espen's view, were not merely held to interpreting the received collections of canons and decrees, but instead had some say over the legitimacy of the particulars of church discipline. Therefore they needed to look at Scripture, the writings of the Fathers and early councils in addition to the *corpus iuris canonici.*[28]

Van Espen's most important contribution was to integrate the "history of ancient discipline" into church law. He transformed the subject from a

---

[24] *Jus Ecclesiasticum Universum* (hereafter *JEU*) is divided into three parts: (1) Of persons (clerics, bishops, congregations, regular clergy, and the duties and rights of these persons; (2) Of things (which in this case includes sacraments, benefices, feasts, cemeteries, etc.); and (3) Of ecclesiastical judgments, crimes, and punishments (civil and criminal jurisdictions, ministers of church courts, trials).

[25] On the significance of the term, see Wiel, *History of Canon Law*.

[26] Van Espen, *JEU*, v.

[27] Van Espen, *JEU*, vi.

[28] In the second section of the preface, Van Espen addressed the question of what use was to be made of the early discipline of the church. He did not intend to restore the earlier discipline, but rather thought that it could serve to illuminate present practice and also to correct it when present practice was based on misinterpretation of earlier rules. *JEU*, vi.

literary concern with the past in which history served the function of critique, to the practical application of that critique in the law. Van Espen harvested the fruits of the genre of literary history – most notably that of the Oratorian Louis Thomassin (1619–1695) – and applied it systematically to the genre of canon law, thus transforming the history of the law into an interpretive principle to be used in courts and legal education.[29]

An example of the way historical interpretation was employed by van Espen is found in the very first title, "On Clerics." The first chapter deals with the tonsuring of clerics, and whether it was necessary for ordination. He notes that in the early centuries of the church, tonsuring was not carried out before ordination, and cites historians supporting and denying this claim. Because of abuses by those receiving the tonsure only to escape civil jurisdiction, the Council of Trent declared that it should be refused to those seeking it for worldly ends.[30] He then proceeds to discuss specific legislation in Belgium (*Belgii*) relevant to questions of determining when tonsure had been received out of desire for worldly benefit.[31] The point of the exercise was to lay out the various approaches to how one decides on the validity of claims to tonsure, which he does by a historical exposition of the problem. Similarly, his treatment of baptism notes that the practice of the rite can be found in the earliest period of the church, even if the external form has changed.[32]

While his subsequent personal history quite clearly demonstrates his own convictions and sympathies for Jansenist positions, the *Jus Ecclesiasticum Universum* itself was not at outright challenge to the ecclesiastical hierarchy. Indeed, it was in some ways the condemnation of his major work that moved him subsequently to more active support of Jansenism.[33] At worst (from a papal point of view) it purported Gallican views, especially in the emphasis on the equal power of bishops and the

---

[29] Van Espen did not cite Thomassin as much as other authors, although Thomassin was widely seen as exemplary. There has also been some controversy as to whether Van Espen merely plagiarized large passages of Thomassin. Leclerc dismisses these accusations, which indeed seem unlikely. Also to be taken into account is the nature of early modern history writing, which relied on frequent and heavy citation of passages from well-known authors. See Leclerc, *Zeger-Bernard van Espen (1646–1728) et l'autorité ecclésiastique. Contribution à l'histoire des théories gallicanes et du jansénisme*, 270–3.

[30] Van Espen, *JEU*, part I, title 1, cap. 1, §iv, 1.

[31] Although there was no such independent state, he uses the term "Belgii" in the title: *Jus ecclesiasticum universum antique et recentiori disciplinae paresertim Belgii, Galiae* [...].

[32] Van Espen, *JEU*, part I, title 2, cap. 3, §1, 23.

[33] See Guido Cooman and Bart Wauters, "*Jus Ecclesiasticum Subversum*. La Condamnation du *Magnum Opus* de Zeger Bernard van Espen par le Saint-Office Romain

insistence that church edicts and laws needed the *placet* of the prince to be binding. In hindsight, it is easy to put van Espen in a lineage that descended from Gallicanism and Jansenism, and then continued after him into the German "Gallicans," the Josephinists, and into the nineteenth-century Catholic dissidents who were always uneasy about, and sometimes outright hostile to, papal legal centralization. While this simplification helps clarify the lineages of ecclesiastical debates from the early modern period into the nineteenth century, it also masks the open-ended possibilities in thinking about the Catholic church around 1700.

Although his innovations have radical implications, van Espen's historicism is tempered by a conservative approach to received law. Van Espen saw his efforts to broaden the scope of the sources of canon law beyond papal decrees as a conservative project. Van Espen wrote at a time when it still seemed possible to work out the proper boundaries between church and state in Catholic Europe. Only later would it become clear that the "perfect societies" of civil society and religious life existed only as theoretical abstractions. Attempts to transform these abstractions into concrete structures of governance involved political, financial, and ultimately military actions that hardened battle lines on all sides. However, it had not yet come to this when van Espen was writing (though the conflict over *Unigenitus* in 1713 was to hint at things to come). Van Espen's brilliance and erudition enabled him to synthesize a vast knowledge of ecclesiastical history and to apply that knowledge systematically to a new organization of church law. As a Netherlandish jurist of Gallican sympathies, he had a certain intellectual freedom that enabled him to draw upon a historical conception of the church without the need to propagate classical papal law. Van Espen's method did not necessarily lead to a break with Rome, for one of the most famous heirs of his historical approach to church law was Benedict XIV. This new historical interest in the laws of the church coincided with a crisis of authority that began roughly at the turn of the eighteenth century. The immediate past of the church – the era of the Counter-Reformation, in short – was coming under intense scrutiny. Yet churchmen of all stripes reached back farther into the ecclesiastical past for models of how to react to the new dispensation. The lessons of history, they would discover, were as different as the political and ecclesiastical viewpoints of the historians. The "ancient constitutionalism" of the German canonists was made an

(1704)," in *Zeger-Bernard van Espen at the Crossroads of Canon Law, History, Theology, and Church–State Relations*, Cooman, Van Stiphout, and Wauters, eds., 70–94.

intellectual possibility by the historical school of canon law. As important was the place of the church in the Empire after Westphalia.

THE GERMAN GALLICANS: CANON LAWYERS AND THE IMPERIAL CHURCH

The historical school of canon law gave the German canonists the intellectual and moral tools to question the Roman monopoly on the law of the church. In addition to this methodological component – which was, in a sense, the universal property of Catholics and arguably applicable to any national context – there was also a specific set of legal and historical problems that were relevant to the German church. As the German canonists challenged the primacy of the pope in establishing the valid law of the church, they turned to the imperial framework to define the German church. As Catholics, the greatest example for the German canonists was the Gallican church, which had by the middle of the eighteenth century fairly well established its "liberties." If German Catholics were to construct an alternative order for the ecclesiastical polity, they would need to elaborate just what exactly the German church was. They did so historically, by looking to the century before the Reformation to the Conciliar era. They thus showed how two fundamental issues were intertwined: first, it was the Reformation (and specifically the politics of the Reformation – that is the struggles between dynasties, princes, estates, and the curia more than dogmatic points) that had prevented the solidification of the German church as a viable ecclesio-political entity. The *Reichskirche* had become a rump of its potential self. The second related point was that the softening of confessional conflict could provide the basis for a reunion of the confessions within Germany. More so than for Protestants, German Catholics elaborated a vision of national unity that depended on the persistence of the old *Germania Sacra*.[34] Fundamental to this Catholic attempt to construe

---

[34] In the classic account of the rise of national feeling among Germans, it is only language (and pointedly not the Empire) that draws Germans together. This is why the late emergence of German as a literary language (late in comparison to the two normative traditions of nation-formation, England and France) supposedly explains the peculiarities of German nationalism – especially its tendency to abstraction and idealization. Herder, who occupies a prominent place in the early history of linkage of German nationalism with culture and language, commented that it was impossible to write a history of the Germans because Germany as such had not yet come into being: "*Kurz, was noch nicht geschrieben ist, zeigt durch sich selbst genugsam, daß es bis dahin noch nicht geschrieben werden konnte. Wenn dies geschehen kann, wirds werden.*" J. G. Herder, "Warum wir noch keine Geschichte der Deutschen haben," in *Neue Deutsche Monatsschrift* 1 (1795): 328.

the collection of German ecclesiastical provinces as a national church was the rehabilitation of the office of bishop.

A monument to this revival of the idea of the episcopate was the multivolume *Concilia Germania* published between 1759 and 1775,[35] the product of the labors of Johann Friedrich Schannat and Joseph Hartzheim.[36] The former, influenced by the Maurist school, began to collect documents in Germany and abroad relating to synods and councils in Germany from the fourth to the eighteenth century. After his death, Schannat's work was continued by the Jesuit Joseph Hartzheim. In his dedication to the patron of the work, the archbishop of Prague, Hartzheim stresses that it is through the bishop that Christ remains with the church. Through the bishop the unity and concord of the faithful is maintained. Because their duty is to correct errors that have crept in, the bishops hold frequent councils and synods.[37] *Concilia Germania* builds, in part, on the legacy of Nicholas of Cusa, the great theorist of Conciliarism who also recognized the need for papal leadership to preserve the unity of the church.[38] Indeed, there was a wider interest in the fifteenth century in the work of the German canonists: the reestablishment of German episcopal autonomy depended on a return to pre-Reformation ideals of the concordance of popes and bishops. This revival could take different forms. As expressed in Hartzheim and Schannat's *Concilia Germaniae*, it was not necessarily anti-papal. Their listing of diocesan synods through the centuries demonstrated how the bishops held together and preserved the *Germania Sacra*. Indeed, their work confirms the thrust of Pope Benedict XIV's *De Synodo Diocesana* (1748), which sought to strengthen the role of the bishop while not undermining the rights of the papacy. *De Synodo Diocesana* was an important work both for the methodical application of new historical techniques to the

---

[35] The index was published in 1790.

[36] See Herman-Josef Sieben, "Die Schannat-Hartzheimische Sammlung der deutschen Konzilien (1759–1790)," *Theologie und Philosophie* 76 (2001).

[37] Essential to the revival of the diocesan synod was Benedict XIV's *De synodo diocesana* (1748).

[38] Raab notes in passing that there was a revival of interest in Nicholas of Cusa, the champion of conciliar principles at Basel who then later sided with the pope in recognition of the need for unity in the church. Interestingly enough, one of the earlier works on Cusa was by a Jesuit named Casparus Hartzheim who may very well have been a relative of Joseph, though I have found no record either way. Casparus Hartzheim, *Vita Nicolai de Cusa* (Trier: 1730; reprint, Frankfurt: Minerva, 1968); Raab, *Die Concordata Nationis Germanicae in der kanonischen Diskussion des 17. bis 19. Jahrhunderts*, 108; Paul Sigmund, *Nicolas of Cusa and Medieval Political Thought* (Cambridge: Harvard University Press, 1963); and Cusa, *The Catholic Concordance*.

discipline of canon law, as well as for its emphasis on the diocesan synod (under the leadership of the bishop) as the surest method for reforming morals, maintaining correct teaching, and tending to the faithful.[39]

How, then, did this revived interest in the office of the bishop take on an anti-Roman tone? True enough, the German canonists looked to history to validate their claims. But that history was open-ended, and it is surely significant that they chose to represent the past of the church in a certain light, one that cast its own shadows on the policies of the Curia. As Heribert Raab has shown, the intellectual *locus* for this debate was in the discussion about the fifteenth century *Concordata nationis germanicae.*[40] To that canon-law discussion we would also need to consider the development of legal historicism in the Empire after the Peace of Westphalia.[41]

This legal historicism developed from the confluence of two strains of legal dispute – canonical and secular. In the minds and practices of early modern jurists and theologians, of course, they were inextricably linked.[42] The canon-law dispute dealt with the jurisdictional supremacy of the pope. While elements of this dispute served as fodder for the Reformers' split with Rome, the resurgence of the papacy in the wake of the Council of Trent only increased tensions among those who remained within the old church.[43]

---

[39] Peter Landau, "Benedikt XIV," in *Juristen. Ein biographisches Lexikon,* Michael Stolleis, ed. (Munich: C. H. Beck, 1995).

[40] Raab, *Die Concordata Nationis Germanicae in der kanonischen Diskussion des 17. bis 19. Jahrhunderts.*

[41] See, most recently, Constantin Fasolt, *The Limits of History* (Chicago: University of Chicago Press, 2004).

[42] Similarly, the evolution of the European *jus commune* is held to evolve from the marriage of Roman and canon law in the eleventh century. See especially the conclusion to Winroth, *The Making of Gratian's Decretum.*

[43] The most well-known irruption of these tensions was with the papacy's struggles with Venice in the beginning of the seventeenth century. Two literary products of that dispute are worth mentioning for their subterranean influence in Catholic thought of the seventeenth and eighteenth century: Paolo Sarpi's *History of the Council of Trent,* and Marc Antonio de Dominis *De republica ecclesiastica libri X* (1617–1622). De Dominis was Archbishop of Split (Spalato), but came into quarrel with Rome over the Venetian interdict, fled to England and was made bishop in the church of England by James I. He published, without authorization, Sarpi's *History of the Council of Trent* (1619). He returned to Rome on the succession of a relative to the papal (see Gregory XV), but then was arrested by the Inquisition after Gregory XV's death. He died in prison, but his remains were burned as a heretic. On Sarpi and Venice, see William Bouwsma, *Venice and the Defense of Republican Liberty: Renaissance Values in the Age of the Counter-Reformation* (Berkeley and Los Angeles: University of California Press, 1968).

The second strain of legal history to be considered here is specific to the development of post-Westphalia German legal consciousness. Against the Emperor's claims to universal sovereignty based on Roman law principles, the Helmstedt jurist Hermann Conring had argued that Roman law was introduced only by gradual use of jurists who had trained in Italy – not, as the legend had it, by some foundational act of sovereignty or law-giving.[44] Conring's argument was aired in 1643, and was therefore very much directed against the pernicious role that Imperial claims had played in fomenting the Thirty Years' War. That other institution with universal claims, the Catholic church, became as much a target for jurists and political theorists such as Conring after it refused to ratify the Peace of Westphalia.[45] This was natural enough for Protestants, who saw in both Imperial (that is Habsburg) and papal claims of universal supremacy a dangerous threat to confessional and territorial peace. The most significant development for eighteenth-century German Catholicism, however, was the gradual acceptance of the very same Westphalian principles the papacy rejected and which enshrined biconfessionalism in the Empire. This German Catholic vision of the national church grew to oppose papal claims of universal jurisdiction. For the smaller and medium-sized Catholic states, it was the Imperial constitution – not the Emperor – which protected Catholicism in Germany. The German canonists' claims to episcopal autonomy adopted similar argumentation about the usurpation of German ecclesiastical rights. And just as for Conring Roman law was introduced by students, so for Hontheim the chief cause of the introduction of Rome-centric canon law was the jurists who had studied canon law at Bologna and subsequently brought it back to Germany.

Thus two intellectual traditions merged to form the anti-curial German school of canon law. The legal sensibility of the historical school of canon law (i.e., that of van Espen and Benedict XIV) was grafted onto the concern with post-Westphalian German legal history by Johan Kaspar

---

[44] Hermann Conring had debunked the so-called Lotharian legend, that Emperor Lothar III (1075–1137) had introduced Roman law into Germany with *De Origine Iuris Germanici liber unus* (1649). See Fasolt, *The Limits of History*; Michael Stolleis, ed., *Hermann Conring (1606–1681): Beiträge zu Leben und Werk* (Berlin: Duncker & Humblot, 1983) and Michael Stolleis, "Conring, Hermann," in *Juristen. Ein biographisches Lexikon*, Michael Stolleis, ed. (Munich: C. H. Beck, 1995).

[45] Konrad Repgen, "Der päpstlicher Protest gegen den Westfälischen Frieden und die Friedenspolitik Urbans VIII," *Historisches Jahrbuch* 75 (1956) and Hermann Conring, *De Pace Perpetua inter Imperii Germanici Ordines religione dissidentes servanda libelli duo, Quorum ultimo in Bullam Innocentii X Papae, quae utrumq. Pacis pactum irritum reddere conata est, animadvertitur* (1657).

Barthel (1697–1771) and his students.[46] In 1727, the prince-bishop of Würzburg, Friedrich Karl von Schönborn, commissioned Barthel to "accommodate" canon law to the peculiarities of the Empire.[47] Barthel had trained with Lambertini in Rome, yet his intellectual lineage drew as much from the Gallicanism of van Espen.[48] Barthel's impact was as much through his teaching as through his writing. While he published smaller tracts throughout his career, his major compendium did not appear until the latter years of his life, and even that was relatively limited in scope. As the regent [*regens*] of the diocesan seminary of Würzburg, he also had great influence over the instruction of the secular clergy and did his best to counteract the influence of the Jesuits.

In his canonistic writing and teaching, Barthel sought the middle ground, and emphasized the need for cooperation between secular and clerical authorities, and between the episcopate and the curia. In his 1762 *Historical-Canonical-Pragmatic Treatise … On the Concordat of the German Nation*,[49] he notes that "the scope of this work is to defend the rights of the German nation while preserving the rights and authorities of the Roman pontiffs."[50] He continues by noting that both "Curialists"

---

[46] The German legal situation is further complicated by the lack of any uniform legal institutions. Indeed, there were two "supreme" courts in the Empire: the Imperial Chamber Court (*Reichskammergericht*), which met in Wetzlar, and the Imperial Aulic Council (*Reichshofrath*), which met in Vienna. See Michael Hughes, *Law and Politics in Eighteenth-Century Germany: The Imperial Aulic Council in the Reign of Charles VI* (Woodbridge, Suffolk: Royal Historical Society, 1988). Hughes notes that cases had become backlogged in Wetzlar, and that the Aulic Council had become a more effective court for resolving dispute. He argues that the Imperial Aulic council took pains to preserve confessional and dynastic neutrality (as far as that was possible in the period) so that the court would be respected by Protestants as well as Catholics. By restraining favoritism in the court, Habsburg policy aimed to increase the prestige of the emperor, which it could only do by acting in an impartial manner.

[47] Karl Otmar Freiherr von Aretin, *Das alte Reich, 1648–1806, II: Kaisertradition und österreichische Großmachtpolitik, 1684–1745,* 4 vols. (Stuttgart: Klett-Cotta, 1993–2000), vol. 2, 396.

[48] On Barthel, see Heribert Raab, "Johann Kaspar Barthels Stellung in der Diskussion um die Concordata Nationis Germanicae. Ein Beitrag zur Würzburger Kanonistik im 18. Jahrhundert," in Raab, *Reich und Kirche in der frühen Neuzeit* (Freiburg, Switzerland: 1989) [Orig: *Herbipolis Jubilans*. Würzburg, 1952, 599–616], 127. For Barthel's influence and a list of many of his student, see Raab, "Der reichskirchliche Episkopalismus von der Mitte des 17. bis zum Ende des 18. Jahrhunderts," in *Handbuch der Kirchengeschichte* V, Jedin, ed. (Freiburg: Herder, 1970), ch. 22.

[49] Full title: *Tractatus Historico-Canonico-Pragmaticus Loco Dissertationis Tertiae de Concordatis Germaniae Specialis Exhibens Commentarium Hermeneuticum ad Eorundem Textum et Literam*, Würzburg, 1762. In: *Opsculorum Recentiorum*, Pars I.

[50] Barthel, *Tractatus*, 1f.

and Protestants have written on this matter, and that he will address the errors of both camps. As the summary of the chapter indicates, the main errors of the "Curialists" are that they neglect the ancient canons and the history of the church. Furthermore, they assume that the princes received all the Decretals without distinction, and they err in that they attribute too much authority to the decisions of the Rota and therefore to the style of the Curia. Moreover, Barthel argues, they follow the assertions of scholars without adequate examination. Though not a major compendium on canon law in the style of van Espen, this collection serves as a supplement for canonists who needed to know specifics about canon law as applied to German conditions. Throughout, Barthel is judiciously restrained on points of controversy.[51] Barthel and many of his generation (e.g., the moral theologian and modernizing scholastic Eusebius Amort[1692–1775]) wrote and acted in an age where compromise and accommodation between Rome and the national churches seemed possible. The tensions between universalism and particularism were problems for the scholars and princes, but it did not yet seem as if they would tear the church apart.[52]

Barthel grafted German legal sensibility and conservatism onto the historical approach to Catholic church law. His method was not inherently anti-Roman: Barthel had studied under the greatest of the papal canonists, and he consciously sought the middle ground on disputed questions. However, as a practical matter, legal historicism in Germany had become linked to episcopalian politics. The sponsors of the historical and legal world were bishops and churchmen intent on establishing their legitimate independence from Roman influence. Much of their theology was inspired by Gallican theories. This perhaps flattered the French ecclesiastics, yet there was one fundamental difference: the French episcopate was constituted as part of a unified French church with the

---

[51] Barthel's student often did not share his restraint. This was a product of the growing tension between German and Roman attitudes toward ecclesiastical authority. Raab indicates that one can also trace the influence of regional conditions in the works of later German canonists. For example, Neller, teaching in Trier, represented an approach suited to the Rhenish conditions and Gregor Zallwein, a Benedictine monk from the abbey Wessobrun in Bavaria, taught at the Benedictine University in Salzburg (the only non-Jesuit University in Catholic Germany), and particularly defended the privileges of the Prince-Archbishop of Salzburg. See Raab, *Die Concordata Nationis Germanicae in der kanonischen Diskussion des 17. bis 19. Jahrhunderts*, 113–8.

[52] Barthel's epigoni included all sorts of canonists, some more radical than others. Georg Chrisoph Neller was perhaps his most significant pupil, for he brought Barthel's ideas from Würzburg to Trier, where they most likely influenced Hontheim.

monarch at its head. The clergy made up one of the three estates in France, and the only one which was allowed to meet on a regular basis (though not in the form of a national synod). For all that external glory, however, church and state were intertwined to such an extent in France that it can plausibly be asserted that the discrediting of that alliance over the course of the eighteenth century was a fundamental aspect in the ultimate fall of the monarchy.[53] Although they never ceased to extol the liberties of the Gallican church, it seemed at times that the German canonists had underplayed the extent to which the church was part of the state in France.

HONTHEIM'S *DE STATU* AND THE GERMAN EPISCOPAL MOVEMENT

Thus it was that the ground had been well prepared by the time Hontheim issued his treatise claiming that German Catholics needed to reclaim their church from papal incursions. Through Hontheim, the German Catholic Enlightenment was able to transform the old canon-law disputes about papal primacy into a greater struggle over the direction and control of the German church. As I stated above, it is misleading to try and grasp the entirety of the German Catholic reform program in Hontheim's *de Statu* because it really only encapsulated the attempt to revive the old episcopal ideal. *De Statu* did not propagate many of the other essential elements of the reform Catholicism in the areas of liturgical change, education of clergy, and so forth. But it was through these claims of jurisdictional autonomy that German Catholics sought to assert their rights to make such reforms, and was the beginning of a process of rethinking the church that would expand in the remaining decades of the century.

A synopsis of Hontheim's argument can be gleaned from the full title: Justin Febronius' Single Book on the state of the church and the Legitimate Power of the Roman Pontiff, Composed for the Reunion of Dissidents in

---

[53] See for example Dale van Kley, *The Religious Origins of the French Revolution: From Calvin to the Civil Constitution, 1560–1791* (New Haven: Yale University Press, 1996), John McManners, *Church and Society in eighteenth-century France*, 2 vols. (Oxford: Oxford University Press, 1998); and Joseph Bergin, *The Making of the French Episcopate 1589–1661* (New Haven: Yale University Press, 1996). Also of major importance was the social split between the upper and lower clergy in France. Though technically bishops and parish priests alike were members of the First Estate, the crucial breakthrough in 1789 occurred when much of the lower clergy, having been alienated by bishops and "abbés" siphoning off ecclesiastical wealth allied with Third Estate.

the Christian Religion. Hontheim had taken the pseudonym from the religious name of his niece, Febronia. While to modern eyes, the book seems long-winded and dense, at about 600 quarto pages it was in fact quite concise by early modern theological standards. The significance of this being a "single book" therefore lies in its polemical and public aim: compared to other works of ecclesiastical history and law, *de Statu* is very accessible, with a clear argument and an organization that is easy to follow. The clarity of its argument and its relatively succinct arrangement was born out by its popularity both in Germany and across Europe. By focusing in the "state of the church," Hontheim indicated that he meant to discuss the governmental structures of the church – though in reality he could not avoid more fundamental ecclesiological issues (i.e., the theological status of differing definitions of the church).

Hontheim tried to restrict his discussion to the "legitimate power" of the pope by distinguishing between the primacy of the pope and what he saw as illegitimately accrued jurisdictional powers over other bishops. While Hontheim can rightly be considered the author of the book, it was "composed" in the sense that much of the work is cobbled together from quotations of other authors whose works had received approbation, such as Bossuet, Fleury, and Gerson. This was done in part to avoid censorship – although no one was fooled, and the work was quickly put on the Index. Finally, Hontheim's claim that he was trying to "reunite" Protestants to the Catholic church was based on the assumption that Protestants had kept away from the Catholic church mainly on account of papal prerogatives.[54] While we should not dismiss the effort as mere cynical rhetoric, the Protestant reaction – lukewarm at best – reveals that Hontheim was more than a bit naive in his understanding of German Protestants. While, as Schilter indicated, they were disturbed at papal claims of primacy, there were also dogmatic issues that Hontheim did not address.

The first seven of the nine chapters of *de Statu* deal with the structures and laws of the church, whereas the final two outline a program for "recovering" the original "liberties" of the church. The first chapter details the "external form of government of the church" as instituted by Jesus Christ. The second chapter discusses the notion of primacy in the church, and "its genuine rights." The third chapter portrays the growth of the rights of Roman primacy, which was "sometimes by accident and unwittingly, sometimes by crime [*tum fortuitis & innocuis tum sontibus*]."

---

[54] An argument supported, in some sense, by one of his Protestant sources, Johannes Schilter's *De libertate ecclesiarum Germaniae* (Jena: 1683).

The fourth chapter discusses the so-called "major cases," that is, jurisdictions supposedly reserved to the pope (such as questions of faith, the confirmation of episcopal elections or the removal and translation of bishops). The fifth chapter discusses the laws of the church, the right to make them for the universal church, and the right of appeal to the pope. The sixth chapter discusses general councils, and the seventh chapter argues that bishops have their authority "from divine law." The eighth chapter outlines "the liberties of the church, the law, and the means to reestablish them." The ninth chapter is similarly titled, discussing the "means to reestablish" the liberty of the church. In this final chapter, though, Hontheim addresses a more general remedy than mere application of canonical procedures, and instead argues that education and vigilance are needed to preserve the "liberty" of the church.

After the requisite dedications to Pope Clement XIII, Christian kings and princes, and the bishops of the Catholic church, Hontheim addresses the "doctors of theology and canon law."[55] He tells these teachers that, "the state of the government of the church, as well as its vicissitudes, is due to you more than one thinks, or at least more than is commonly acknowledged."[56] The canon lawyers and theologians are responsible for propagating a vision of the Catholic church as a monarchy, a vision which is set forth in the Decretals, the Clementines, and the Extravagantes. "Gregory IX, Boniface VIII, and John XXII," Hontheim argues:

did not promulgate these collections solemnly in the form of laws, but instead sent them to the doctors of the University of Bologna, so that they could be taught in their schools, and by this means was established the basis of the sacral monarchy."[57]

The University of Bologna served a key role in spreading the idea of a papal monarchy. Hontheim states:

From the thirteenth and fourteenth centuries, the study of both kinds of law flourished at Bologna. Young people from all over the civilized world came there, as if coming to a market of civil and ecclesiastical wisdom. Upon return to their fatherlands, they ascended to high civil and ecclesiastical offices. They then brought into practice and custom the principles of this jurisprudence they had

---

[55] Hontheim was taken to task for his cheekiness in dedicating a work to the pope that subsequently proceeded to attack the papacy's privileges. Yet in Hontheim's defense, it could be said that he was employing the classic strategy of appealing to a ruler against the corrupt ministers and advisors surrounding him – in this case, the Roman Curia.

[56] Hontheim, np [author's dedication].

[57] Hontheim, np.

just learned. And thus the Monarchical State [of the church] was established without difficulty, and through these doctors of law, it was received as natural throughout all of the West.[58]

Hontheim thus had a very specific thesis to explain how the papal monarchy assumed its current role. He laid the blame not only on the Curia and the partisans of the pope, but also on the learned men of Europe, who imbibed at the well of papal jurisprudence at Bologna and then subsequently assumed positions of influence in civil and ecclesiastical institutions all over Europe. He continued by noting that the papal system was especially propagated by the regular clergy in Italy and Germany, who passed on their ideas to generations of students.[59]

While one could dispute veracity of Hontheim's interpretation, the significant point is that *de Statu Ecclesiae* in large part seeks to redress false historical development by appealing to the canon lawyers of Europe.[60] A large part of Hontheim's thesis is not merely that the false decretals of Isidore were indeed false. Papal supporters, while perhaps not admitting that the decrees were forgeries, did not try to base the legitimacy of their positions on them. What is significant is how much the impact of this falsification comes to the fore in *de Statu* as *the* main cause for all subsequent developments (over all other possible moments of papal infringement). The importance is placed not just on the law *per se*, but on the overwhelming significance of right knowledge about the law. In Hontheim's view, the canon lawyer belongs to those whose duty is to be concerned about the public law of the church. By commenting on the law, the canon lawyer cannot avoid contemporary church politics. Hontheim's preface makes it clear that lawyers are both the root of the problem and the key to the solution. Legal discourse, however, draws its legitimacy from a supposed neutrality. By legalizing theological and political disputes about the role of the church in German society,

---

[58] Hontheim, np.

[59] See Brundage, *Medieval Canon Law*, 44f and Berman, *Law and Revolution: The Formation of the Western Legal Tradition* (Cambridge: Harvard University Press, 1983).

[60] Evidence of the widespread scholarly interest in canon law can be seen in Philip Anton Schmidt's publication of seven volumes containing the best dissertations on canon law. Much like collections and anthologies in our day and age gather scholarly articles from obscure or limited circulation journals, Schmidt made accessible otherwise hard to find treatises on canon law. See Schmidt, Philip Anton, *Thesaurus iuris ecclesiastici: potissimus germanici, sive Dissertationes selectae in ius ecclesiasticum* ... (Heidelberg: Goebhardt, 1772–1779). Cf. J. F. Schulte, *Die Geschichte der Quellen und Literatur des canonischen Rechts*, vol. 3 (Graz, 1956), 248.

Hontheim at once politicizes canon law and yet tries to remove church reform questions from theological polemic.

Two types of historical awareness are operative in Hontheim's work. First, the school of diplomatic study developed by Mabillon and the Benedictines of St. Maur used critical study of language to reveal the truth or falsity of particular documents. The basis for this historiography lay in philology and detailed scrutiny of competing accounts. Second, Hontheim propounds a theory of historical causation, whereby one key misinterpretation (or willful deceit, perhaps excusable by contemporary circumstances) supplies a vital link in a subsequent unfolding of events. The forgeries of Pseudo-Isidore laid the groundwork for later misrepresentations by generations of law students streaming to Bologna. This theory of historical causation implies that concerted action may be able to reverse earlier mistakes. Having acknowledged their earlier participation in the subversion of the original church constitution, Hontheim exhorts his scholarly colleagues to make amends and restore the church to its original condition. There is what might be called a "republican" element to Hontheim's work, in the sense that the active ecclesiastical citizen-scholar is engaged in the work of vigilance and dedication to his church.[61] He says as much in the final chapter when he declares that "since learning is the strongest rampart for both the Republic and the church against highly dangerous superstition and fanaticism, scholars ought to be considered the *natural defenders* of ecclesiastical and secular authority."[62]

The stated purpose of Hontheim's book is to demonstrate the legitimate power of the pope – which means, of course, denouncing its present condition as illegitimate. The basis of his argument is that supporters of papal infallibility maintain that the church is monarchical in form, with the pope at its head. The supporters of papal absolutism, Hontheim claims, misinterpret scripture. For example, Jesus' admonition in John 21 to "feed my sheep" is commonly taken by monarchists to have been addressed to Peter alone, which would mean that the successor of Peter – the bishop of Rome – had inherited Peter's primacy. Hontheim states that instead, Jesus addressed these words to all the apostles, and therefore the

---

[61] In *Venice and the Defense of Republican Liberty* (Berkeley and Los Angeles: University of California Press, 1968), William Bowsma suggests that Paolo Sarpi fit the mold of the republican humanist – concerned not just for the Serene Republic of Venice, but also for a Church he thought was threatened by papal despotism.

[62] "Cumque scientiae fortissimum sint repagulum adversus superstitionem & fanatismum, Reip. & Ecclesiae adeo exitialem, vere Eruditi debebunt censeri *nati defensores* Sacerdotii & Imperii." Hontheim, IX, §2, 2, 562.

entire episcopate – as descendants of the apostles – was given its authority by Christ.[63] He accuses the "lawyers" [*advocati*] of the Roman Curia – especially Robert Bellarmine – of intentionally misusing scripture to argue that the church has a monarchical form. Hontheim quotes Bossuet to the effect that one should not use mere reasoning to derive the essential structures of the church, but should rely instead on Scripture and tradition.[64] Since Scripture is silent on this point, we should doubt the proposition that the entire church should be in the hands of one person. It is unlikely, Hontheim argues, that Christ would have intended to found an absolute monarchy and then left only unclear statements about the matter.[65]

Hontheim does not doubt that the papacy enjoys primacy in the church, and indeed that this position is necessary for the unity of the church. There needs to be someone in the church to keep watch over innovations and heresy. The pope executes church laws and has the right to send ambassadors to help him with the primatial duties.[66] Yet, Hontheim argues, Roman primacy has ballooned into a set of other rights and privileges. This often occurred because people had turned to Rome in difficult circumstances, thus increasing that see's standing.[67] It was in precisely such a set of difficult circumstances that the false Isidore Mercator forged his decretals. The problem is that, according to Hontheim, these false decretals are still used by the papacy to support its claims to absolute authority.[68] Lest the dispute over papal prerogatives become too abstract, Hontheim proceeds to outline the specific jurisdictional questions that the papacy had "reserved" to itself.[69] Hontheim argues that the right of the papacy to confirm episcopal elections is a recent invention. Hontheim tries to show that rights now claimed by the papacy such as the deposition of bishops and the creation of new dioceses in fact originally belonged to provincial synods. This latter right was not expressed in any written law, but grew out of custom.[70]

Hontheim does not directly address the general question of dispensations in this section. However, these jurisdictional questions affected the

---

[63] Hontheim, 15.
[64] Hontheim, 16f.
[65] Hontheim, 18.
[66] Hontheim, 46; 72; 83.
[67] Hontheim, 125.
[68] Hontheim, 176f, ch. 3, §11.
[69] Hontheim, 190.
[70] Hontheim, IV, §8, 202; IV, §ix, 207.

general structure of the episcopate in the Old Regime church. Whether a bishop was nominated by a king – as in France – or elected by a cathedral chapter – as was the case in most of the German dioceses, the papacy could still refuse to grant the provision allowing the elected bishop to be ordained. Hontheim's concern over papal control over election and confirmation of bishops reflects a larger concern over the social role of the episcopacy. The system of dispensations was one of the key tools in the hands of the papacy. While the rules laid down at the Council of Trent forbade, for example, plurality of benefices and required a minimum age for episcopal ordination, the papacy could and did grant dispensations. These dispensations were essential to the functioning of the Old Regime church. Without them, many of the men who occupied episcopal sees throughout Europe would have been unable to receive ordination.[71]

In order to argue that bishops and synods need to be returned to their rights, Hontheim tries to show that church laws are only valid insofar as they are promulgated in each diocese.[72] He denies universal and autonomous legislative authority to the pope in the same way that he rejects the idea that the papacy is a monarchy. Hontheim notes that dispensations from the rules of the church are sometimes needed and useful.[73] Yet, the right to dispense originally belonged to all bishops in the church, and just like the "major" cases, was progressively monopolized by the papacy. The point of this entire exercise is to argue that the bishops are more or less "sovereign" in their dioceses.[74] Hontheim argues that Christ created the episcopate and made the bishops (as successors to the apostles) equal in authority.[75]

Hontheim tries to undermine the pope's authority to create law of his own accord. For example, Hontheim claims that the Gratian's Decretal is a "compilation ... made by a private individual, who was not given any ecclesiastical authority."[76] This is in fact true, in the sense that Gratian's *Concordance of Discordant Canons* was an attempt to present church

---

[71] See Stephen Kremer, *Herkunft und Werdegang geistlicher Führungsschichten* (Freiburg: Herder, 1992), 66f and Hans Erich Feine, *Die Besetzung der Reichsbistümer vom Westphälischen Frieden bis zur Säkularisation, 1648–1803* (Stuttgart: Ferdniand Enke, 1921; reprint, 1964).

[72] Hontheim, V, §3.

[73] Hontheim, Editio tertia, V, § 5, n. 2, 318.

[74] This strong position of episcopal sovereignty was problematized by the epsicopalist claim that metropolitains and provincial synods should have more power. The tension between bishops and metropolitans would actually play out in the events leading up to the Ems Congress of 1786.

[75] Hontheim, VII, §1, 441.

[76] Hontheim, V, §3, n. 1, 236.

law as a series of decrees whose contradictions could be resolved through reason, but was not legislation as such.[77] Hontheim further criticizes Gratian's work because its errors and confusions had become institutionalized as it had been used in schools and tribunals alike.[78] In a later edition, Hontheim further notes that Pope Nicolas I avowed that the authority of decrees does not come from the fact that they are found together in a collection, but because they are issued by the bishop of Rome.[79] Yet even purported papal authorship does not, in Hontheim's view, automatically render decrees obligatory. A core tenet of Gallican, and then later German, canon law was that universal church laws were only valid once they had been promulgated in each individual diocese. This theory was the legal corollary of the doctrine of episcopal sovereignty – indeed, the next two chapters of *de Statu*, "On General Councils" and "On the Authority of Bishops by Divine Law," explicitly challenge papal jurisdictional authority over the rest of the episcopate, and assert the fundamental equality of all bishops.

Hontheim contends that more recent church law, particularly the decrees of the Council of Trent, had been used by the papacy to consolidate its control over local churches. One of the chief culprits in this process had been the Council Congregation, which was set up under Pius IV in 1564 to apply and interpret the reform decrees of the Council of Trent. Its decisions are issued not by men drawn from the province from which its cases arise, "but instead are issued by men preoccupied by the prejudices of the court of Rome, making their rules according to Roman practices and Pontifical constitutions that have not been generally received elsewhere." Even more egregious, the council sometimes "extends its decisions beyond the propriety of the words and against the letter and sentiment of the council and makes new law."[80] Hontheim continues that the same process applies to the decisions of the Rota, which has adopted the style of the Curia and makes law where it should only decide on individual cases.[81] Hontheim's general argument is, first,

---

[77] See, most recently, Winroth, *The Making of Gratian's Decretum*. Scholars see Gratian's *Concordia discordantium canonum* as ushering in the "classical" period of medieval canon law, which ranged from about 1140 to 1375. See Brundage, *Medieval Canon Law*, 44ff.

[78] Hontheim, V, §3, n. 1, 237.

[79] Hontheim, third edition, V, §3, n. 1, 290.

[80] Hontheim, V, §3, n. 7, 240 and third edition, V, §3, no. 7, 294f.

[81] Hontheim, third edition, V, §3, n. 9, 296. On the Rota, see Lefebvre, Pacaut, and Chevailler, *Les Sources du Droit*, 173–7. The basis of Hontheim's complaint is that the Council Congregation applies the prejudices and ideas of the Roman Curia to cases

that since the days of Gratian the papal decrees have unjustly acquired the status of common law and been used to resolve disputes where they really have no competence. Second, this trend toward papal centralization has only worsened since the Council of Trent. Notably, it is not the Council itself, or even its particular resolutions, that Hontheim attacks. Rather, it is the practice by which those rules are applied and interpreted that Hontheim considers faulty. The Council Congregation, in Hontheim's analysis, was a tool in the hands of the papal Curia aimed at undermining the rights of particular churches.

As part of a more generalized critique of Roman ignorance of German conditions, Hontheim – quoting directly from Johann Kaspar Barthel – refers to an argument by the Jesuit Adam Contzen (1571–1635), the confessor of Elector Maximilian I of Bavaria.[82] In his *Politicorum libri decem* – one of the classic Counter-Reformation political treatises justifying the alliance of church and state – Contzen remarked that "many errors have been committed on account of ignorance of the Republic." He continues:

For it is not easy that strangers could know much about other people, everything about the vast assemblage of provinces of the Empire, and all that belongs to the state of the Empire, above all the diverse religions and their free exercise. How many Italians believe that the Bishops of Germany resemble them in their external government? They are comparing fir trees to tamarisk bushes. How many imagine that the Empire is a vast city? A certain Gentleman demanded if the Emperor had many villages.[83]

Contzen more concisely states the differences between the Italian and German church in the pithy marginal summary: "German Bishops are princes, Italians are not." [*Germaniae Episcopi principes sunt, non Itali.*][84] Indeed, that was the basic problem faced by the German bishops,

arising from distant regions and different customs. The Congregation, it should be noted, was not technically a court, and did not have any jurisdictional authority *per se*. Since it was charged with interpreting the decrees of Trent, however, its opinions more and more carried the force of law, an evolution which the papacy tried to formalize. See Lefebvre et al., *Les Sources*, 161f. The Concil Congregation became the main rival of the Rota. See *Lexikon für Theologie und Kirche* 5:1345, "Kardinalskongregationen."

[82] Robert Bireley, *The Counter-Reformation Prince. Anti-Machiavellianism or Catholic Statecraft in Early Modern Europe* (Chapel Hill: University of North Carolina Press, 1990).

[83] Hontheim, third edition, "Appendix Prima," ad V, §3. n. 7, 788. He quotes directly from Barthel, *Dissertatio Praeliminaris Historico-Publico-Canonica de Concordatis Germaniae ...* (Würzburg, 1740). The quotation is on page 115 of the second part, caput II, Sectio III, § iii. Hontheim and Barthel both miscite the passage as cap. 36.

[84] Contzen, 418.

for they felt that the drive toward systemization and uniformity based in Rome did not take into account the special conditions of the Empire.

Hontheim's critique – as that of the German canonists generally – claimed that the papacy asserted its universal jurisdiction over ecclesiastical courts to level and attack individual and regional privileges. In this he was entirely correct, for indeed the eighteenth-century papacy – especially under the reign of Benedict XIV – had re-invigorated its campaign against particularism. Much of the older scholarship on Febronius and history of German Catholicism tended to fall short on this, however, as it usually accepted its sources' claim that they were victims of a backward or hidebound Curial regime. Instead, the contentiousness and passion of the German movement was not the logical outgrowth of centuries of accumulated "gravamina," but rather a response to more immediate shifts in the Roman Catholic legal and administrative system.[85]

The immediate consequences and impact of Hontheim's publication of *de Statu Ecclesiae* can be recounted rather briefly. Soon after its appearance, translations appeared in several languages (including German, French, and Italian). Subsequent editions were published with additions. The first edition was placed on the Index, and many notable Catholic theologians penned refutations, such as the Jesuit F. A. Zaccaria's *Antifebronio*. Several prominent German theologians, notably Eusebius Amort and Martin Gerbert, were each suspected of being the author based on their earlier works, though both quickly repudiated the arguments of *de Statu*.[86] Under intense pressure, Hontheim recanted in 1778, though he later issued an "explanation" of his recantation that seemed to reconfirm his original arguments. *Febronianism* as an ideology took on a scope far broader that the actual issues raised by Hontheim's book.[87] The two stated concerns of *de Statu* were for a constitutional reform within the Catholic church (i.e., the restoration of the rights of the bishops), and for a reunion with Protestants. This latter goal became overwhelmed by the constitutional controversy within the German church and the international Catholic church. *Febronianism* came to imply the association with Jansenist and later, anti-clerical, Enlightenment ideas, and the evolution of the slogan

---

[85] Charles Lefebvre, Marcel Pacaut, and Laurent Chevailler, *L'époque moderne (1563–1789): les sources du droit et la seconde centralisation romaine* (Paris: Éditions Cujas, 1976).

[86] In 1761, Gerbert had published *De communione potestatis ecclesiasticae inter summos ecclesiae principes pontificem, & episcopos*, a work that was hardly an attack on papal privileges, but which did emphasize the sharing of power within the church.

[87] Volker Pitzer, "Febronius/Febronianismus," in *Theologisches Realenzyklopädie* (1983).

shows how ecclesiastical and religious-cultural politics became polarized by the end of the eighteenth century.

In terms of church politics, the most notable outcome of "Febronian" ideas in the Empire was the conference of the four German metropolitans – the archbishop-electors of Trier, Cologne, and Mainz, and the prince-archbishop of Salzburg – at the German spa town of Ems in 1786. They hoped to form a coalition against the exercise of jurisdictional authority by papal nuncios in the Empire.[88] Their 22-point statement capped more than a century of complaints about the authority of the nuncios ever since the establishment of the Cologne nunciature in 1643. These complaints had recently intensified following the establishment of a Munich nunciature in 1785. According to the Ems Punctuation, the nuncios should only be diplomatic representatives of the papal Curia to the Empire. They should not intrude into the ordinary jurisdiction of the German church hierarchy; they should not hear any appeals in their tribunals; marriage and other dispensations until now issued by the nuncios, as well as the special "faculties" (delegated pastoral powers), should now revert to the local bishops. Instead of the Concordat of Vienna (1448), the Ems document claimed that the principles of the Council of Basel and the Aschaffenburg agreements of 1439 and 1448 should be the rule for the Empire. Resignations "in favorem" (by which the holder of a benefice or church office could name his own successor) should be forbidden, and the minimum age for ordination to sub-deacon should be set at 22 years. The bishop's oath, as laid out in the Decretals of Gregory IX, was declared incompatible with the duties of an imperial prince. The Ems decrees repeated age-old calls to end annates and pallium taxes sent to Rome.[89] The political ambitions of each archbishop precluded any meaningful common action, especially because they did not have support of the other bishops of the Empire, who saw little benefit in

---

[88] This summary follows the entry by Leo Just in the *Lexikon für Theologie und Kirche*, vol. 3 (Freiburg: Herder, 1959). They met from July 25 to August 25. The result of the meeting was the so-called "Ems Punctuation." The 22 articles of the document were signed by the suffragan Bishop von Heimes for Mainz, the Augsburg vicar general J. L. Beck for Trier, the ecclesiastical councilor G. H. von Tautphaeus for Cologne, and the consistory councilor J. M. Boenicke for Salzburg.

[89] The signatories called on Emperor Joseph II for support. He delayed and finally answered on November 16, 1786 that the archbishops should come to agreements with their suffragans. Pius VI answered with a 426 page rebuttal published in 1789. The first to withdraw was Cologne Archbishop Clemens Wenzeslaus. With the outbreak of the French Revolution in 1789 the German archbishops pulled back from their innovations.

having papal "usurpations" replaced with increased control by their metropolitans.

Papal diplomats skillfully exploited differences among German sovereigns and prelates, and did not hesitate to turn to Prussia for help. Like the Empire itself, the constitution of the *Reichskirche* was eminently suited for factional politics and the dispersion of power; it did not aid in the creation of grand coalitions. More important for the actual legal and constitutional changes wrought by Febronianism was the way in which the dispute shaped the consciousness of a generation of German Catholics. For them, the struggle for control was nothing less than a struggle over the organizing principle of culture and society, of church and nation.

Finally, the coincidental fact that Hontheim's *de Statu* was published in 1763, the same year that the Seven Years' War came to an end, is worth considering. Coincidence it may have been, but this fact points toward two important developments in the Empire that were to decisively shape the German Catholic reform program. First, while the war had ended in a draw, it nevertheless settled once and for all the stability of Protestantism in the Empire and confirmed Prussia's status as a great power. No longer concerned with Habsburg aggression or the threat of re-Catholicization as a force for instability, German Protestants like Friedrich Carl Moser turned to questions about German unity and the character of the German nation.[90] More than anything else, exhaustion seemed to guarantee the peace.

The second related development to the aftermath of the Peace of Hubertusburg was the attempt on the part of the territorial states in the Empire to come to grips with the reality that modern warfare required modern finance and economic reorganization.[91] Prussia had already made great strides toward the complete mobilization of its economic and human resources in the interest of building up military power. The need to catch up prodded the major Catholic states in the Empire to look inward for sources of wealth. This meant, on the one hand, that the inherited religious wealth of the ecclesiastical foundations in, especially, Bavaria and the Habsburg territories, was no longer safe from the

---

[90] Moser, *Vom Teutschen Nationalgeist*. This point is suggested by W. R. Ward, *Christianity under the Ancien Régime, 1648–1789* (Cambridge and New York: Cambridge University Press, 1999). It should also be noted that Moser was paid by Joseph II.

[91] P.G.M. Dickson, *Finance and Government under Maria Theresia, 1740–1780*, 2 vols. (Oxford: Clarendon Press, 1987).

all-too-visible hand of the state. On the other hand, the drive toward fiscal and economic rationalization also set the major states qualitatively ahead of both the ecclesiastical states and the minor German secular principalities. This had the consequences that supporters of the major Catholic princes sought to revise their understanding of the prince's role as the *advocatus ecclesiae*. Moreover, Catholics and Protestants in the Empire began to question the viability of the ecclesiastical states given the rise of the newly powerful secular state. In other words, new conditions required a rethinking of the church in relationship to the state – as a concrete legal institution as well as an abstract concept – and to the Empire.

The following chapters will address this development by focusing on three particular themes: the question of the wealth of the clergy in relation to the state, the problem of ecclesiastical immunity (legal and fiscal) in German states, and the question of the fate of the ecclesiastical estates and their relationship to the German idea of liberty – both national and ecclesiastical.

3

The German Church and the Absolute State

True ecclesiastical and secular public law and the *Concordia sacerdotii et imperii* must be sought in the acts of Jesus, in the teaching of the apostles, and in the tradition of the church. This must teach us how the justification for both church and state – each in its proper boundaries – can exist next to each other without collision.

– Peter von Osterwald, 1766[1]

In the wake of the Seven Years' War, German states, Catholic and Protestant alike, needed to come to terms with the new fiscal and economic pressures brought about by modern war-fighting and modern bureaucracy. For Catholic states, this process required a wholesale rethinking of political theology. This rethinking occurred within the larger European intellectual context of the mutual redefinition of the church and the state. The development of legal, fiscal, and administrative tools and infrastructures in the eighteenth century represented an intensification of a process that had begun in the sixteenth century.[2] The conceptual elaboration of the state, as

---

[1] Veremund von Lochstein (Peter Osterwald), *Gründe sowohl für als wieder die Geistliche Immunität in zeitlichen Dingen* (Strasbourg, 1766), 195.

[2] P.G.M. Dickson, *Finance and Government under Maria Theresia, 1740–1780*, 2 vols. (Oxford: Clarendon Press, 1987); Michael Stolleis, *Geschichte des öffentlichen Rechts in Deutschland. 1: Reichspublizistik und Policeywissenschaft 1600–1800* (Munich: Beck, 1988); Dietmar Willoweit, *Rechtsgrundlagen der Territorialgewalt: Landesobrigkeit, Herrschaftsrechte und Territorium in der Rechtswissenschaft der Neuzeit* (Köln: Böhlau, 1975); Andreas Schwennicke, *"Ohne Steuer kein Staat." Zur Entwicklung und politischen Funktion des Steuerrechts in den Territorien des Heiligen Römischen Reichs (1500–1800)* (Frankfurt: Vittorio Klostermann, 1996); and Michael Stolleis, *Staatsdenker im 17. und 18. Jahrhundert: Reichspublizistik, Politik, Naturrecht*, second, expanded edition (Frankfurt am Main: A. Metzner, 1987).

Quentin Skinner has argued, marked something new in the history of early modern political thought. This new view of political life held that "our duties are owed exclusively to the state, rather than to a multiplicity of jurisdictional authorities, local as well as national, ecclesiastical as well as civil."[3] The emergence of this new idea of the state also required a new ideological justification, and conditions in Catholic Germany meant that the process of rethinking would occur somewhat differently than in other parts of Europe.[4] First, on account of the nominal sovereignty of the Emperor, German princes and their supporters made their claims in a more subtle rhetorical register, given that earlier elaborations of state supremacy in Western Europe had been articulated against Imperial claims. Second, Catholic dynasts whose families had sought legitimacy by claiming to protect the church needed to show how their actions – likely seen as disruptive of the church – were in fact a continuation of historical advocacy for the Catholic cause. The prevalence of these concerns serves to situate the ideological work eighteenth-century state ministers needed to do to justify their proceedings in the face of church opposition.

As part of this new justification, the language of utility became linked to claims of serving the common good. In itself, the turn toward utility was not that radical. However, state ministers and their supporters also sought to appropriate authority, functions, and, above all, wealth, that had previously been devoted to religious purposes. Partly, the states were motivated by a desire to rationalize resources for the purposes of warfare and state-building. Even if church property was not to be directly appropriated, the state would still benefit from taxing any increase in economic activity resulting from the liberation of ecclesiastical wealth. However, such practical and economic interest did not preclude a genuine desire to reform ecclesiastical institutions – notably in the fields of education and parish organization. Indeed, for most reformers, these programs went hand in hand. The conflicts over these programs of economic and legal reform recast the ways in which the state justified its authority over the church.

---

[3] This idea pervades his work, but a brief account is "From the State of Princes to the Person of the State," in *Visions of Politics. Volume 2: Renaissance Virtues* (Cambridge: Cambridge University Press, 2002). The quotation is from page 368.

[4] See, among others, Reinhart Koselleck, *Critique and Crisis: Enlightenment and the Pathogenesis of Modern Society* (Cambridge: MIT Press, 1988); Quentin Skinner, *The Foundations of Modern Political Thought*, 2 vols. (Cambridge: Cambridge University Press, 1978); and Gerhard Oestreich, *Neostoicism and the Early Modern State*, trans. David McLintock (Cambridge: Cambridge University Press, 1982).

Lay Catholic princes sought to justify their incursions into areas traditionally dominated by the ecclesiastical hierarchy, an especially delicate endeavor because the dynastic reputations of these lay lords rested on a commitment to the church. They therefore also appealed to new understandings of piety and devotion. These moves should not necessarily be seen cynically: one could properly attack as "superstition" or "outworn" practices and endowments even as the proceeds from abolishing them would accrue to the state (often to be redirected toward charity, education, or new parishes).[5]

In the eighteenth century, religious justifications for state power began to be supplanted by an emphasis on utilitarian definitions of the common good. This is not to say that princes and ministers universally rejected religion or the religious principles by which they had been raised. However, a generation that had been educated reading Pufendorf and Thomasius was ready to propound immanent and non-theological definitions of political authority. While certain conservatives, such as Anselm Desing (discussed below), would see this embrace of Protestant natural law theory as inherently anti-Catholic, there certainly was something in the theories of Pufendorf and Thomasius that had appeal to moderate Catholics.[6] By rethinking the church and the state in such a way that they could not touch each other, these moderate Catholic princes and ministers sought to open up room for maneuver so as to adapt both to new times.

THE POLITICAL ECONOMY OF GERMAN CATHOLICISM

Even if they bore the same external form, Catholic and Protestant states differed in their political theologies. This was a result of the Reformation and Counter-Reformation, and was rooted in the ways in which the different religious parties justified the role of the "prince" in reforming the church. Lutheran theology initially propagated the idea that the prince was the "emergency" bishop (*Notbischof*), and therefore stepped in to reform the church where the normal hierarchy had failed.[7]

---

[5] For a discussion of the process in sixteenth-century Protestant Germany, see Christopher Ocker, *Church Robbers and Reformers in Germany, 1525–1547: Confiscation and Religious Purpose in the Holy Roman Empire* (Leiden: Brill, 2006).

[6] Anselm Desing, *Juris Naturae Larva Detracta compluribus libris sub titulo Juris Naturae Prodeuntibus* (Munich: 1753).

[7] Which is not to say that this was Luther's original position, especially as put forth in his 1523 treatise on "weltlicher obrigkeit." Rather, it evolved over the course of the Reformation and subsequent years. See W. D. J. Cargill Thompson, *Political Thought of*

Subsequently, the prince, in Lutheran territories, was held to be the supreme bishop of the church. While, in principle, Reformed (i.e., Calvinist) church discipline placed the authority in the hands of the consistory, in practice, German Reformed territories – for example, the Palatinate – saw the prince assume the leading role in religious affairs. The political theology of Catholic states was different in the sixteenth and seventeenth centuries: the prince cast himself as the traditional "protector" of the church, which meant that he committed himself toward the preservation of the Catholic hierarchy. Of course, despite the rhetoric of pious cooperation, Catholic princes were often in conflict with both the local bishops and the Roman curia. Nevertheless, the Counter-Reformation alliance of church and state proved a useful convenience for both from the onset of the Reformation into the eighteenth century.

In response to Machiavelli's challenge that Christianity and politics were incompatible, theologians and political philosophers elaborated a theory whereby the prince did indeed serve the common good in a way that included the highest end, salvation. This ideology could function across confessional lines in a similar manner in the seventeenth century. However, it unraveled in quite different ways in Protestant and Catholic territories. This was mainly because the Lutheran prince, as *summepiscopus* did not need to wage the same type of institutional struggles as were required of his Catholic counterpart.

The classic Lutheran statement of the view of the prince as protector of true religion was Veit Ludwig von Seckendorff's *Teutscher Fürstenstaat*, originally published in 1656.[8] The purpose of princely government was the pursuit of the "common good and prosperity in spiritual and secular matters. The final end indeed of all human activities and deeds should be the honor of God, for which the human race was created." The authorities (*obrigkeit*) "which are God's deputies on Earth" are to see that the honor of God is secured in all things. They do this through the "loyal and diligent exercise of their office and vocation, which is appropriate to the

---

Martin Luther (Brighton, Sussex: Harvester Press, 1984); and Manfred Rudersdorf, "Die Generation der lutherischen Landesväter im Reich. Bausteine zu einer Typologie des deutschen Reformationsfürsten," in *Die Territorien des Reichs im Zeitalter der Reformation und Konfessionalisierung: Land und Konfession 1500–1650. Band 7: Bilanz, Forschungsperspektiven, Register*, Walter Ziegler and Anton Schindling, eds. (Münster: Aschendorff, 1997).

[8] Stolleis, *Staatsdenker im 17. und 18. Jahrhundert*, 148–71.

divine word as well as the natural and customary laws, all of which aim toward the promotion of spiritual and physical well-being."[9]

The German Counter-Reformation vision of the prince's role was aptly articulated by Adam Contzen (1573–1635), the Jesuit confessor to Maximilian I of Bavaria. According to Contzen, the state was not only to secure order and tranquility, but also to assure that its subjects achieved their higher ends, namely a Christian, moral life.[10] The purpose of state (*respublica*) is the happiness of each individual as well as the whole: "Beatitudo singulorum hominum, atq. Universae Reipublicae finis est."[11] The term *beatitudo* can be used in a mundane sense to imply happiness and well-being, but can also imply "blessedness." The state must assure that *felicitas* is not merely worldly, but reaches toward God. Accordingly, Contzen states "the earthly republic must not be separated from the church, but it is necessary that the heads of each be conjoined. For the natural good and moral virtues are not to be obtained without the aid of divine grace."[12] Indeed, the "civil magistrate is the advocate and defender of the priest [*sacerdotum*]."[13] In the eighth book, "*Potentia*," Contzen outlines the tools the prince needs, ranging from taxation, to fortresses, to the need to supervise the economy.[14] Above all, however, "the resources of the Republic consist in piety and virtues."[15] Contzen's political theory was constructed to justify a strong prince, but even the strongest means and tools were subordinated to the higher purpose of the state, which was inseparable from that of the church.[16]

---

[9] Veit Ludwig von Seckendorf, *Deutscher Fürstenstaat: samt d. Autors Zugabe sonderbarer u. wichtiger Materien*, seventh edition, *Verbessert, mit Anm., Summarien u. Reg. vers. von Andres Simson von Biechling* (Jena: 1737 (1656); reprint, Aalen: Scientia Verlag, 1972), 37–8.

[10] Contzen Lib. VI, C. III, §3, 337. Cf. Ernst-Albert Seils, *Die Staatslehre des Jesuiten Adam Contzen, Beichtvater Kurfürst Maximilian I. von Bayern* (Lübeck, Matthiesen, 1968), 51ff and Wolfgang Weber, *Prudentia gubernatoria: Studien zur Herrschaftslehre in der deutschen politischen Wissenschaft des 17. Jahrhunderts* (Tübingen: Niemeyer, 1992), 118.

[11] Contzen, Lib. II, C. II, §1, 63.

[12] Contzen, Lib. II, C. II, §5, 65. "Hinc sit, ut seperari non debeat terrena Respublica ab Ecclesia, sed oporteat summam esse utriusque coniunctionem. Neque naturale bonum quisquam obtinebit, & virtutes morales, sine divinioris gratiae adiutorio."

[13] Contzen, Lib. III, 3, 10, 330.

[14] Contzen, Lib. 8, C. XI, 570.

[15] Contzen, Lib. 8, 4, 1, 552. "Vires Reipublicae in pietate, & virtutibus consistunt." See Robert Bireley, *The Counter-Reformation Prince. Anti-Machiavellianism or Catholic Statecraft in Early Modern Europe* (Chapel Hill: University of North Carolina Press, 1990), 143.

[16] For a brief discussion of Contzen's position in relation to Spanish Scholasticism and the teachings of Robert Bellarmine, see Ernst-Albert Seils, *Die Staatslehre des Jesuiten Adam Contzen*, 56f. See also F. X. Arnold, *Die Staatslehre des Kardinals Bellarmine*

There were two very different models of the Catholic state. First, the *geistlichen Stifte* were the territories under the secular jurisdiction of the Imperial bishops (as well as a few large abbies). Second, there were principalities with lay lords,[17] of which the Bavarian and the Habsburg territories were the most prominent.[18] These two different models of lordship were put under pressure by the problems that accompanied the rise of the modern state.

This new view of the role of the state with respect to religion can be glimpsed in the work of one of the foremost "cameralist" writers of the day, Johann Heinrich Gottlob Justi (1717–1771).[19] Not unlike political writers from previous generations, Justi emphasized that good morals (*Sitten*) were needed for the strength of the state. "The moral conditions of the subjects forms one of the most important objects of policy," Justi wrote in his 1760 *Die Grundfeste zu der Macht und Glückseligkeiten der Staaten, oder ausführliche Vorstellung der gesamten Polizeiwissenschaft.*[20] A chief concern for the monarch, however, was to pay close attention to his role as a secular ruler, leaving aside questions of religion that did not affect his worldly rule and responsibilities. Justi defined the goal (*Endzweck*) of civil (as opposed to ecclesiastical or religious) society: "religion is not the final purpose of men, when they join together in a civil society. Their goal with this act is solely directed toward temporal felicity. On the other hand, religion has an entirely different purpose, namely eternal felicity."[21] Justi voiced an idea that had its

(Munich, 1934); on the Spanish Scholastics, see Skinner, *The Foundations of Modern Political Thought.*

[17] "Principality" is used here as a generic term. The "prince" could be an elector, a duke, and so forth.

[18] It should be emphasized that the Catholic territories did not develop along any uniform path in the wake of the Reformation. Those territories that remained in the "old faith" engaged the process of internal reform and revival in very different ways. See Walter Ziegler, "Altgläubige Territorien im Konfessionalisierungsprozess," in *Die Territorien des Reichs im Zeitalter der Reformation und Konfessionalisierung: Land und Konfession 1500–1650. Band 7: Bilans, Forschungsperspektiven, Register* (Münster: Aschendorf, 1997). For a brief overview of Bavaria and the Counter-Reformation, see Walter Ziegler, "Bayern," in *Die Territorien des Reichs im Zeitalter der Reformation und Konfessionalisierung: Land und Konfession 1500–1650. Band 1: Der Südosten,* Walter Ziegler and Anton Schindling, eds. (Münster: Aschendorff, 1989).

[19] Keith Tribe, *Governing Economy. The Reformation of German Economic Discourse 1750–1840* (Cambridge: Cambridge University Press, 1988).

[20] Johann Heinrich Gottlob Justi, *Die Grundfeste zu der Macht und Glückseligkeiten der Staaten, oder ausführliche Vorstellung der gesamten Polizeiwissenschaft,* 2 vols. (Königsberg and Leipzig: 1760; reprint, Aalen: Scientia Verlag, 1965), 21.

[21] Ibid., vol. 2, book 9, 15.

immediate roots in Pufendorf and Thomasius.[22] There was of course a longer history to this idea, especially with regard to the claims of temporal power and wealth of the church. Much of the language could be found in various mutations reaching back to Marsilius of Padua. The idea that "civil society" was to be distinguished from "religious society" was one of the most powerful intellectual tools of the nascent early modern state in its efforts to draw a restrictive boundary around religious institutions, and therefore is hardly novel in Justi's book. Indeed, its appearance in Justi's work – directed toward use in the university and in state administrations – shows that it had become commonplace.

Justi's work and the theories behind it were not particular to Catholic or Protestant states. This indeed seems to be one of the most significant developments in German political thought in the eighteenth century. The withering away of religious justifications for the exercise of state power also brought a certain confessional leveling in the perceptions of the state. These new ideas and justifications for the state had permeated certain segments of German Catholic political thought.

Accompanying this declining zeal for defending the Catholic hierarchy was the view that elements of the Catholic religion were themselves a drain on the economy, and therefore on the basic power of the state. This, at least, was the view put forward by a pseudonymous pamphlet that has been attributed to Johann Adam Ickstatt (1702–1776), a Bavarian minister and educational reformer.[23] Writing as Christian Friedrich Menschenfreund, Ickstatt raised the following question in the title of his essay: *Why is the Wealth of the Protestant Lands so much greater than in the Catholic Lands?*[24] Ickstatt professes that he was raised to believe in the church, but that the church does not teach that one must hold that Catholicism is the most useful (*erträglich*) for the

---

[22] See, among others, Ian Hunter, *Rival Enlightenments: Civil and Metaphysical Philosophy in Early Modern Germany* (Cambridge: Cambridge University Press, 2001).

[23] On Ickstatt see Karl A. Schleunes, *Schooling and Society: the Politics of Education in Prussia and Bavaria 1750–1900* (Oxford: Oxford University Press, 1989); Fritz Kreh, *Leben und Werk des Reichsfreiherrn Johann Adam von Ickstatt: 1702–1776; ein Beitrag zur Staatslehre der Aufklärungszeit* (Paderborn: Schöningh, 1974); Gerhard Wilczek, "Johann Adam Freiherr von Ickstatt und die Hohe Schule zu Ingolstadt," *Ingolstädter Heimatblätter* 32, no. 1 (1969); and Notker Hammerstein, *Aufklärung und katholisches Reich. Untersuchungen zur Universtitätsrefrom und Politik katholischer Territorien des Heiligen Römischen Reichs deutscher Nation im 18. Jahrhundert* (Berlin: Dunker & Humblot, 1977).

[24] Christian Friedrich Menschenfreund [Ickstatt, Johann A.], *Untersuchung der Frage: Warum ist der Wohlstand der protestantischen Länder so gar viel größer als der catholishen?* (Salzburg und Freisingen, 1772).

state.[25] Indeed, he notes, it seems that among the Christian peoples, the Protestants seem to be the better-off.[26] Ickstatt declares:

The Catholic religion is the cause of this. No one will deny it. Only the reasons remain to be explained. For we share with these people [the Protestants] the same five senses, and their rulers have the same rights in secular matters as ours. Between us there are no other differences than those of religion. Therefore it follows that it is only religion that can be at the source of such a great difference in wealth [*Wohlstand*].[27]

Ickstatt justifies this claim with the argument that the trappings of Catholicism are a drag on the economy and that monastic foundations, chapels, pilgrimages, and the other expenses of Catholic devotion remove money from circulation. Moreover, Protestants must work harder because they do not have the option of placing their children in cloisters. Fasting can be expensive, especially in Southern Germany, where the fish has to be imported from Hamburg, England, Norway, and Holland.[28]

Two central aspects that arise from Catholic doctrine come in for special rebuke. First, he criticizes the belief in purgatory. Ickstatt argues that the dying Catholic, filled with the fear of final judgment at the last moments of life, can only hope that additional gifts to the clergy and charitable foundation earn him eternal rest. This money then does not go to one's wife and children. Ickstatt is not opposed to the idea of charity per se, as he praised the Protestant foundations. It is rather the supposed haphazardness induced by the fear of death that he criticizes.[29]

The second major element of Catholicism that is seen as hindering economic development are the institutions of celibacy and monasticism:

How many more happy subjects would our Catholic Princes have, if the monks and nuns had not sworn off the sacrament of holy matrimony? What power would these princes then not have against the Protestants? How many armies could we not form out of our monks? How many upstanding housewives would our nuns not therefore supply? How many scholars, merchants, manufactures, artists, artisans and farmers would we then not find among their children?[30]

---

[25] Ickstatt, 3.
[26] Ibid., 7–8.
[27] Ibid., 7.
[28] Ibid., 9–20.
[29] Ibid., 46–7.
[30] Ibid., 85.

Ickstatt here articulates a common criticism of the role of monastic institutions and clerical celibacy in the economic life of the state.[31] The ideas articulated here had been important in the wave of monastic reforms and suppressions starting in the 1760s and 1770s throughout Catholic Europe, and would only sharpen as the century progressed.[32] The discussion of the types of wealth appropriate to church institutions was therefore not merely theoretical. Moreover, while Ickstatt and, as we shall see, Osterwald were concerned in the short run with the place of Catholic institutions within the territorial state (i.e., not with the *reichsunmittelbar* ecclesiastical states), their questions aimed at a core problem in the question of church wealth. At stake was an essential element of the settlement of 1648. This settlement had tried to resolve the disputes over the ownership of church property. After all, it was Ferdinand II's Edict of Restitution (1629), aimed at reversing Protestant seizures of church property since 1555, that had galvanized Protestant powers to fight the emperor and assured that the Thirty Years' War would assume the intensity that it did. As the Secularization of 1803 would bear out, however, the legal guarantees of Church property set out at Westphalia provided a latitude that proved fatal once Catholic sovereigns lost the political will to assure the security of property for ecclesiastical institutions.[33] At stake in the debate over amortization and the wealth of the Church was the legitimacy of a certain type of Catholicism, and consequently of a certain type of society.[34]

---

[31] For a recent overview of the importance of monastic institutions in Catholic Europe, see Derek Beales, *Prosperity and Plunder: European Catholic Monasteries in the Age of Revolution, 1650–1815* (Cambridge: Cambridge University Press, 2003).

[32] In the Habsburg lands, for example, at least 600 monastic houses were dissolved under Joseph II. See Dickson, *Finance and Government under Maria Theresia*, vol. 1, 77. On the Austrian Church reforms, see Derek Beales, *Joseph II: In the Shadow of Maria Theresa, 1741–1780* (Cambridge: Cambridge University Press, 1987); Harm Klueting, ed., *Der Josephinismus: ausgewählte Quellen zur Geschichte der theresianisch-josphinischen Reformen* (Darmstadt: Wissenschaftliche Buchgesellschaft, 1995); Ferdinand Maass, ed., *Der Josephinismus, Quellen zu seiner Geschichte in Österreich 1760–1850,* 5 vols. (Vienna: Verlag Herold, 1951–1961); and Helmut Reinalter, *Der Josephinismus: Bedeutung, Einflüsse und Wirkungen* (Frankfurt am Main, New York: Peter Lang, 1993).

[33] Rudolfine Freiin von Oer, "Der Eigentumsbegriff in der Säkularisationsdiskussion am Ende des Alten Reichs," in *Eigentum und Verfassung. Zur Eigentumsdiskussion im ausgehenden 18. Jahrhundert,* Rudolf Vierhaus, ed., *Veröffentlichung des Max-Planck-Instituts für Geschichte 37* (Göttingen: Vandenhoeck & Ruprecht, 1972).

[34] It should be kept in mind that the attack on monastic wealth was often quite separate from questions of income and endowments for diocesan clergy and parishes. Indeed, it was proposed that the financial need of the secular clergy be met by reapportioning wealth from monastic institutions (and of course the endowment of the suppressed

ECCLESIASTICAL IMMUNITIES AND STATE TAXATION

"Sine tributis nullus status" [Without taxation there is no state]

– Justus Lipsius[35]

In 1766, the Bavarian Ecclesiastical Councilor Peter von Osterwald (1717–1778) unleashed a heated public discussion concerning the authority of the state over the temporal goods of the church with a treatise entitled *Veremund von Lochstein's Gründe sowohl für als wieder die Geistliche Immunität in zeitlichen Dingen* [*Veremund von Lochstein's Reasons for and against Ecclesiastical Immunity in Temporal Matters*].[36] Osterwald's tract became a touchstone for a set of issues regarding the interaction of temporal and secular power.

Osterwald's responsibilities as a government minister meant that his treatise essentially put forward the state's position in its assault on the accumulated temporal privileges of the church in Bavaria. Osterwald, who had converted to Catholicism as a young man, studied in Halle, Leipzig, Jena, and Strasbourg, was briefly a Benedictine novice before leaving the order and becoming a tutor in Augsburg. After serving in the cabinet of Bishop Johann Theodor of Freising and Regensburg, Osterwald was ennobled and became a privy councilor in the government of the Hochstift of Freising. In 1761, Osterwald entered the service of Elector Maximilian III Joseph of Bavaria. He was an important founding member of the Bavarian Academy of Sciences, and eventually became a lay director of the Ecclesiastical Council (*Geistlicher Rat*) in 1768.[37] The Bavarian Ecclesiastical Council made great strides toward increasing state control over the church, especially in civil jurisdiction over marriage, amortization laws, control over religious orders, censorship, education, and the reduction of feast days.[38]

Society of Jesus). The question was, what political or legal entity had the right and the authority to carry out such reforms.

[35] Lipsius, *Politica*, 1589, Antwerp, lib. II, cap. XI, 114. Cited in Schwennicke, *"Ohne Steuer kein Staat." Zur Entwicklung und politischen Funktion des Steuerrechts in den Territorien des Heiligen Römischen Reichs* (1500–1800), 129.

[36] Peter Osterwald, *Veremund von Lochstein. Gründe sowohl für als wieder die Geistliche Immunität in zeitlichen Dingen* (Strasbourg, 1766). A second edition was published in 1767 with minor changes. Because the libraries I used had different editions, I will quote from both the first and second edition. To my knowledge, they are essentially the same, yet for accuracy's sake, I will note when I am using the second edition.

[37] The council had both lay and clerical members. On the council, see Richard Bauer, *Der kurfürstliche gesitliche Rat und die bayerische Kirchenpolitik, 1768–1802* (Munich: 1972).

[38] Biographisch-Bibliographisch Kirchenlexikon VI (1993), 1319–22. See also *Lexikon für Theologie und Kirche* 7, 1284–5.

Osterwald's treatise is divided into two sections of unequal length. The first section purports to lay out the reasons for ecclesiastical immunities and the second section explains the reasons against. As is to be expected, however, Osterwald undermines the reasons for immunity even in the first section. He starts by noting that if one accepts the premises of papal bulls and canon law, then there can be no question that the territorial lord could ever exercise authority over the temporal goods of the church.[39] He separates ecclesiastical goods into three types: in the first order are church buildings, vestments, holy vessels, and other things "which through consecration and benediction are tools dedicated to worship." To the second group belongs the temporal goods of churches and benefices which are not consecrated or blessed, the income of which however the "blessed donors" willed toward the support of the church, its hierarchy and servants, "and that which remains should be given to the poor." This second category also includes the tithe, sacrifices, and stole fees. The third category of ecclesiastical goods (*Patrimonialen*) belongs to ecclesiastical persons not because of their relationship to the church, but rather according to their secular title (inheritance, purchase, etc.) The income a priest receives from his ecclesiastical benefice would belong to the second category, whereas wealth he inherits from a relative would fall into this third category of purely personal property.[40] Osterwald's categories of church property are fairly standard, though the categories themselves do not matter as much as the results one draws from them.

Osterwald states that the canonists teach that all three types of ecclesiastical property are immune from secular jurisdiction.[41] When the secular authorities wanted to tax or otherwise exercise authority over ecclesiastical goods, express permission of the pope was required. So stated, at least, the Bull *In coena domini*. This Bull was read every year on Holy Thursday (hence the title, "At the Lord's Supper"). In it, the pope reserved the right of absolution for those who – among other infractions – assaulted church property.[42] As the Bull was a source of tension, it was often not allowed to be published in Gallican France. Perhaps the most contentious element of the Bull was the automatic excommunication it proclaimed (*latae sententiae* – "a sentence already imposed") on those

---

[39] Osterwald, second edition, 1, §1, 3.
[40] Osterwald, second edition, 1, §3, 5.
[41] Osterwald, second edition, 1, §4, 5.
[42] The practice dated back to the fourteenth century. The Bull had assumed it final formulation with Urban VIII in 1627. See *Lexikon für Theologie und Kirche* 1:32.

who violated church property. By reserving to himself the right to absolve, the pope in essence assured that he would make final decisions concerning exceptions. In fact, state taxation of church property was quite common. At issue was whether the state needed to get authorization from the papacy before it levied taxes. As with Old Regime law in general, the right to grant privileges and exceptions was often the most powerful tool a secular or ecclesiastical authority could possess. Two issues therefore lay at stake: first was the question of whether the state needed permission from the church at all to make use of temporal property, and second, whether the state needed permission from the pope, a local bishop, or simply the user of the property in question. Thus the question was not just about relations between the church and the state, but about the constitution of authority *within* the church as well.

While papal rhetoric was forceful, in practice the state did tax the church on a regular basis. Osterwald outlines the canonists' line of reasoning in justifying this taxation. First, a great need must be demonstrated that affects both secular and ecclesiastical estates, such as an attack by enemies or a heretical movement which threatens to overturn the state. Second, the wealth of the secular estates must be insufficient to cover the need. Consequently, the property of these secular estates must be examined to determine that they do not have enough to meet the emergency. The judgment about the emergency need of the state must be left to the bishops and clergy, and they must deliberate about it; it is not enough for the prince and his ministers to say there is a need. Some canonists, Osterwald writes, argue that the bishop and all the clergy must deliberate, others that just the bishop and his chapter must agree. This condition can be problematic, Osterwald notes, when territorial and diocesan boundaries do not coincide, since those chapter members in the land concerned will want to give money, but probably not the others; thus the prince is obliged to accept anything at all with gratitude, recognizing it as a free gift.[43] In order to ensure that the contribution occurs without any coercion, it must be executed by the bishop, not by secular authorities. The pope must consent, and although he formally requires the agreement of the bishop, in practice the pope's consent alone is all that is needed.[44]

Osterwald notes that the canonists make no exceptions to these conditions, except in the case of extreme emergency. When danger is imminent and there is not time to receive consent from the pope or bishop,

[43] Osterwald, second edition, 3, §2–4, 31.
[44] Osterwald, second edition, 3, §6, 33.

secular princes may presume that church officials would not be opposed to the action.[45] In this, Osterwald argues:

it seems to us as if the interpreters of ecclesiastical laws contradict themselves, and do not follow their own principles. For they seem to admit that ecclesiastics, at least in certain cases, are legally obliged to be taxed for the common good. But this can only be interpreted to mean that they are indeed part of the general community [*gemeinen Wesens*].[46]

This admission, Osterwald contends, undermines the canonists' own arguments for ecclesiastical immunity from secular authority. For they claim that ecclesiastics form a separate society; even if they do contribute to the secular authorities, they do so out of free will, not out of obligation. If the clergy is not subjected to the secular authority, then at no time may that authority impose its will in them. Yet by acknowledging that in times of crisis the state may impose taxes on the clergy without the prior consent of the bishops or pope, the canonists also recognize a higher natural law to which ecclesiastical and lay society alike are subjected.

Osterwald concludes:

once one admits that the clergy are member of the general community, natural law completes the argument to show that they are obliged to promote the happiness and welfare of the secular state just like other members, no matter how great or small the need, and no matter the circumstances.[47]

This passage is very significant, for Osterwald makes his point in the first part of the treatise, where he is supposedly laying out the reasons *for* ecclesiastical immunity, and claims to derive the arguments from the texts of the canon lawyers. Here, by showing that the canonists make an exception in case of emergency, he argues that they have undermined their position by an appeal to natural law. For if immediate need requires that the canon law of the church (as regards proper procedure) be suspended, then the canonists admit there is a higher law governing the situation. Osterwald and like-minded thinkers would build the case for state supremacy over the temporal goods of the church on this principle of natural law.

Osterwald next pursues the implications of the fact that, despite the clergy's supposed immunity, there do exist taxes on church property even when there is not apparent or immediate danger. In Bavaria, he notes, it is

[45] Osterwald, second edition, 3, §7, 33.
[46] Osterwald, second edition, 3, §7, 33
[47] Osterwald, second edition, 3, §7, 33.

known that the *Prälatenstand* pays as much in normal taxes (*ordentlichen Landsteuern*) as the other estates. The secular clergy pay taxes on property that belong to their benefices, which in principle belong to the second class of ecclesiastical goods mentioned above.[48] He observes that no mass excommunications – as threatened by *In coena domini* – have taken place. By pursuing clerical claims *ad absurdum*, Osterwald hopes to overturn their fundamental assertion that the church was not only separate from the rest of society, but that its interests were necessarily of a higher order than secular institutions.

The second section of *Veremund von Lochstein* lays out the reasons *against* ecclesiastical immunities in temporal matters. The arguments that Osterwald musters are very similar to those discussed in the previous chapter on Hontheim's *de Statu*, yet he goes further in that he is concerned not only with authority within the church hierarchy, but also with the relationship between secular and ecclesiastical law. Osterwald states that the canonists' position on immunity assumes that the pope and councils have a law-giving power which is set over the secular lords.[49] Yet, he continues, "according to the principles of French and other canonists, who are as Catholic as ours as well as those on the other side of the mountains," papal constitutions, decrees of councils, and so forth, which extend to the dominion of the church over temporal things, have no binding power on secular states. Ecclesiastical immunity is not derived from "divine law," but rather from "positive human law" in the sense that those immunities which the church possesses are the result of privileges granted by the secular rulers. These privileges, however, were granted "as far as the rulers could and willed, and insofar as no disadvantage to their states or their successors developed from them."[50]

An essential part of Osterwald's argument is that both secular and spiritual power should be entirely separate (an assertion, however, in which the determination of boundaries was highly contested). Neither is dependant on the other in those areas proper to their authority: "there are two powers by which humans in this world are ruled, namely the spiritual [*geistliche*] and secular."[51] Dominating this assertion is the theme that the state is now recovering authority which it had lost to the clergy, a point which is backed up by historical examples and the usual references to the

[48] Osterwald, 35.
[49] Osterwald, 52.
[50] Osterwald, 56.
[51] Osterwald, 57.

early church. Osterwald states that "with regard to its main task, the secular power has always stayed within its boundaries. Only the spiritual authority has overstepped its bounds. One cannot deny that the secular princes are in good part themselves to blame." First, Osterwald faults secular powers for granting exemptions to the clergy in civil courts; once given this little bit, the clergy kept on grabbing more. Second, the clergy was unreasonably enriched which then allowed it to take a large part in state affairs and make the secular authority fear it. Third, the princes entrusted clergy with important court service since lay people were not able to handle the tasks. Finally, the princes were too submissive, and too subject to "the gruesome ignorance and superstition of the middle centuries."[52]

In making assertions about secular power, Osterwald also defines what he means by spiritual authority. So there will be no confusion, Osterwald lays out his own understanding of ecclesiastical authority. "As for the sovereignty of the spiritual powers, we do not mean despotic authority, as if it were bound by no laws. Rather, we mean that in the exercise of its authority it depends on no other worldly authority."[53] Furthermore, Osterwald argues, one may say that the church is a sovereign power set above the state, but this is only true as far as its spiritual function. This does not abolish the sovereignty of the state in temporal matters, since the state does not allow the church to step in on its functions. With regard to the temporal goods of the church [*Temporalien*], the state "regards it as a private community, or as a *collegium* [society] within the state."[54] Osterwald's interest is in drawing a clear line between church and state, though when it came to so called "mixed" affairs, the state was given priority. Therefore religious ceremonies or practices which could be seen to adversely affect the economy (like pilgrimages or feast days) were considered as falling under the jurisdiction of the state.[55]

In the first section of *Veremund von Lochstein* Osterwald had tried to show that the canonists' arguments would fall apart under their own weight. In the second section, Osterwald tackles a different problem when he notes that the canon law *per se* should only be valid as the private law of the Church. Although states and princes have had canon law taught at

[52] "Gräuliche Ignoranz und und Superstition der mittleren Jahrhunderten." Osterwald, 61.
[53] Osterwald, 58, footnote.
[54] Osterwald, 179.
[55] Karl Hausberger and Benno Hubensteiner, *Bayerische Kirchengeschichte* (Munich: Süddeutscher Verlag, 1985), 256

their universities, and have even let it take the place of Roman law in civil courts, they have done so only out of expedience. The acceptance of certain canonical principles and laws in civil courts does not, according to Osterwald, imply a general submission to canon law or an admission that canon law stands over civil laws. Osterwald distinguishes *jus canonicum* – the private law of church – from a more general *jus publicum ecclesiastico-seculare* [ecclesiastical and secular public law].[56] Although Osterwald claims that he seeks only to restore church and state to their proper boundaries, he must appeal to religious authority to make his point:

> true ecclesiastical and secular public law and the *Concordiam sacerdotii et imperii* [Concordance of sacred and secular authority] must be sought in the acts of Jesus, in the teaching of the apostles, and in the tradition of the church. This must teach us how the justification for both church and state – each in its proper boundaries – can exist next to each other without collision.[57]

Those things which are contrary to these boundaries, he continues, whether through ignorance, false conceptions, or prejudice, are abuses.[58] Osterwald argues that the clergy's claim to the tithe from divine law is based on the biblical injunction that the Levites should get a tenth of the harvest. He suggests that this was reasonable at the time because the Levites, after all, were one of the 12 tribes, so this was more or less a proportional amount. However, in addition to the tithe, the clergy also receives gifts, stole fees, and other payments. These possessions it does not claim by right of divine law. In some lands, Osterwald continues, ecclesiastical property may amount to as much as a third of all landed property, while the clergy only amount to 1% of the population. In such a situation, the clergy is given more in temporal goods than the Levites.[59]

Osterwald's core legal argument is that those immunities that the Church possessed were granted by the state, implying that what the state granted, the state could also take away. He writes: "clerical immunity in temporal matters had its roots nowhere else but in the civil laws of the first Christian emperors, and these [immunities] stretched no farther than the exemption of clerical persons from civil jurisdiction."[60] He continues that the main benefit of their immunity was that the clergy was freed from

[56] Osterwald, 196.
[57] Osterwald, 195.
[58] Osterwald, 195–6.
[59] Osterwald, 246.
[60] Osterwald, 238.

"extraordinary and disdainful service toward the community."[61] In other words, the State granted exemptions out of its concern for the common good. According to theological justifications for ecclesiastical wealth, after the needs of the clergy had been met surplus income from church property was to go to the poor. While the clergy clearly did enjoy the surplus income, this could not be said to come from divine law: "divine law only provides for the reasonable upkeep of the clergy. Everything that they possess beyond that – since it no longer belongs to the poor – can only be by right of human law."[62] Therefore the clergy must follow the dictates of the civil law like all the other citizens.

In earlier times the state did not tax the Church because it would only be taking money from the poor. If the clergy now keeps the surplus wealth for itself, then the state has no interest in protecting this accumulation, especially since there are poorer members of society who are being taxed. It is unfair for the burdens of state – which are fixed – to be disproportionably distributed.[63] Taxes on Church property – when there is a surplus beyond the immediate needs of the clergy – are well within the bounds of reason, he claims. Osterwald pushes this conclusion even farther to suggest that the common good is harmed by a buildup of ecclesiastical property. He states:

History shows us that morals were never more decayed than in those times when the pious foundations [*milden Stiftungen*] were at their most frequent. And we see today many countries that have plenty of gold and silver in their ornate churches, but so much the less in private houses. They are rich in church treasures, but very poor in people and money, and – which is the most irritating – they are very poor in Christian virtues.[64]

While he does not overtly advocate that the clergy should be stripped of its wealth, he does note that the desire to return the church to its early poverty is a "pious wish" [*pia desideria*].[65]

As the passages quoted above indicate, Osterwald's argument is built upon a subtle but significant shift in the concept of "common good." While the state did not tax church property in earlier times out of a concern for general well-being, times had changed so that the taxation of church property at the present time would in effect benefit the public. Having rejected the principle that ecclesiastical immunities derive from

---

[61] "Verächtlichen und außerordentlichen Diensten." Osterwald, 238.
[62] Osterwald, 260.
[63] Osterwald, 260–1.
[64] Osterwald, 245.
[65] Osterwald, 259.

canon law, Osterwald places the power to determine the scope of public good in the hands of secular authorities. Given the obvious wealth of monastic institutions and other ecclesiastical foundations, it was not too much of a leap for the state to try to redistribute ecclesiastic wealth.

Much of what Osterwald puts forward here – at least with regard to the relative limits of church and state authority – is directly indebted to the Gallican Bossuet and de Marca. Moreover, his arguments are in line with the development of European political and religious thought since before the Reformation. To a certain extent, his ideas rely on arguments put forth by Marsilius of Padua and by theologians and canonists writing in the wake of the Franciscan poverty dispute.[66] Why did his tract create such a stir when it appeared, given that many of Osterwald's complaints arose from age-old questions about the privileges of the church. His focus on ecclesiastical immunities from civil jurisdiction was part of an attempt to legitimize the increasing economic and political pressure that state authorities – and specifically Bavarian authorities – were putting on church institutions and church wealth. Yet the tract was also read in *stiftische* Germany, where political, economic, and ecclesiastical conditions were very different from those in Bavaria. The general public interest in *Veremund von Lochstein* was in large part due to a growing conception that the apparent wealth of the church no longer served an appropriate function. Yet this conviction depended on certain ideas about common good and church organization, not to mention the question of the role the state should play in reforming the church. The question of reform was pursued on different levels. Of immediate concern was the need to pay priests and to organize diocese properly. Even where the state wanted to step in and take over from either the bishops or the pope, these reforming efforts were often undertaken by ministers with religious aims. On a larger level, however, the amount of ecclesiastical wealth led many to question not just its redistribution for church purposes, but also whether a religious organization had any right to such wealth.

"IS THE WEALTH OF PRIESTS HARMFUL TO THE STATE?"[67]

The question of the potential damage of ecclesiastical wealth was brought to the fore by a second pamphlet, this time by the pseudonymous Johann

---

[66] See Francis Oakley, *The Western Church in the Later Middle Ages* (Ithaca: Cornell University Press, 1979).

[67] Anselm Desing, *Opes Sacerdotii Num Reipublicae Noxiae? Ex Rerum Natura, Sana Politica et Communi Sensu Generis Humani Examinatum*, 1753. Also in German:

Georg Neuberg's 1768 *Abhandlung von den Einkünften der Klöster und dem Amortizationsgesetze* [*Treatise on the income of the cloisters and the amortization laws*].[68] The author of this pamphlet, who may have been Osterwald, or possibly his successor at the ecclesiastical council Anton Eisenreich, sought to defend the Bavarian amortization law of 1764, the goal of which had been to limit monastic wealth and indeed to claim some of that wealth for the state.[69]

While the following section deals with the debate over ecclesiastical wealth in Bavaria and attempts by the electors to claim part of the vast wealth of ecclesiastical institutions – notably through amortization laws and the suppression of monasteries – the issue of amortization was not restricted to Bavaria. In the prince-bishoprics, even the bishops themselves did not necessarily have free power over collating benefices or even rearranging church wealth due to legal restrictions on ecclesiastical property.[70] Thus the overall issue was one in which secular and ecclesiastical authorities felt that the wealth of the church was constrained and tied up by an inherited political and legal system that was no longer appropriate to the times. Proponents of amortization laws continually decried the fact that land and money given to ecclesiastical institutions was in the "dead hand" of the church. This phrase could be colored according to one's interests and particular concern: in a more restricted sense, property willed to the church in earlier centuries was still controlled by the testament of a long-dead benefactor. Accordingly, reformers tried to argue that the pious wishes of earlier generations should be respected in spirit, but not literally. The key to this argument was the assertion that piety manifested itself differently over time: a nobleman who left an endowment for masses would today rather fund a hospital or educational institution. More broadly, the "dead hand" of the church was

---

Staatsfrage: Sind die Güter und Einkünfte der Geistlichkeit dem Staate schädlich oder nicht? Beantwortet und Lochstein und Neubergern entgegen gesetzt (Munich, 1768).

[68] *Johann Georg Neubergers juris utriusque licentiate Abhandlung von den Einkünften der Klöster und dem Amortizationsgesetze*, 1768. See also the third edition, 1769. I cite both the first and third editions because different libraries had only one or the other edition. Citations from the third edition enclosed in brackets.

[69] Bauer and Andreas Kraus, "Probleme der bayerischen Staatskirchenpolitik," in *Katholische Aufklärung – Aufklärung im katholischen*, Kleuting, ed. (Hamburg: Meiner, 1993), 130 list Eisenreich (1735–1793) as the author of the pamphlet, while others trace it to Osterwald.

[70] The Prince-Bishopric of Mainz passed a particularly strong amortization law in 1746. T. C. W. Blanning, *Reform and Revolution in Mainz, 1743–1803* (Cambridge: Cambridge University Press, 1974), 104.

regretted by reformers because they saw a certain portion of the national wealth removed from commerce – both literally, on account of the inability for holders of church offices to sell the land ("alienate"), and metaphorically because church institutions were seen as promoters of laziness and inactivity. In this latter sense, the "dead hand" of the church was holding back national prosperity.

In today's usage, amortization normally refers to the extinguishing of debt or loan. However, it was used quite differently in medieval Europe. Feudal lords were normally entitled to a variety of payments and taxes when tenures and fiefs changed hands. These payments could vary significantly, and they were by no means as predictable as other taxes. Yet when tenants died or sold their leases, the lord could expect some type of payment. Once property passed to the church, however, the lord lost forever his right to collect these dues. This was, first of all, because the church, as a moral person (as opposed to a physical person), was immortal. Second, church law did not allow the alienation of its property, so once it possessed certain lands, they could not be sold, and therefore feudal lords could not collect the payments which would normally accrue to transfers. The lord could try to reduce his losses by limiting tenure to a year and a day or by fictively placing the tenure in the hands of a living person, upon whose death certain dues were to be paid. A third practice was amortization, whereby the lord was paid a certain sum as indemnity against future losses in return for the lord's consent that the property was now in mortmain.[71]

Postmedieval amortizations, on the other hand, were an invention of absolutism. French lawyers devised a theory whereby it was argued that an ancient law prohibited ecclesiastical institutions from acquiring property, but that the king could grant exceptions. These would of course require payment: the French monarchy was thereby able to retroactively tax the vast ecclesiastical wealth of the realm. In a declaration of 1639, a slate of "nonpaid amortizations" was announced, and in 1689 payment of 18 million *livres* was demanded on amortization considered 43 years in arrears.[72] These laws continued to be strengthened in the eighteenth

---

[71] According to the *Dictionaire de Droit Canonique*, medieval amortizations were seen as the rights of seigneurs and were enacted only by monarchs insofar as they were also seigneurs, and not necessarily for the entirety of their realm. "Amortissement," *Dictionnaire de droit canonique*, R. Naz, ed. (Paris: Letouzey et Ané, 1935–1965), 468–71.

[72] Ibid., 470–1 and John McManners, *Church and Society in eighteenth-century France*, 2 vols. (Oxford: Oxford University Press, 1998), vol. 1, 142. See Jean Tournyol de Clos, *Les amortissements de la propriété ecclésiastique sous Louis XIII, 1639–1640* (Paris: M. Giard & E. Briere, 1912).

century. Laws against mortmain were further tightened in 1749. Not only new acquisitions, but also improvements or new leases required payment to the crown.[73] The French amortization laws therefore functioned in two different ways: the first was directly financial in that it proclaimed certain sums and taxes due to the state by church institutions as compensation for a loss of future revenue. The second practical effect of the laws was to limit the amount and types of property that could transferred into ecclesiastical hands.

The Bavarian amortization law of 1764 was primarily aimed at limiting new acquisitions by ecclesiastical foundations. However, it also applied to mobile assets as well as to real estate and even to monetary gifts over 2000 Gulden.[74] This 1764 amortization law differed from earlier attempts to limit church property in Bavaria in that the state was seeking not only to acquire church land, but also to shape its economic activity.[75] The practical aim of the law was not strictly financial. Rather, it was one of macroeconomics. Whereas the secularization of mediated cloisters was a direct attempt to redistribute church wealth (sometimes for religious or charitable purposes, sometimes not), the amortization laws had as their expressed goal the preservation of the civil economy.

Such, in any case, is the argument of Neuberg's *Abhandlung*. In the first few chapters the author acknowledges that monastic orders have been useful in the past, and that they had converted the German nation from paganism.[76] He also admits that priests serve an important function and deserve the protection of the state. Yet, he continues, while we may be thankful for past achievements of the orders, we are not obliged to let "our money" continue to flow to them, especially through the further creation of ecclesiastical foundations.[77] Neuberg proceeds to a pointed critique of the buildup of ecclesiastical wealth throughout the centuries and states that the cloisters' "daily growth" of temporal goods is damaging. The thrust of Neuberg's argument is summarized in the title of the fourth chapter: "The daily growth of the cloisters' temporal goods and wealth causes great harm

---

[73] McManners, *Church and Society in eighteenth-century France*, vol. 1, 115.

[74] Romauld Bauerreiss, *Kirchengeschichte Bayerns, 7. Band (1600–1803)* (Augsburg: Verlag Winfried, 1970), 408.

[75] This point is indebted to Dietmar Stutzer, *Klöster als Arbeitgeber. Die bayerischen Klöster als Unternehmenseinheiten und ihre Sozialsysteme zur Zeit des Säkularisation 1803* (Göttingen: Vandenhoeck & Ruprecht, 1986), 23.

[76] Because the precise authorship is unclear, and does not directly affect my emphasis on the evolution of concepts in public debate, I will retain the pseudonym.

[77] Neuberg, *Abhandlung*, 40f.

to the state and ultimately, its ruin."[78] The state's role is to assure that no estate dominates the others. "The welfare of the state," according to Neuberg, "demands that no estate (*Stand*) become inordinately wealthy and swallow up the others." The "productive civil estate (*bürgerliche Nahrungsstand*)" is slowly loosing ground and risks being "swallowed up by the cloisters." However, "the civil productive estate is vital to the temporal welfare of the state."[79] The state must guarantee the rights of each estate against the others.[80] Moreover, the state must specifically assure that money circulates among the members of the state. He asserts that

> it is in the best interest and highest concern of the state that money circulate among its members, and that it does not fall into "dead hands" (*ad manus mortuas*). ... Money is the nourishing juice and the blood of the body of state. This body can only have life and activity when this 'blood' circulates – otherwise it stands still and the body falls into weakness and lethargy.[81]

Neuberg continues that the salesmen and manufacturers put the money to use and pass it on in the form of goods, which in turn beget more goods, yet the "surplus money of the cloisters remains mainly in cashboxes, which is like letting blood out of a body and putting it in the corner."[82]

By way of response specifically to the treatise, but more generally to the attitudes it represented, Anselm Desing (1699–1772), a Bavarian Benedictine and polymath published a German tract in 1768 defending the wealth of ecclesiastical institutions.[83] Desing had earlier, in 1753, published the treatise in Latin under the title *Does the Wealth of Priests Harm the State?*[84] At that time, the question seemed somewhat abstract because

---

[78] Neuberg, *Abhandlung*, 92 [50].

[79] "Nun nimmt der bürgerlichen Nahrungsstand so viel ab, als die Klöster an bürgerlichen Mitteln reicher werdern, folglich müßte endlich mit der Zeit der bürgerliche Stand gänzlich in Ruine kommen, und von den Klöstern verschlungen werden, wenn die Klöster immer an zeitlichen Gütern und Reichthümern zuehmen," Neuberg, *Abhandlung*, 92 [50].

[80] Neuberg, *Abhandlung*, 96. He also cites the example of the Venetian amortization laws of 1333, 1536, and 1605. Neuberg, *Abhandlung*, 95 [51].

[81] Neuberg, *Abhandlung*, 102f. [55].

[82] Neuberg, *Abhandlung*, 102f. [56]. Compare Hobbes' extended comparison of the state to the human body in chapter 24 of *Leviathan*, including the pithy marginal note: "Mony the bloud of a commonwealth." Thomas Hobbes, *Leviathan*, Richard Tuck, ed., revised student edition (Cambridge: Cambridge University Press, 1991, 1996), 179.

[83] Anselm Desing, *Staatsfrage: Sind die Güter und Einkünfte der Geistlichkeit dem Staate schädlich oder nicht? Beantwortet und Lochstein und Neubergern entgegen gesetzt* (Munich, 1768).

[84] Anselm Desing, *Opes Sacerdotii Num Reipublicae Noxiae? Ex Rerum Natura, Sana Politica et Communi Sensu Generis Humani Examinatum* (Pedeponti, 1753). Missing in

the Bavarian state had not yet started its program of appropriating church property in earnest. The author's answer to this question was of course that such wealth was not harmful.[85] The significance of the German edition is that while the earlier Latin tract had belonged to a type of armchair sociology – refuting Montesquieu and providing an intellectual defense of the wealth of the church – the new German edition was shorter, restricted to German conditions, and, most importantly, accessible to readers who did not read Latin. There was a new urgency, since it seemed that those who would justify further restrictions on church property were gaining ground in Germany. Osterwald's and Neuberg's treatises represented attempts to justify state limitations on ecclesiastical wealth, a matter which had seemed more pressing in the wake of the Seven Years' War. Not only was the state's ability to tax important, but also the awareness was growing that the need for cash – as opposed to payments in kind or other contributions – was now a permanent one as large, well-trained standing armies became a requirement for survival.

Desing's quarrel with partisans of a strong state has to do with the latter's definition of the common good.

One hears nowadays so many complaints that the income of the clergy is detrimental to the state, that in order to set things in proper perspective, it must first be established what is meant by the word 'State' or 'Common Good.[86]

Focusing on the income of the clergy, Desing continues, misses the mark: for certainly ecclesiastical institutions are not the only ones who draw wealth from the common good.

How many do not also complain about the harmful agglomeration of nobles, soldiers, councilors, lawyers and merchants, etc.? Either such people are in error, or everything that draws from the common good must be harmful – most of all the ruler who demands taxes from his subjects. For he who takes, harms.[87]

the 1768 German edition was the entire second section that dealt with the issue of the wealth of priests in an almost sociological manner. Desing questions the role of wealth used for religious purposes by ancient Greeks and Romans, Mayan priests, and in the Ottoman Empire.

[85] The polymath Desing, a Benedictine from the abbey of Ensdorf, was most famous for his *Juris natura larva detractata* (1753), in which he argued that the natural law of Pufendorf, Wolf and Thomasius was dangerous to Christian principles, despite the avowals of the natural lawyers to the contrary. For more on Desing, see Manfred Knedlik and George Schrott, eds., *Anselm Desing (1699–1772). Ein benediktinischer Universalgelehrter im Zeitalter der Aufklärung* (Kallmünz: Michael Laßleben, 1999).

[86] Desing, *Staatsfrage*, 2.

[87] Desing, *Staatsfrage*, 2.

Desing continues by stating that a prelate could just as well argue that a private individual with vast land and castles, or a merchant or money changer with millions does not bring anything to the country [*Land*] and that this property should be taken away and turned toward the common good. A peasant [*Bauer*] might complain that the thousands spent on the salary of a staff officer would easily support 20 peasants [*Landleute*] with wives and children.[88] Desing is not singling out soldiers and aristocrats, but rather trying to say that this type of thinking – which singles out the clergy – is not productive, because every estate [*Stand*] would wind up questioning the privileges and possessions of the others. Indeed, Desing's point seems to be that the property of each estate must be protected and that jealousy might undermine the cohesion of civil society.[89]

Insisting on the preservation of the rights of the estates, Desing accuses his opponents of equating the common good with the treasury of the prince.[90] He contends that full coffers do not mean that the state has real power. The true treasury of the state is the trust and dedication of the citizens, who gladly give the prince money when he needs it.[91] Servants of the common good are not only the soldiers that defend the state, but also those who contribute money and provisions.[92] The wealth of the clergy, Desing continues, cannot be considered to be in a "dead hand," because the clergy contributes more than its share toward the state in taxes and other payments.[93] Yet Desing refuted only one version of the "dead hand." His arguments about mortmain did not respond directly to Osterwald's complaints. This is because Desing still sees the role of the wealth of the church as steady and established – based in land, not commerce. Ecclesiastical foundations and lands, Desing suggests, serve as great reserves for the state and make up a bulwark of the national wealth.[94] The problem from the perspective of state-builders and

---

[88] Desing, *Staatsfrage*, 3–4.
[89] Desing, *Staatsfrage*, 4. "Jeder Stand der bürgerlichen Gesellschaft könnte andere Beschwerdniße vorbringen, wenn dieser Irrthum zu denken sich einschleichen sollte." In his "Gespräche über die Soldaten und Mönche," Lessing indicates that there is little difference between them: "If a peasant sees his crops destroyed by slugs and mice, what does he think is dreadful about it? That there are more slugs than mice? Or that there are so many slugs and mice." Cited and translated by Beales, *Prosperity and Plunder,* vi.
[90] Desing, *Staatsfrage*, 4–5.
[91] Desing, *Staatsfrage*, 7.
[92] Desing, *Staatsfrage*, 87.
[93] Desing, *Staatsfrage*, 89.
[94] Sophie de la Roche made a similar observation, though with much more ominous – and prophetic – overtones: "Die geistlichen Stifter und Länder sind Sparpfennige unserer

ministers was that even if the estates [*Stände*] were reliable and could be counted on to contribute when called, there was not enough ready cash for the state without increased taxes and other payments.

Desing admits that the clergy enjoys a surplus, which means that it controls more wealth than is needed for its immediate physical needs. But it does not follow from this that such a surplus is harmful to the state or to the common good. He emphasizes that the church redistributes its surplus to the needy. Significantly, Desing does not make a point of defending the use of the surplus to fund contemplative activities or the endowment of masses for the dead. Desing also notes that even those who claim that the wealth of the church is harmful to the common good still hope for ecclesiastical offices for their children.[95] Desing thereby points out one of the most significant social roles of the Church in German Catholic society, namely as a place where families could be sure that their children would be provided with a decent living. While the highest offices went to the scions of the great dynasties and families, even modest bourgeois could hope to see their sons or daughters in a well-endowed abbies, and, with talent and luck, sons of the middle classes and lower nobility could become abbots of important institutions (indeed, there were even sons of peasants who rose to the rank of abbot). The problem cannot be merely one of surplus: for even if it is granted that the clergy lives too richly, this does not mean that the state is thereby harmed. Though he does not endorse it, Desing refers to Mandeville's argument that even supposedly useless opulence benefits the artisans who are hired to create luxury items. More to the point, Desing resents that fact that the luxury of the clergy is singled out, when by rights the same criticism should apply to the wealthy *Bürger* and nobility as well.[96]

While the discussion thus far has focused on the contest for legitimate control over church property and wealth, it is important to recall this wealth was by and large based in agriculture. Abstract discussions of state revenue and commerce were bound up in real issues of agrarian reform. Neuberg's comments about the uselessness of the cloister and the benefits of the "productive civil estate" were common enough in the cameralist literature of the day. Yet were they really true for Bavaria, indeed, for most of Catholic Germany? It is notable that the examples Neuberg gives

---

großen weltlichen Fürsten, die sie bei der nächsten großen Gelegenheit angreifen und teilen werden." Cited in Aretin, *Das Reich*, vol. 3, 244.
[95] Desing, *Staatsfrage*, 31.
[96] Desing, *Staatsfrage*, 58–9.

of "productive" uses of money all involve industry or trade. But what of agriculture, which formed the major part of the German economy in the eighteenth century? Neuberg's critique of the uselessness of monastic wealth was part of a larger attack on monasticism and monastic culture. While Neuberg's assumption that money in the hands of a salesman or weaver would be more "productive" than if it were given to ecclesiastical institutions seems to make sense in the industrial age, it is important to remember that the economy of Germany was predominantly agricultural far into the nineteenth century. As Desing's treatise shows, the embrace of commerce as means of growth rather than a service of common utility was not universally accepted. An agricultural economy, however, is not a static one. Even those who did not embrace commerce and manufacturing could still criticize laws that restricted the sale of church land, since such restrictions tied up a large amount of property in an age when agricultural improvement was all the rage. As state ministers, Osterwald and Eisenrich (the possible author behind Neuberg's tract) were specifically interested in Bavaria. Desing's reply would seem to apply mainly to mediate cloisters and institutions (i.e., those institutions that did not have a seat in the Reichstag and fell under the lordship of another prince). Yet in a larger sense, both authors addressed a German public interested in general questions of the role of ecclesiastical wealth and the common good. Thus questions about the agrarian economy of Germany transcended the Bavarian context in which Desing, Osterwald, and "Neuberg" argued.

Finally, Desing specifically criticizes the notion that the church's lands should be freed up for commerce. He states that "some strongly suggest trade and commerce, and maintain that this is the best means" to foster the common good. "However, I think quite differently," he continues:

and believe instead that forced commerce leads to the poverty and need of many, and this in many states today that almost all complain of their need and weakness. Certainly this need will show itself even stronger, the more one tries to increase commerce.[97]

While Desing does not give any particular evidence for his claim – nor does he really explain what he means by commerce – the significant point is that he is trying to defend the viability of a certain type of economy in which the landed wealth of the ecclesiastical institutions would still have a major social role. Yet his vision of stability and security also implied that the estates of the nation would act in harmony to defend the state

[97] Desing, *Staatsfrage*, 110.

against aggressors and in times of need. Such a vision was incompatible with that of absolutist princes who needed dependable sources of tax revenues to support their military and bureaucratic apparatus.[98] Moreover, it is a vision in which commerce is not an end in itself, but a way of assuring just distribution of wealth and surplus. Accordingly, it was an economic and political worldview that refused to separate questions of morality from those of economy. While no one stated their positions in these exact terms, behind differing definitions of the common good lurked divergent views of political economy: those which saw Germany's strength in its rural nature and in the guaranteed rights of the *Stände* versus those which favored increased commerce, standing armies, and a strong state.

---

[98] See also John Brewer, *The Sinews of Power: War, Money, and the English State, 1688–1783* (New York: Alfred A. Knopf, 1989).

4

Church and Empire in the Eighteenth Century

"GERMANIAE EPISCOPI PRINCIPES SUNT"

"The bishops of Germany are princes," the Jesuit Adam Contzen laconically declared in 1621. "Italian bishops," he continued, "are not." With the exception of the papal states, in which even Hobbes recognized the pope as sovereign, that temporal power was invested in the bishop was indeed the distinguishing characteristic of the German episcopate. This peculiarity meant as well that any realignment of the church in Germany would also touch the fundamental structure of the Empire. Issues of Catholic reform were of general interest because the fate of the *Reichskirche* was inseparable from the fate of the Empire itself.

The bishops were endowed with ecclesiastical foundations (*Stifte*) over which they ruled – in conjunction with the cathedral chapter – as lay lords.[1] Ideally, territorial independence assured that a bishop would not be hindered in the exercise of his sacred office. In reality, wealth and power in the hands of these bishops was often a source of criticism and rebuke ever since the later Middle Ages, and complaints had sharpened considerably at the time of the Reformation.[2] Moreover, a bishop's spiritual and secular jurisdictions did not necessarily coincide. This meant, for example, that a bishop would at times have to rely on the goodwill of a neighboring lay prince – or possibly even another bishop – to enforce his religious authority,

---

[1] Not all the German bishops ruled independently over ecclesiastical foundations. There were several diocese, for the most part in the east and in Austrian territories, that did not exist as independent ecclesiastical states.

[2] Thomas A. Brady, Jr., *The Politics of the Reformation in Germany. Jacob Sturm (1489–1553) of Strasbourg.* (Atlantic Highlands, New Jersey: Humanities Press, 1997), 22–4.

whereas he may have subjects under his territorial jurisdiction who belonged to a different diocese.[3]

The ecclesiastical principalities were the Empire's oldest institutions. Medieval emperors had endowed bishops and other churchmen with secular authority in areas where these ecclesiastics were the only viable powers. By the late Middle Ages, the church had become the strongest support of the Empire. The emperors sought backing in the Church, which prayed for the ruling dynasty and supported it financially and militarily. In return, the church was rewarded with endowments and the temporal rights that eventually became the basis for the ecclesiastical states. The role of these states had been altered by the Protestant Reformation as the papacy sought to strengthen the German episcopate. The papacy was able to survive the Protestant Reformation in Germany in part by relying on both the large dynasties as well as the lesser nobility.[4] These noble families provided a bulwark against Protestantism where they were able to control the cathedral chapters that were responsible for electing bishops.[5] The political strategy of the church called for a strong independent basis of power that would enable the Catholic church to survive threats to its existence from Protestant dynasties. This made the German Catholics bishops unlike their counterparts in other kingdoms.

German bishops were elected by a cathedral chapter, though these elections needed to be confirmed by the pope. While election by chapter did not mean that bishops were always chosen on the basis of pastoral ability or spiritual commitment, it did mean that those families – by and large from the ranks of the imperial knights (*Reichsritterschaft*) – who traditionally controlled the chapters held significant bargaining chips in dealings with the emperor, the papacy, and the large German dynasties.[6]

---

[3] For detailed maps see Anton Schindling and Walter Ziegler, *Die Territorien des Reichs im Zeitalter der Reformation und Konfessionalisierung: Land und Konfession 1500–1650*, 7 vols. (Münster: Aschendorff, 1989–).

[4] Thomas A. Brady, Jr., *German Histories in the Age of Reformations, 1400–1650* (Cambridge: Cambridge University Press, 2009), ch. 14.

[5] By comparison, French and Spanish kings had the right to nominate directly, which enabled the French monarchy in particular, to wield enormous influence in the shaping of the Gallican church. See Joseph Bergin, *The Making of the French Episcopate 1589–1661* (New Haven: Yale University Press, 1996).

[6] There were a few significant exceptions to the *Ritterschaft* pre-eminence, notably the election of Clemens Wenzeslaus of Saxony (1739–1812) as Archbishop-Elector of Trier (r. 1768–1801) and bishop of Augsburg (r. 1768–1812), and the appointment of Maria Theresa's son Maximillian Francis (1756–1801) to the sees of Cologne and Münster. In general, see Peter Hersche, "Adel Gegen Bürgertum? Zur Frage der Refeudalisierung der Reichskirche," in *Weihbischöfe und Stifte. Beiträge zu reichskirchlichen Funktionsträgern*

From the emperor, the knights wanted constitutional guarantees of their rights. For their part, the Habsburgs were able to court *Ritterschaft* influence by sometimes supporting their candidates for episcopal sees to undermine rival dynasties, notably the Wittelsbachs.[7]

While the papacy (which still had to confirm appointments, and, as important, to issue dispensations from canonical rules) could in theory refuse particular candidates, in fact it rarely did so.[8] Although the emperors certainly would have liked to have such powers (and indeed tried to claim them), the German lesser nobility held on to its privileges and consequently limited the growth of centralized power in the Empire.[9] The Habsburg policy of appeasing the smaller powers as a counterbalance to the larger dynasties took advantage of a key strength in the structure of the Empire: corporate solidarity. While it is an open question how long the Empire would have survived had there been no Napoleon, it is nevertheless true the mid-level states (e.g., Württemberg, Bavaria, and Saxony) progressively abandoned – in spirit if not in law – imperial constraints on aggrandizement.[10] Since this abandonment was partly due to the rising costs of warfare and the bureaucratic rationalization of the

---

der Frühen Neuzeit, Friedhelm Jürgensmeier, ed., *Beiträge zur Mainzer Kirchengeschichte Vol 4* (Frankfurt: 1995) and *Die deutsche Domkapital*, 3 vols. (Bern: 1984).

[7] One of the most significant families of imperial knights – the Schönborns – succeeded so well that they were raised to territorial sovereignty. Schönborn power was at first fostered by Ferdinand III, who helped John Phillip von Schönborn attain the see of Mainz in 1647. John Philip was active in bringing about peace after the Thirty Years' War, and concentrated on preserving the independence of the knights and indeed the Empire itself. However, by 1694, the sees of Bamberg and Mainz were in the hands of Lothar Franz von Schönborn, which led Emperor Leopold I (1648–1705) to try and check that family's power. Being elevated to territorial sovereignty only further committed the Schönborns to the Habsburgs and the imperial constitution as the guarantee of their new rights while it effectively removed them from a leadership position among the knights. In principle, this practice is no different than that of French kings insofar as they sought to consolidate their power among the nobility by ecclesiastical appointments. Ever since the Concordat of 1516 the French monarchy had a powerful tool at its disposal, since it could nominate candidates to some 800 offices with their respective benefices. Lawrence G. Duggan, "The Church as an Institution of the Reich," in *The Old Reich. Essays on German Political Institutions 1495–1806*, James A. Vann and Steven Rowan, eds. (Brussels: 1974); 159–62 and John McManners, *Church and Society in eighteenth-century France*, 2 vols. (Oxford: Oxford University Press, 1998), vol. 1, 48.

[8] For example, many, if not most, of the nominees for powerful and wealthy ecclesiastical offices in France could rarely claim to meet all of the requirements of age, celibacy, or proof of ordination.

[9] Duggan, "The Church as an Institution of the Reich," 158.

[10] Peter H. Wilson, *War, State and Society in Württemberg, 1677–1793* (Cambridge: Cambridge University Press, 1995), 10–25.

modern state, it was questionable how much longer the smaller principalities could compete. However, the ecclesiastical politics of the *Reichskirche* [Imperial church] remained a core element of the dynastic and
aristocratic balance of power down to the end of the Old Regime.
Therefore, the discussion about the fate and status of the ecclesiastical
states in the eighteenth century was also about the political and social
position of the Catholic church in Germany.

This concern about the social and political place of a landed and
powerful church was sharpened by developments in the 1780s in Catholic
Germany. In July and August of 1786, deputies of the four German
metropolitans – the archbishop-electors of Trier, Cologne, and Mainz,
and the prince-archbishop of Salzburg – met in the German spa town of
Ems to form a coalition against the exercise of jurisdictional authority by
papal nuncios in the Empire. One critical observer, the Belgian ex-Jesuit
François Feller, dissected the bishops' claims and traced them to their
interest in asserting the social and political primacy of the German aristocratic bishops.[11] Feller's criticism of the Ems program falls into three
general categories. First, he argues that the German archbishops would
undermine the unity of the universal church if they enhanced their own
power at the papacy's expense. Second, Feller takes issue with the Ems
program's understanding of canon law and its historical status. Third –
and most trenchantly – Feller accuses the archbishops of merely serving
their own worldly ends, and of having little real interest in the condition
of the church.

The Ems meeting had been organized primarily in response to the
creation of a nunciature in Munich. The Ems declaration stated that papal
legates worked to undermine the authority of the bishops and weakened
the church. Feller argues that the legates preserve unity under papal primacy.[12] The reformers – who, following Hontheim, desired to create a
"Gallican" church for the Empire – "confuse the liberties of the Gallican
church with the ecclesiastical anarchy of Febronius' treatise."[13] A basic

---

[11] Feller (1735–1802) is also one of the "enemies of the Enlightenment discussed in Darrin
M. McMahon, *Enemies of the Enlightenment: the French Counter-Enlightenment and
the Making of Modernity* (New York: Oxford University Press, 2001).

[12] François Feller, *Coup d'oeil sur le Congres d'Ems, Tenu en 1786 par Quatre Députés
des quatre Métropolitains d'Allemagne* (Dusseldorff: Kauffmann, 1787), 51. Feller
quotes the Austrian canonist Johann Joseph Nepomuk Pehem, *Praelectiones in jus
ecclesiasticum,* part 1, §268–9. Pehem was in fact a partisan of Joseph II's church
policies, yet in this case, it would seem that the supporters of papal centralization and
the ecclesiastical politics of the territorial princes share the same arguments.

[13] Feller, 104.

complaint of the episcopal movement was that papal centralization ever since the days of Gregory VII had deprived them of their rights and liberties. Have the bishops of Germany forgotten, Feller asks, that it was always to the See of Rome that they owe their protection, and that it was Gregory VII who had contributed the most to the status of the episcopacy in Germany? In an earlier age, Feller notes, the bishops were often at the mercy of the lay powers:

has the Archbishop of Mainz forgotten the catastrophe of his predecessor Arnold, whom Frederick I condemned to carry his dog [...]? Has the Archbishop of Salzburg forgotten that in 965 Herold, one of his predecessors, had his eyes stomped out by order of Emperor Otto?[14]

Feller's defense of papal prerogatives is based ultimately on political rather than strictly theological or historical arguments. He argues that the authority of the "head of the church" is a "fulcrum" upon which rests the authority of all the bishops and metropolitans. If unity which arises from this authority is lost, Feller asks:

where would the German church then be? Can one believe that she would preserve the shadow of her prerogatives and privileges? Will they [the church's privileges] not be swallowed like the Anglican church and reduced to the most humiliating servitude to the arbitrary and absolute power of the civil authority?[15]

Indeed, he continues, is this not already the case, since the archbishop-electors, even with their temporal powers, have appealed to the Emperor for protection?[16]

This first category of Feller's criticism is essentially rhetorical: he seeks to undermine the reformers' claim that they wish only to preserve harmony in the church by resolving contentious issues between the papacy and the German bishops. Both sides, in fact, were claiming the same rhetorical ground, namely, that the liberty of the church was at stake. The German canonists saw the liberties of the German church under attack, whereas Feller and supporters of the pope contended that only a strong papacy with real jurisdictional powers could preserve the liberty of the universal church. The partisans of the *Reichskirche* did not see any contradictions between the liberties of the universal and the particular churches. Would anyone doubt, they might ask, the Catholicity of the Spanish and the French churches – both in possession of extensive privileges?

---

[14] Feller, 133.
[15] Feller, 135f.
[16] Feller, 135.

The second category of Feller's critique touched on two related concepts: the legal history defining the relationship between the metropolitans and their suffragans, and the German canonists' assumption that ancient church discipline was better church discipline. To the Ems proclamation that the archbishops' "rights" had been violated, Feller responds that the relationship between the nuncios and the archbishops was the same as it had been for centuries.[17] Feller's point relies on the principle of prescription: given that certain actions had been tolerated for years, they were to be assumed to be accepted as valid by all sides. Feller also takes issue with the archbishops' appeal to an imperial rescript. Could such a rescript regulate the spiritual authority between the pope and the bishops?[18] Feller points out that the metropolitans merely want to arrogate to themselves the very same powers they resent in the papacy. He accuses them of trying to resuscitate "not episcopal authority, but the ancient empire of the metropolitans, which had been so fatal to the episcopate."[19] Indeed, claims Feller, the very Pseudo-Isidore, whom the German canonists blame for papal usurpation was in fact trying to free the German bishops from metropolitan overreaching.[20] In any case, it is by no means clear that Pseudo-Isidore's falsification actually changed the nature of the ecclesiastical hierarchy.[21] As Feller notes, the dignity of the metropolitan is of human creation (the papacy he presumes was created by Christ, and the bishops descended from the apostles and disciples).[22] The archbishops had claimed that "those reservations against German liberties introduced by the Roman Curia after the Concordats are void."[23] Feller replies that "it is impossible to conceive that the Curia would have been able to introduce any type of reservation without the consent of the nation, its head, and the tribunals of the Empire."[24] Once again, Feller is here appealing to a principle similar to prescription, namely that the historical fact that the papacy could introduce new reservations meant that they were at least implicitly accepted by the public authorities.

The archbishops' general complaint about curial "innovation" rested on a repeated appeal to the "ancient discipline" of the church. The claim

[17] Feller, 88.
[18] Feller, 88–9.
[19] Feller, 94.
[20] Feller, 97.
[21] Feller, 98.
[22] Feller, 93, footnote "a."
[23] Feller, 209.
[24] Feller, 209.

that the earlier organization of the church was necessarily better was a common refrain of the reform movement. Its most powerful advocate in the field of canon law was the Louvain jurist van Espen. Feller rejects the equation of antiquity with superiority:

is it reasonable to want to reduce all things to their condition in the first centuries? If someone proposed that for a monarchical state, or for any political state, he would be taken for insane. But the folly is even more marked in the idea of such a regression with respect to the Catholic church, in whom the Holy Spirit directs not only the teaching, but also the practices, law, and discipline.[25]

It is absurd, he continues, to presume that Jesus would have structured his church without giving it the flexibility to adapt over successive ages for different historical and political conditions.[26]

The third category of Feller's critique extends to the legal and social pretensions of the archbishops. He views their jurisdictional aim skeptically and reserves even more sarcasm for what he sees as their preoccupation with worldly ends. The bishops had claimed that they should have power of dispensations (this would include, for example, the right to accumulate multiple benefices). The bishops also wanted to end the practice whereby members of the cathedral chapter would resign their post in favor of another – usually, of course, a family member or client. The effect of these reforms, Feller argues, would be to turn the bishops into petty despots, whose actions would be unchecked by a cathedral chapter of their own creation. With the powers they claim, states Feller, "the Archbishop or bishop will have ... the entire chapter completely dependent on him, a dependence of interest, flesh and blood, which is not one of hierarchy."[27] He continues to note that in the future, no one will hesitate to enter the chapter and receive orders, secure that when the time comes, the bishop will grant them the necessary dispensations (regarding, for example, residency or university degrees). In return, the chapter will no longer serve as a check on the bishop, and the bishop can always force out an uncooperative canon by refusing a dispensation.[28] Feller was especially alarmed at the metropolitans' desire for the right both to collate prebends and to dispense from the prohibition against plurality. If the bishops were to be granted these powers, Feller concludes, "one sees that the entire servitude of the chapters was decided at Ems."[29]

[25] Feller, 94.
[26] Feller, 95.
[27] Feller, 166.
[28] Feller, 166.
[29] Feller, 167.

Feller – though perhaps without recognizing it – was showing that those trying to claim "Gallican" style liberties for the German church would also wind up with the same French system of benefices, sinecures, and creatures – that is the potential subservience of the Church to the social hierarchy.[30] Feller finds it ironic that the bishops were trying to assert more control over their diocese, claiming that, "according to the nature of the primitive constitution of the church, every person in a diocese is, without distinction, subordinated in internal and external affairs of religion."[31] Feller responds to this claim by noting that the bishop himself is subordinated to the pope and the laws of the universal church. Without this subordination, the danger of schism increases.

Finally, the bishops claim that once they have "recovered" their rights, they will then be able to proceed with much-needed reforms. They imply that their political struggle against the papacy has prevented them from undertaking reform. Feller's reply deserves quotation:

This situation [of decayed morals and religion] will continue until the metropolitans are masters of their own domain as well as over their suffragans, without any dependence on the pope. Then, according to the promise of the prophets of Ems, things will change completely. In the future, we will no longer see either archbishops or bishops living like crooks and gamblers, running with packs of dogs, with coiffured hair and splendid carriages. No longer will they hit the streets without really having any destination, nor will they absorb in their sumptuous palace the wealth of the church and the state, etc. No, none of that will take place any more. We will see them taking great care and instructing themselves in order to instruct their flock and edify by example. They will visit their dioceses in person, supervise the pastors and spread their immense revenues among the poor. We will no longer see their courts occupied by mountebanks, castrati and charlatans. No more ... O what a beautiful project, and moreover very consoling. It is only too bad that it will not be put into place until the pope, the bishops, the general councils, the validity of marriages, solemn vows, and so forth, are put at the arbitrary disposition of the metropolitans.[32]

Dismissing the metropolitans' assertions, Feller has also put his finger on a weakness in their position. As secular princes, the four metropolitans – like many of the other bishops of the Empire – did not hesitate to assume the lifestyle of the territorial prince. Of course, partisans of a papacy residing in the baroque splendor of Rome would be treading on thin ice to

---

[30] See also Feller, 213, where he states that under the Ems program, each bishopric will become a little "oriental state."

[31] Feller, 139.

[32] Feller, 270–2.

claim that secular comforts undermined the spiritual legitimacy of a bishop. Nevertheless, Feller, an ex-Jesuit who had no reason to be sympathetic to the German aristocratic church, pointed to the *religious* problem that the ecclesiastical states presented. Already at the time of the Reformation (and earlier), the inappropriateness of bishops living like princes was cause for religious critique. Could it not be that Catholics like Feller did not see the need for these strongly independent bishops? Did they no longer serve their original purpose, the physical and political independence – *libertas* – of the Catholic church? These questions were also raised, *mutatis mutandis*, about the viability of the ecclesiastical states in the Empire.[33]

THE ECCLESIASTICAL STATES AND THE EMPIRE IN THE EIGHTEENTH CENTURY

In his three-volume *Historical Development of the Current Constitution of the German Empire*, the prominent Göttingen professor of Imperial law and history Johann Stephan Pütter noted that the ecclesiastical states were born out of the decline of the Carolingian empire in the wake of northern invasions. Weakness of royal power led to the law of the feud and the devolution of power.[34] Quite often it was ecclesiastical institutions that were in the best position to assume power in troubled areas. According to Pütter, no distinction was made between clerical and lay powers. The important factor was merely that those who had land and resources naturally assumed power.[35] Pütter continues that this was not without negative results for the interest of religion:

Under such conditions there was now little attention paid to the enlightenment of the people, especially since cloisters and foundations that should have been dedicated to the education of youth now concentrated more on matters of war than on schooling. All the worthy foundations that Charlemagne had created or had at least started became quite fruitless. [...] Those who dedicated themselves to the clerical estate received only as much training in reading and writing as was

---

[33] The ex-Jesuit Benedict Stattler raised similar doubts about the influence of the aristocratic constitution of the church in Germany. Benedikt Stattler, *Wahre und allein hinreichende Reformationsart des katholischen gesammten Priesterstandes, nach der ursprünglichen Idee seines göttlichen Stifters* (Ulm, 1791), vii. Stattler's essay is discussed below in Chapter 7.

[34] Johann S. Pütter, *Historische Entwicklung der heutigen Staatsverfassung des Teutschn Reichs*, 3 vols. (Göttingen, 1786), Book I, ch. 7, ix., 87.

[35] Pütter, Book I, ch. 7, ix, 82.

needed for their purpose. And yet they still had an advantage over the entirely ignorant, which meant that the importance of the clergy over the secular estates from this point on grew disproportionately.[36]

The growing power of the clerical estate [*geistliche Stand*] is a major theme of Pütter's account. When the emperor had been strong, he lavished wealth on the church to foster culture and learning. But the collapse of central authority and the growth of feudalism meant that those institutions that had been the benefactors of imperial largesse were by necessity turning to more worldly affairs. Because they had a monopoly on learning, the clerical estates made themselves indispensable to the monarchy, and used their power to assure their privileges. Pütter implies that the power of the clerical estates – established at a time of crisis only because there was no better option – had not only long outlived its usefulness, but was also positively harmful to the further development of civil society.[37] He suggests that this power would wither away of its own lethargy. Nevertheless, Pütter did not advocate in any way the abolition of the ecclesiastical estates or the power of the *geistliche Stand*, for he was more than aware that the corporate solidarity on which the Empire rested depended on these states and the imperial knights. However, by showing that the *geistliche Stand* had amassed more power than was its due, Pütter could also express confidence that the relative weakening power of this estate was not in itself fatal to the constitution of the Empire.[38]

Recent scholarship has shown that the ecclesiastical principalities were not simply remnants of a darker time but rather had been purposefully built up first by the emperors and then later fostered by a papacy threatened with the loss of Catholic Germany to the Reformation.[39] Nevertheless, eighteenth-century Germans began to realize that the small state was becoming unsuitable – or more precisely unviable – in a world of

---

[36] Pütter, Book I, ch. 7, xiv, 87–8.

[37] Compare the remarks of J. G. A. Pocock on the role of "civil society" in Enlightenment historiography. J. G. A. Pocock, *Barbarism and Religion. Volume I: The Enlightenments of Edward Gibbon* (Cambridge: Cambridge University Press, 1999), 4. This topic will be addressed at length in Chapter 9.

[38] For a discussion of reform projects for the Empire after 1648, see Wolfgang Burgdorf, *Reichskonstitution und Nation. Verfassungsreformprojekte für das Heilige Römische Reich Deutscher Nation im Politischen Schrifttum von 1648 bis 1806* (Mainz: Philipp von Zabern, 1998). On the image of the Empire among scholars of Imperial law in general, see Bernd Roeck, *Reichssystem und Reichsherkommen: die Diskussion über die Staatlichkeit des Reiches in der politischen Publizistik des 17. und 18. Jahrhunderts* (Stuttgart: F. Steiner, 1984).

[39] Brady, *German Histories in the Age of Reformations, 1400–1650.*

power politics and standing armies. As a spiritual lord, the bishop had religious authority over his diocese and could claim certain "spiritual" taxes and fees, such as annates and the tithe. In reality, however, very little of his income came from these spiritual sources. In the diocese of Constance, for example, only about 1% of the bishop's income came from the "fiscus episcopalis." The rest came from his direct holdings as landlord and through the taxation he could collect as secular lord.[40] While the numbers would of course vary by diocese, the key point is that centuries of agreements, concordats, princely mandates, and custom had taken their toll on the amount bishops could collect from spiritual sources. The bishops therefore depended on their secular power and the wealth of their respective *Stifte* for the exercise of their functions. Toward the latter half of the eighteenth century, the viability of these states began to be questioned in journals and pamphlets.

The weakness of the ecclesiastical states was of great concern even to those so-called *Reichspatrioten* [imperial patriots] who feared that these smaller states were necessary to preserve the corporate solidarity of the Empire.[41] In 1785, a Catholic journal solicited essays on the topic of whether the constitution of the ecclesiastical states was responsible for their weakness:

Given that the states of the ecclesiastical imperial princes are elective, and are among the most blessed provinces of all Germany, they should rightly enjoy the wisest and happiest governments. If they are not as fortunate as they should be, then the fault lies not with their rulers but with their internal constitution.

The prize essay question, therefore, was posed: "what are their actual deficiencies, and how can these be corrected?"[42]

The most radical solution was proposed by Carl Friedrich von Moser (1723–1798), who advocated that the office of bishop be separated from the temporal rule of the ecclesiastical states. These states should retain

---

[40] Rudolf Reinhardt, "Gründe für den wirtschaftlichen Niedergang der Reichskirche in der Neuzeit, dargestellt am Beispiel Konstanz," *Zeitschrift für Kirchengeschichte* 103 [Fourth Series, XLI] (1992), 230. With an average yearly income of 55,600 fl., the bishop received only 570 fl. from the "fiscus episcopalis," that is, from the Constance bishop's position as spiritual lord. The numbers and proportions would vary significantly, and it should also be noted that Constance had a rather small *Stift* (foundation) in comparison with the size of the diocese.

[41] P. Wende, "Die Gesitliche Staaten und Ihre Auflösung im Urteil der Zeitgenössichen Publizistik," *Historische Studien* 396 (1966).

[42] *Journal von und für Deutschland*, 12 Stück, 1784–, 552. The question in quotation marks was to be the basis of the essay.

their elective character, however, since that was the feature that assured they would be always wisely ruled and that the regent would not use his office to further the interests of his family alone. In Moser's words they would become "elective aristocratic republics."[43] Moser's suggestion, as he was well aware, never had a chance since it would have eliminated the ecclesiastical nature of the states. Nevertheless, his essay is indicative of the feeling that these small aristocratic states provided a bulwark both against centralization in the Empire, and, perhaps more importantly by the later eighteenth century, against domination by the large dynastic states.

The winning essay, by the imperial councilor Joseph Sartori (1750–1812), was more in keeping with the moderate reform proposals of the later eighteenth century: namely that these states needed to "modernize" their governmental apparatus and foster industry. Sartori's tract, entitled *Statistical Treatise on the Deficiencies in the Constitution of the Elective Ecclesiastical States, and on the Means to Correct Them*, reflects typically practical concerns.[44] Sartori notes that many of the weaknesses are indeed external and cannot be related to constitutional flaws. For example, many problems of these states are due to wars and dealings with neighbors. Sartori also considers the sums that must be paid to Rome upon the election of a new bishop a harmful external factor: "a hard fate for a free state, which upon the death of its ruler must purchase the next with a heavy sum."[45] It is an "external" problem in that these payments had more to do with the structure and governance of the Catholic church than with the administration of the lands of the prince-bishop or abbot. This was a common refrain of Catholic reformers.[46] Furthermore, pluralism meant that money was lost to a nonresident bishop, who may reside in his other see. Also beyond their control was the fact that the

---

[43] Friedrich Karl Moser, *Über die Regierung der geistlichen Staaten in Deutschland* (Frankfurt am Main, 1787). See Max Braubach, "Die kirchliche Aufklärung im katholischen Deutschland im Spiegel des 'Journal von und für Deutschland' 1784–92," *Historisches Jahrbuch* 54:1 (1934). On the discussion over imperial reform see Burgdorf, *Reichskonstitution und Nation*.

[44] Joseph von Sartori, *Staatistische Abhandlung über die Mängel in der Regierungsverfassung der geistlichen Wahlstaaten, und von den Mitteln, solchen abzuhelfen* (Augsburg, 1787).

[45] Sartori, 13.

[46] See the anticlerical *Magazin für Geschichte, Statistik, Litteratur und Topographie der sämtlichen deutschen geistlichen Staaten* (Zürich, 1790) by Winkopp and Höck, which lists the costs of the pallium and other fees required for confirmation of an episcopal election.

ecclesiastical princes contributed financially to imperial wars, but even then had to subsidize external powers to guarantee their freedom.[47]

The most recent problem, according to Sartori, seemed to be a shortage of money:

only since the Seven Years' War in Germany, which particularly in the ecclesiastical states brought with it an undeniable shortage of cash, can one sense a noticeable weakening of the foundation lands (*Stiftland*), on top of which comes the export of cash due to plurality.[48]

Accordingly, Sartori's suggestions orient themselves on questions of economy in the ecclesiastical states. He suggests that spinning institutions and weaving factories (*Strumpfstickerey*) be set up.[49] He cites the example of the princes of Thurn and Taxis, who set up a weaving shop from which the postal agents were clothed.[50] More important was the overall awareness of economic conditions on the part of the ruler, who could then foster trade:

Every ecclesiastical prince, if he had an exact knowledge of the strengths and weaknesses of his state, the conditions of his land, and if he examines the needs and relations of his neighbors, can find an area of trade for his land that would occupy his subjects, would fix his neighbor's interests in his own, and would unleash a monetary circulation that is otherwise lacking in almost every German ecclesiastical principality.[51]

One of the main reasons for this lack of monetary circulation and general economic weakness, Sartori believes, is that industry has not been fostered in the ecclesiastical principalities. The fact that these states enjoy high population does not make them prosperous. If these state were sparsely populated but nevertheless encouraged their subjects to work hard, "then they would be much happier than they actually are, despite their high population, given that the largest proportion is made up of the lazy and of beggars." He continues by arguing that "the art of begging has reached the highest level of perfection in the German ecclesiastical principalities.[52] This harms all the other German provinces as well" since the

---

[47] Sartori, 13.

[48] Sartori, 18.

[49] Sartori, 42.

[50] Sartori, 43.

[51] Sartori, 44.

[52] Peter Hersche notes that almost all enlightened critics noted the high percentage of beggars in Catholic lands. However, he continues, beggars had a different function in those states, and were not seen as shameful. Prelates and Catholic nobles resisted the centralization of poor-houses, and so forth, because they needed the beggars to demonstrate their

beggars and "lazy people" (*Mußigänger*) unsettle the neighboring states.[53] In sum, the main failures of these principalities have been that they do not work to release the "inner forces" (*innere Kräfte*), do not foster industry and trade, or do not focus on education as the motor of prosperity.[54]

While there is certainly an element of truth in Sartori's criticism, the more significant question is why these principalities in general did not undertake the kind of wholesale economic and social reorganization that their larger neighbors – notably Austria and Prussia – did? One major exception to this inactivity was Mainz. Yet Mainz, though small, had a significant constitutional role in the Empire, and the archbishop-electors harbored political ambitions.[55] Mainz's military and diplomatic expenses in fact did encourage the electors to sponsor industry and reorganize the education system.[56] The Mainz exception in essence proves the rule: it was power politics and warfare that drove the attempts at economic and social reorganization in the German dynastic states. The smallest ecclesiastical principalities were instead committed to preserving the status quo, and moreover, the system of election by chapter meant that any one ruler could not change the state into a hereditary principality for his family.[57] The ecclesiastical states were by their very nature conservative, and this bothered not a few people. However, an odd intellectual alliance of smaller Catholic dynasties and *Reichspatrioten* saw that the independence of these states underpinned the structure of the Empire.

THE EMPIRE AND THE LEGAL FOUNDATIONS OF THE CHURCH

The security of the Catholic church was, in principle, guaranteed by Imperial law. Yet what would seem to be a rather straightforward task – namely locating and identifying the role of the Catholic church in the

giving of alms, whereas in Protestant lands – especially in Holland – poor were whisked away into work-houses. Peter Hersche, "Intendierte Rückständigkeit: Zur Charakteristik des geistlichen Staates im Alten Reich," in *Stände und Gesellschaft im Alten Reich* [Veröffentlichen des Instituts für europäische Geschichte, Bd. 29], Georg Schmidt, ed. (Stuttgart, 1989), 142f.

[53] Sartori, 48.

[54] Sartori, 67.

[55] See T. C. W. Blanning, *Reform and Revolution in Mainz, 1743–1803* (Cambridge: Cambridge University Press, 1974).

[56] Although still bishops, the electors still ran into significant difficulties when they secularized monastic institutions and used the income to reform the university. See Ibid.

[57] On this issue in general see also Peter Hersche, "Intendierte Rückständigkeit."

Imperial constitution – is actually one of great complexity. The controversy over Hontheim's *de Statu*, as well as over the later efforts of the four German metropolitans to assert their independence from Rome highlighted the particularities of the *Reichskirche* [German Imperial church]. The *Reichskirche* is a term that in its most restricted usage refers to the legal standing of the church in Imperial law. In this sense it covers both the bishops and other prelates with a seat in the Reichstag, as well as the imperial guarantees of ecclesiastical property.[58]

"Church" itself was a fluid concept whose meaning varied according to the assumptions of each particular party. It was simultaneously a metaphysical and spiritual concept as well as one with very specific institutional connotations. This very ambiguity was enshrined in the Westphalian settlement itself. In order to appreciate the complexity of this question, we must consider the different ways in which the church and Catholic practice could be conceived of as being protected in the Empire. For example, did the survival of the religion depend on a powerful episcopate – that is on bishops with temporal authority? Were the ecclesiastical states the best guarantee of an institutionalized role for the church in German society? Consequently, was the church's best support the very existence of the Empire? Or was the church's greatest support to be found in papal agreements with the most powerful princes – principally the Habsburgs, but also the Bavarian electors – even when such alliances could undercut the interests of the bishops? A more fundamental question had to do with what, precisely, was to be protected. Was it the security of property held by the church, or was it ecclesiastical independence in appointing bishops, ordaining clergy, teaching correct doctrine and administering the sacraments? In this latter sense, church property was secondary and served only to assure material support for the officers of the church.

One of the most significant guarantees of the Peace of Westphalia was that church property would not be seized. Canon law also forbade the

---

[58] Gerhard Benecke has noted that the *Reichskirche* was "a unifying concept, not an actual institution of the Old Reich." This is a useful way of thinking about the status of the church in the Empire because, to a large degree, the story of the episcopal movement told in the preceding chapter was one of trying to define and rationalize this "unifying concept" and to turn it into a functioning reality. The episcopalists appealed to Imperial law, yet as we shall see "law" itself was not (nor is now) a mechanical function but instead a legitimating principle of action. The assertion of legal right does not necessarily mean results, especially when conflicting legal principles – in this case metaphysical ones – are involved. Benecke, "The German Reichskirche," in *Church and Society in Catholic Europe of the Eighteenth Century*, W. J. Callahan and D. Higgs, eds. (Cambridge: Cambridge University Press, 1979), 78.

alienation of the goods of the church. Yet, as Rudolfine von Oer has pointed out, there was a fundamental ambiguity in the Westphalian guarantee. This ambiguity was introduced as a way of achieving a confessional compromise over the status of church property. The compromise had to do with competing definitions of "church." While the legal principle was acknowledged that "church" property should not be alienated, it made quite a difference if one meant by "church" the visible hierarchy (the Catholic interpretation), or rather a broader definition that included "religious ends," and that would eventually include piety and charity. As the Secularization of 1803 would bear out, the legal guarantees of church property set out at Westphalia provided a latitude that proved fatal once Catholic sovereigns lost the political will to assure the security of property for ecclesiastical institutions.[59] It was the principle of confessional parity that enabled the peace to succeed, but that very principle allowed contradictory interpretations of the fundamental term "church."

The principle of non-alienation of ecclesiastical property survived the Reformation, albeit with great difficulties, in Protestant lands.[60] What had changed in Protestant countries was the role and authority of the ecclesiastical hierarchy – which was ultimately what mattered when it came to the distribution and control of ecclesiastical property. Neither theories of communal property nor the interests of the secular authorities left room for the ecclesiastical states. The Religious Peace of Augsburg in 1555 (§18 and §19) recognized that those ecclesiastical states already secularized would remain so. The Imperial law's protection of church property was thus broken on pragmatic grounds. As Johannes Heckel states:

the untouchability of church property was grounded in the essence of the Empire as a secular–spiritual unity. Even the recognition of the Protestants as a religious party did not alter that fact. The Religious Peace of Augsburg simply declared

---

[59] Rudolfine Freiin von Oer, "Der Eigentumsbegriff in der Säkularisationsdiskussion am Ende des Alten Reichs," in *Eigentum und Verfassung. Zur Eigentumsdiskussion im ausgehenden 18. Jahrhundert*, Rudolf Vierhaus, ed., *Veröffentlichung des Max-Placnk-Instituts für Geschichte 37* (Göttingen: Vandenhoeck & Ruprecht, 1972).

[60] Ibid., 200. This paragraph is indebted to Oer's sketch. See also Christopher Ocker, *Church Robbers and Reformers in Germany, 1525–1547: Confiscation and Religious Purpose in the Holy Roman Empire* (Leiden: Brill, 2006). Ocker agues that the Protestant Reformers were conservative in their approach to church property. They did not merely hand over all rights to the territorial lord, but elaborated legal and theological arguments in keeping with traditional notions of the autonomy of the church and Church property.

that those cases in which Protestant princes had broken that protection were not punishable, and moreover could not be prosecuted either in court or outside of court – to the disadvantage of the Catholic church property.[61]

Imperial protection of church property remained; what was disputed was how to define the church. Where the Reformation succeeded, the right to oversee ecclesiastical property fell to the territorial prince. The prince was supposed to make sure that church property was used for its original purpose. Thus in principle, it could be argued that church property was not alienated, since Protestants would argue that those things given to God long ago would still be applied to godly work, whether for worship, clergy, charity, or hospitals.[62]

In 1555, this principle of broadening the definition of "ecclesiastical," as applied to the use of goods, was used to overcome confessional differences. It was a pragmatic solution that developed into a legal principle. It also found its way as a means of preserving parity into the *Instrumentum pacis osnabrugense* (IPO) in 1648, one of the two treaties ending the Thirty Years' War.[63] In the section on Secularization and the Normal Year (1624), Oer notes:

it was not the church or the churches that were the objects of the guarantee of possession. For this would have meant that Imperial law would have had to make a dogmatic pronouncement about the truth claims of the major confession, which was precisely the type of decision that the principle of parity was supposed to avoid.[64]

For how could it guarantee the Catholic church its ownership without recognizing the Catholic church's own definition of itself and its hierarchy? Alternatively, to adopt a Protestant definition and to declare that each parish or community owned its property would drive a wedge between the local priests and bishops, not to mention the papacy. Instead, the object of the IPO's guarantee was the Imperial Estates and the church property of their area of rule *(Herschaftsgebiet)*. Each individual territory was affected only insofar as it could make the Normal

---

[61] Johannes Heckel, "Kirchengut und Staatsgewalt," in *Das blinde, undeutliche Wort "Kirche." Gesammelte Aufsätze*, Siegfried Grundmann, ed. (Cologne: Böhlau, 1964), 335.

[62] This, for example, was Martin Bucer's point. See Ocker, *Church Robbers and Reformers in Germany*.

[63] Incidentally, as Heckel notes, it is here that the word "secularization" appears for the first time to mean the transformation of ecclesiastical property by the state. Heckel, "Kirchengut und Staatsgewalt," 336.

[64] Oer, "Der Eigentumsbegriff in der Säkularisationsdiskussion am Ende des Alten Reichs," 201.

Year apply to it. Imperial law therefore did not decide among the concepts of property. This was one of the reasons why the Curia did not recognize the Peace.[65]

The papacy could not officially support the Peace and thereby endorse confessional parity. But it could and did consider indirect dealings with Protestant powers under Urban VIII. However, as Konrad Repgen has shown, the election of Innocent X in 1644 resulted in a harder line and in the ultimate rejection of the Peace with the bull *Zelo domus dei*. As Repgen puts it, "the Roman 'No' signified a renunciation of effective influence over political life" and a refusal of the necessary conditions that were the price of such power.[66] While papal diplomats had been working to assure a peace settlement, the change of policy resulted in a symbolic act that questioned the very legitimacy of the German constitution.[67] This struggle over legitimacy informed much of the Catholic response to the Westphalian settlement as Catholic states that had built their foundations on Counter-Reformation principles now had to find new ways to justify their activities. It is certainly true that on the level of *realpolitik*, church–state relations did not change overnight, nor did the church suddenly find its property under threat of seizure after 1648. However, its guarantees were only in an Imperial law that assumed a different definition of "church" than did the Catholic hierarchy. By the later eighteenth century, this legal ambiguity had developed into a full-scale threat, as princes and ministers on the one hand resorted to utilitarian and natural-law principles, while on the other hand, they sought to define Catholicism in such a way that they could honestly claim to be defending its essential nature.

[65] Ibid.

[66] Konrad Repgen, "Der päpstlicher Protest gegen den Westfälischen Frieden und die Friedenspolitik Urbans VIII," *Historisches Jahrbuch* 75 (1956), 97.

[67] The papal refusal to recognize the peace has been characterized as "inevitable" in some sense because the peace treaties enshrined a concept of confessional parity that denied fundamental Catholic claims to universality. Konrad Repgen takes issue with this view, and has shown how, over the course of the peace negotiations, the curia was willing to accept some form of confessional parity in Germany. While the papacy never planned on giving its explicit approval to such a situation, it does not follow that in practical terms; the curia did not envision a settlement that allowed secularized property to remain in Protestant hands. For this argument, see Ibid. For the full study with supporting documents from papal archives, see Konrad Repgen, *Die Römische Kurie und der Westfälische Friede. Idee und Wirklichkeit des Papsttums im 16. und 17. Jahrhundert*, 2 vols. (Tübingen: 1962–).

Since it was the estates themselves that were protected by the West-phalian settlement, Church property was safe only so long as the estates adhered to Catholic principles. Johannes Heckel notes that

the IPO did not concern itself with the church, but rather with the opposing religious parties. In order to secure political peace, each party must be allowed to develop its own concept of church [*Kirchenbegriff*], and therefore also its own definition of church property for each respective territory.[68]

This meant that each party was entrusted with the care of its religion, so that Catholic and Protestant lords would be applying different inter-pretations to the key concepts like *bona ecclesia*. Significantly, as Heckel states, the protections of the IPO were not directed against the territorial secular power as such, but rather against the *ius reformandi* in the hand of a territorial lord of a different confession. This is why the IPO needed to declare a Normal Year (1624) to determine what would be considered the religious status quo in any particular territory.[69]

After the Reformation, lay Catholic princes still claimed that they had the duty to act as the "protector of the church" (*advocatus ecclesia*). But the papal conception of its universal lordship over ecclesiastical property depended on the good will of the local users. This held – though certainly not without fissures – throughout the Counter-Reformation. However, once conceptions of the church itself begin to diverge, even Catholic estates broke from papal conceptions and applied their own ideas to church property. Bavarian and Habsburg princes were able to justify their sup-pression of cloisters because they had developed a new notion of church property (one that was tellingly similar to that adopted by Protestants in the sixteenth century). While the seizure of Jesuit property in Germany after 1773 was a blow to the papacy, it did follow a papal letter of sup-pression. Legally, therefore, the seizure of Jesuit properties occurred just inside the threshold of the old guarantee of ecclesiastical property. But as the debates over immunities and amortization laws shows, the alliance between the papacy and secular Catholic monarchs was no longer work-ing, and at the heart of the debate were diverging notions of the common good, the nature of law, and the justification for secular power.

---

[68] Heckel, "Kirchengut und Staatsgewalt," 341.
[69] Ibid.

5

Collegialism: The Rise of the State and the Redefinition of the Church

PUBLIC LAW AND THE CHURCH

As Hobbes realized, rethinking the state required rethinking the church. The elaboration of a sphere of secular power in opposition to the church was an act of mutual redefinition. The rise of the state was as much an intellectual phenomenon as it was an institutional one. Earlier, we have seen how Catholic princes and their supporters altered ideas about the common good. Given the tradition of Catholic political thought, with its strong commitment to the alliance of church and state, how did absolutist princes legitimate their exertions of financial and legal pressure on the church? One of the ways in which they did this was by subsuming parts of church law under the category of public law (*öffentliches Recht, ius publicum*).[1] Because of the prominence of public law literature in early

---

[1] The discipline of public law owed its origins to the rise of the modern state, and the development of public law (some times called "constitutional law") can be traced alongside the creation of the institutions and concepts of the modern secular state. As Michael Stolleis notes, that the division of the *ius civile* (civil law) into *ius publicum* (public law) and *ius privatum* (private law) goes back to antiquity. Private law referred to affairs between individuals or groups, in which the state did not have a major interest, whereas public law could include criminal law, constitutional law, and any area where the state had an interest in assuring the common good. Hanns Gross argues that the discipline of public law was particular to Germany because the nature of the Empire raised questions about the locus (or loci) of sovereignty. In other words, while the various terms (public law, *ius publicum*) were employed in other national legal traditions, they never assumed the importance they did for the Empire. He further notes that Bodin's emphasis on the "marks" of sovereignty were taken up as a challenge by German thinkers, particularly since Bodin's emphasis on majesty meant that he did not consider the Empire to be a monarchy. This problem of course cannot be separated from the religious

modern Germany, conceptualizations of the church were shaped by legal discourse.

The discussion and teaching of public law affected the church's law in two ways. First, the legal reasoning employed in distinguishing public from private law migrated into canon-law literature. Initially, the application of new terms like "public church law" was a neutral development and reflected more a shift of language than any radical new theory of the church. In other words, scholars of church law could organize their subject into private and public church laws without necessarily favoring curialist, conciliar, or Erastian positions.[2] The expression *ius publicum ecclesiasticum* could be employed to refer to concordat law or particular state–church law. It could also be used, as the Austrian jurist Josef Johann Nepomuk Pehem would, to distinguish legal matters within the church. In this sense, public church law would refer to the organization of the hierarchy, the status of governing bodies within the church, and the ways in which its laws obliged. Private church law regulated affairs between individuals, persons, benefices, and so forth. Though in principle the ecclesiastical use of "public" and "private" was a neutral terminological distinction, this usage reflected the general shift by which "canon law" came to mean only pure Roman Catholic church law.[3]

The second, more far-reaching, way in which the discourse of public law affected church law was more contested, as public lawyers tried to broaden the competency of the civil authority. "It was in *jus publicum*," Michael Stolleis notes, "that both the range of state influence over ecclesiastical property and law, as well as the reach of ecclesiastical power in secular affairs was to be determined."[4] There was an important difference between the way these things were seen by Protestant and Catholic jurists, given that Protestants recognized the territorial prince as the head of the church. Toward the end of the eighteenth century, Catholic

and political fragmentation of Germany in the Thirty Years' War, in which the authority and nature of the emperor was thrown into question. As recent scholarship has emphasized, the discourse of public law was central in the Empire because the problem of sovereignty and authority was contested. See Michael Stolleis, *Geschichte des öffentlichen Rechts in Deutschland. 1: Reichspublizistik und Policeywissenschaft 1600–1800* (Munich: Beck, 1988), 44–5 and Hans Gross, *Empire and Sovereignty. A History of the Public Law Literature in the Holy Roman Empire, 1599–1804* (Chicago: University of Chicago Press, 1973), xviii.

[2] Willibald M. Plöchel, *Geschichte des Kirchenrechts. Band V: Das kathlische Kirchenrecht in der Neuzeit. Dritter Teil* (Munich and Vienna: Velag Herold, 1969), 358.

[3] Plöchl, 359.

[4] Stolleis, 50.

jurists were borrowing the arguments of their Protestant colleagues to justify their advocacy of increased state authority in ecclesiastical affairs.

This borrowing points to a shared discourse relevant to the administration of the state, namely cameralism. As the art and science of good government and administration, cameralism was an outgrowth of the practical aspect of politics.[5] This was, in principle, confessionally neutral. As we have seen in the writings of Adam Contzen, the prince had every right to mobilize resources as part of the higher calling of protecting the church. Yet underlying cameralist ideology were principles drawn from natural law tradition. Thus to understand the evolution of concepts of the church in relation to the state we must also examine how the growth of the state changed understandings of natural law.

Another way of putting it is to look at how the theoretical side of cameralism concerned itself with questions of happiness and the common good, as well as at how public authority should be structured so that justice was preserved.[6] This latter discipline, Hanns Gross notes, was often pursued in terms of universal natural law.[7] The question facing political and legal writers, therefore, was how these ideas applied to the church. In order to discuss the church in the context of a public law that had already adopted the principles of rational natural law, the theorist needed to develop, at least provisionally, a definition of church that did not depend on revelation.

Such a development differs subtly, but significantly, from the theories of natural religion that had been masterfully employed by the Spanish scholastics and Jesuit missionaries in the New World.[8] The Catholic proponents of natural religion argued that all human societies had religious practices, even if "idolatrous." Providence had thereby bestowed upon them the ability to receive revelation. This theory was employed both to justify the activities of missionaries in the New World and to refute Lutheran and Calvinist conceptions of human inability to act virtuously without grace. However, an examination of Church laws based

---

[5] Gross, xxiv.

[6] Gross, xxv.

[7] Gross, xxiv.

[8] Quentin Skinner, *The Foundations of Modern Political Thought. Volume 2: The Age of Reformation* (Cambridge: Cambridge University Press, 1978); Leonard Krieger, *The Politics of Discretion: Pufendorf and the Acceptance of Natural Law* (Chicago: University of Chicago Press, 1965) and Anthony Pagden, *The Fall of Natural Man. The American Indian and the Origins of Comparative Ethnology* (Cambridge: Cambridge University Press, 1982).

on principles of rational natural law in the wake of Pufendorf and Grotius assumed that there was a church law that could be known through reason, and that these laws were in a sense independent of belief in the church itself.[9] Given the acceptance of natural law, the way was opened for the entry of social contractual ideas into definitions of the church.[10] Furthermore, those elements that were based on reason – instead of revelation – could be more easily seen as subject to the state. The public lawyer intent on expanding the authority of the secular power in ecclesiastical affairs used arguments from reason to establish that the role of the state was to ensure justice and establish the common good. He next needed to draw the boundaries – based on universal reason – between church and state to establish their respective roles.

THE AUSTRIAN CANONISTS

The intellectual development toward separating church law from public law became academic reality in Austria after 1767, when seminarians were first required to hear their lectures in canon law not in the theological faculty, but in the faculty of law.[11] What had previously been an academic debate over the sources of the canon law now obtained official sanction. The implication was that the competence of the faculty of law was broader than that of the canonists in the theological faculty. The concept of "universal church law" (*ius ecclesiasticum universum*) was interpreted by some – notably van Espen – to mean not just the internal laws of the church – the canons themselves – but also the laws of the state that affected the church. Requiring students to learn their canon law from the secular law faculty therefore was a significant practical step because it not only implied this broader conception of church law, but also meant that the instructors were not under ecclesiastical discipline.

The first important Austrian jurist to lay the groundwork for what would become Josephine church policy was Paul Joseph Anton Riegger

---

[9] Plöchel, 358.

[10] Along similar lines, David Hempton has recently noted Methodism's "ecclesiology based on the principle of association." The various disputes over membership and authority within the movement "are essentially the preoccupations of a voluntary association, not a confessional church with its apparatus of clerical authority, historic confessions of faith, and hallowed traditions." David Hempton, *Methodism: Empire of the Spirit* (New Haven: Yale University Press, 2005), 52.

[11] William Bowman, *Priest and Parish in Vienna, 1780–1800* (Boston: Humanities Press, 1999), 120.

(1705–1775). Riegger was professor of public law, German history, and natural law at the University of Innsbruck for 16 years after getting his doctorate in Freiburg in 1733. In 1749 Riegger became professor in the Ritterakademie in Vienna, where he taught Imperial law, Imperial history, and natural law and the law of nations, as well as church law and public law at the Collegium Theresianum. After 1753, he also taught church law at the reorganized University of Vienna. The University reached high international standing, particularly because of the presence on the law faculty of Riegger, Karl Anton Martini (Austrian legal reformer and writer, 1726–1800), and later Joseph von Sonnenfels (ca. 1732–1817), the famous cameralist writer. Riegger's four-volume *Institutiones Iurisprudentiae Ecclesiasticae* (1765, reissued 1777) was contested by the bishops as a textbook, although it was still approved by Maria Theresa.[12] The first volume represents essentially a theoretical approach to church law and the sources of the law, whereas the latter three volumes are organized under the titles of the Decretals of Gregory IX.[13] Riegger begins by establishing the centrality of human desire for happiness (*felicitas*) and the role of religion in achieving it. This first section deals generically with religion, natural religion, and the "natural church." He continues by stating that "when men agree in natural religion, a society is produced, which is called a church. This society is hypothetical, and it can be either equal or unequal."[14] "Equal" and "unequal" refer to the relative status of the members of the society to each other. Riegger then goes on to establish that authority over this natural church falls to the "majesty," but that it can be separated from the "majesty" as well. In other words, even though the civil authority originally has power over this hypothetical religious society, that society may also establish its autonomy. But, Riegger emphasizes, the state never gives up its authority "around" (*circa*) sacred affairs.[15] This same theme is developed with particular skill by Riegger's pupil and successor, Josef Johann Nepomuk Pehem (1740–1799).[16]

---

[12] "Riegger, Paul Joseph," in *Biographisch-bibliographisches Kirchenlexikon VIII* (1994), 310–3.

[13] Riegger, while using the titles of the Decretals, follows a tradition established by earlier canonists in challenging orthodox interpretations of canon law while employing the received form.

[14] Paul Joseph Riegger, *Institutionum Iurisprudentiae Ecclesiasticae*, vol. 1, second ed. (Vienna, 1777–), Part I, §XVI, 13.

[15] Riegger, *Institutiones*, Part I, §XIX, 15.

[16] Pehem and Riegger share the same fundamental ideas about natural law and the role of the state in religion. Indeed, Pehem employs similar phrasing as Riegger (sometimes with, sometimes without, attribution). I have chosen to focus on Pehem, however,

Pehem's *Praelectionum in Jus Ecclesiasticum Universum* comprises three volumes. The first volume treats public church law (*jus ecclesiasticum publicum*), while the second discusses private church law (*jus ecclesiasticum privatum*). The third volume is a treatise of the particular laws and customs of the Catholic church in Germany, which deals with the same issues as had Barthel, Hontheim, and the other German canonists.[17] Pehem's division of the entire law of the church into public and private laws reinforces his argument that the church and the State occupy separate spheres. Pehem's ability to model his church law on the distinction between public and private laws shows how the Catholic church could be rethought on the model of the modern secular state.

Throughout his lectures on church law, Pehem argues for a spiritualization of the church's role and a consequent devolution of many traditional church powers to the state. He defines both the church and the State according to their "ends":

One must derive the boundaries of a particular power from its purpose. From this comes the conclusion that whosoever possesses the right and duty to achieve a certain purpose also has the right to employ all appropriate means through which this purpose can be achieved. Conversely, whosoever has no right or duty to achieve a certain end is therefore denied the use of those means which would be appropriate and necessary for the achievement of that purpose.[18]

Pehem then goes on to define the universal purpose of human activity as one of trying to attain inward and outward happiness [*felicitas, Glückseligkeit*]. Inner happiness is described as being "eternal," while external happiness is "temporal."[19] These qualities are also defined in terms of their purposes: inner happiness has as its purpose the well-being of "our soul in a future life, whereas the latter has as its goal the assurance

---

because in breaking with the method of the Decretals, Pehem organizes church law into public and private in such a way as to emphasize the manner in which the church mirrors the state. But it mirrors the state in an absolute sense: their spheres and powers are to be so totally separated that they never touch. Furthermore, because his lectures were part of the official plan of study until 1810, Pehem influenced a great number of seminarians in Austria. Pehem's lectures on church law sketch a theory of the radical separation of church and state power. In itself this is not novel, but he states this goal with remarkable clarity. On the seminary reforms, see William Bowman, *Priest and Parish in Vienna,* 120.

[17] Josef Johann Nepomuk Pehem, *Praelectionum in Jus Ecclesiasticum Universum, Methodo Discentium Utilitati Adcommodata Congestarum* (Vienna, 1788). See also the German translation: Pehem, *Vorlesung über das Kirchenrecht. Aus dem Lateinischen übersetzt.* 4 vols. (Vienna, 1802–1803).

[18] Pehem, I §635.

[19] Pehem, I §636.

of unimpeded progress in the perfection and satisfaction of this life."[20] From these two principles follows the creation of a church and a state – two entirely distinct institutions constructed according to specific needs. Religion is defined as "a self-determined way in which to honor God." Since "inner happiness cannot be obtained without true religion ... societies were created to honor God in this ordained manner." Such a society is called a "church," and from this it follows that churches were created for the purpose of attaining inner happiness.[21]

The state was created according to Pehem in a similar manner:

When humans still lived in a scattered condition and were singly too weak to achieve the happiness of this life, danger taught them that they needed to come up with means to solve these weaknesses. But no other means were available than to give up the rights of freedom, equality and independence as far as necessary, and to come together in a great number under a single rule.[22]

Pehem borrows from Karl Anton Martini *Positiones iure civitatis* (1768), which maintained that civil society was created by families (specifically the *paterfamilias*) to overcome the difficulties of anarchy. Martini insisted that the state (*civitas*) did not owe its origin to nature or to God, but to reason.[23] He emphasized that his treatment of the state is philosophical rather than historical, which means that he treats the theory of the state and its goals, as opposed to how it actually was formed.[24] Pehem applies the same logic to his definition of the church: by asserting its goals, Pehem then derives what form the church should take, bypassing its actual historical development. Pehem sees the centrality of the institutions of church and state born out in their prevalence throughout the world:

church and state are therefore two societies that are so fundamental to common happiness that humanity cannot do without them. Therefore it is not surprising that almost no human group in the entire world is found without both civil and religious societies.[25]

Pehem presents this definition of the state as a society to make a point about the absolute independence of the state from the church. This

[20] Pehem, I §636.
[21] Pehem, I §637.
[22] Pehem, I §638.
[23] See Karl Anton von Martini, *Positiones de Iure Civitatis in ususm auditorii vindobonensis* (Vienna, 1773), Chapter 1.
[24] Martini, c. 1, §XXVII, 14.
[25] Pehem, I §639.

separation is founded on his definition of church and state according to their "ends" and the means appropriate to achieving those ends. The priesthood, concerned as it is with helping humanity achieve eternal happiness, should be able to employ only spiritual means to attack moral and irreligious evil.[26] Conversely, Pehem argues that religious sentiments are outside of the purview of physical coercion.

> The needs of our souls and the changing of their conceptions cannot be accomplished without reason and consideration. Any attempt to do this by coercive means is an attack on the doctrine of the spirituality of our souls. . . . The power of the ruler therefore does not extend to the thoughts of his subjects.[27]

Pehem thus argues that the very definition of the soul depends on establishing fully separate spheres for religious and secular activities. Otherwise, one would wind up denying the duality between spirit and body.

Pehem resorts to a hypothetical origin of the church to show the limitations of church power.

> Let us first look at the church power without resorting to revelation. Assume that several 'patresfamilias,' who up to this point did not form any sort of civil union entered into a church society. One could not find anyone outside of that union who would acknowledge its power [over them] because of the nature of its origin.[28]

In other words, church power is an internal matter; it rests on the implied consent of those members who have joined it to attain a certain end. But it may not infringe on the power of another society – the state – whose ends are of a different order. This separation is fortuitous:

> because of [the separation] there is not created a *State in the State*, which would be a political monster [*monstrum politicum*]. This would occur when two rulers, though having different purposes, were to exercise the same type of power over the same people.[29]

Even though clergy and bishops make up the society of the church, they are also part of civil society under control of the state. The problem is to

---

[26] Pehem, I §641.
[27] Pehem, "Historisch-Statische Abhandlung von Errichtung, Ein- und Abtheilung der Bisthümer" [1790], in *Der Josephinismus: Ausgewählte Quellen Zur Geschichte Der Theresianisch-Josphinischen Reformen*, Harm Klueting, ed. (Darmstadt: Wissenschaftliche Buchgesellschaft, 1995), 395–6.
[28] Pehem, I §645.
[29] Pehem, I §650.

be resolved, says Pehem, not by "melting" church and state into one society, but to see them as two separate societies with radically differing goals. Augustine's City of God has been recast in light of Protestant natural law theory.[30]

Having established the nature of the church in terms of its "end" and its nature as a society, Pehem moves to outline the power of the ruler in spiritual matters. He deals with this issue through the twin concepts of *jus in sacra* and *jus circa sacra*, which may be translated as the rights "in sacred affairs" and "around sacred affairs" respectively.[31] *Jus in sacra* is seen as the absolute sphere of the church, dealing only with those things necessary to salvation, while *jus circa sacra* has more to do with external governance and organization, and as such may affect the security or functioning of the state. Pehem stresses that the ruler has rights only *circa sacra*. He also does not cite any authorities for his arguments in the initial discussion of these concepts. Instead, most of his points are made based on earlier statements about the role of secular authority, the nature of the church, and the essence of religion.

Despite the subtleties made by writers such as Pehem in distinguishing between matters essential and peripheral to salvation, Josephine reformers increasingly arrogated to the sphere of the prince's responsibility matters that were traditionally seen as subject to the church's concern for salvation. The establishment of the rights and duties of the prince in Pehem's lectures brings us back to the "ends" of civil rule and to the means given to the prince for attaining them. Principle among these was "majesty" [*majestas*].[32] "The creation of a civil society [*constitutio societatis civilis*] is foreordained by natural law, and any activity which is opposed to the completion of this end is also against the law of nature."[33]

---

[30] Moses Mendelssohn's *Jerusalem* likewise borrows much from Protestant legal theory. See especially Alexander Altman's commentary to Moses Mendelssohn, *Jerusalem: or on Religious Power and Judaism*, trans. Allan Arkush, with introduction and commentary by Alexander Altman (Waltham, MA: Brandeis University Press, 1983).

[31] Pehem notes that even the terminology itself is contested:

On this power of the territorial prince there has been much difference of opinion and dispute. There are those who have such a tender conscience that they do not even allow the use of the expression [*ipsum nomen ferant iniquius*], because they confuse the prince's authority over spiritual matters with ecclesiastical authority itself [*jus circa sacra confudentes cum potestate ecclesiastica*].

Pehem I, §752.

[32] Pehem I, §758.

[33] Pehem I, §754.

Therefore the prince has the right to ensure that church activities do not impede the functioning of society:

> although the power of the church is great, it is limited only to those activities which have to do with the proper mode of worshipping God. It is therefore not within the power of the church to propagate an arbitrary method of honoring God which the ruler finds harmful. True piety was just as well expressed in other manners in other times.[34]

Here things begin to get delicate, for according to Pehem's system, the regent is now able to decide about the appropriateness of particular forms of worship and to make judgments about the validity of pious practice in earlier times. He may also limit *accidentialia religionis* – nonessential aspects of the faith – such as pilgrimages, processions, and brotherhoods.[35] Thus, even though the prince is restricted to exercising a *jus circa sacra*, he is actually increasing his influence in the practice of religion.[36]

The prince's largest concern, in Pehem's view, is to assure the proper functioning of civil society. "Civil society" here refers to those individuals who come under the rule of the prince (i.e., everybody in his territory) and whose worldly good he is supposed to be fostering. Solely from the perspective of a prince wishing to benefit society – that is, not as an obedient Catholic monarch – the prince would recognize that religion in general, and not just Catholicism, is beneficial to society. It is the prince's duty, therefore, to tolerate those religions that honor God and encourage obedience and virtue, while those who adhere to no religion and are not pious are unlikely to care much for the general good.[37] On account of his "majesty," the prince has the right to inspect the church to know

---

[34] Pehem I, §757.

[35] Pehem I, §792.

[36] This gradual encroachment of the worldly power into the practice of religion leads to an important point, namely the process by which religion comes to be understood more and more in terms of practice rather than doctrine or belief by certain reformers. Religious practice was seen as affecting the life of the subject in possibly detrimental ways. Conversely, a reform of practice can lead to a general improvement in the character of the individual – an improvement which manifests itself in the spheres of obedience and labor. This point was recognized – albeit from a different perspective, by nineteenth-century Catholics who emphasized the importance of inculcating religion by making devotional practices part of everyday life. See Anon., "Religion als Sitte," *Der Katholik* NF 2 (1850). The idea is discussed in Wolfgang Brückner, "Zum Wandel der religiösen Kultur im 18. Jahrhundert. Einkreisversuche des 'Barockfrommen' zwischen Mittelalter und Massenmissionierung," in *Sozialer und kultureller Wandel in der ländlichen Welt des 18. Jahrhunderts*, Ernst Hinrichs and Günter Wiegelmann, eds. (Wolfenbüttel: Herzog August Bibliothek, 1982).

[37] Pehem I, §759.

whether anything that could damage the state is happening without his knowledge.

An example of the practical application of these ideas can be seen in Josephine policy toward monasteries. The prince's authority over monastic affairs arises from his concern with civil society. According to Pehem, he is right to shrink the number of monks, since the state is hurt when the high number of monks prevents them from working for "defense or nourishment" (i.e., agriculture).[38] The state also exercises a certain jurisdiction over the vows sworn by monks, for their vows are twofold. In the first instance they are promising to join the order and follow its rules. But the oath is also between the monk and the state, whereby he abjures any rights to inheritance, civil occupations, or contracts. The state, for its part, promises to secure his right to live out the cloistered life he has chosen. But, according to Pehem, the monk still has duties as a citizen.[39] During the Investiture Controversy, the world was cast as comprised of the "perfect societies" of church and state. With the world divided into clergy and laity, individuals were kept institutionally apart by means of separate jurisdictions and authorities.[40] Now each person was himself divided into Christian and citizen, and was subject to both authorities simultaneously in their separate spheres.

IUS CIRCA SACRA: PROTESTANT CHURCH LAW
AND MODERN NATURAL LAW

Pehem's lectures in church law drew from two related, yet distinct, intellectual traditions: rational natural law and Protestant church law. Pehem, as we have seen, applied theories of the social contract to define the role of the church in society. As significant was the Protestant provenance of the concepts *ius in sacra* and *ius circa sacra*.[41] Protestant

---

[38] Pehem I, §804. In an earlier era, their prayers may have been seen as beneficial, but such a justification was unlikely to carry much weight in the later eighteenth century.

[39] Pehem I, §798.

[40] In principle, clergy would be tried in ecclesiastical courts for crimes that had nothing to do with their clerical role.

[41] It is clear from Pehem's writings that he had read the Protestant jurists, in particular Justus Henning Böhmer (1674–1749). For example, in a passage on the origins of excommunication in divine law, Pehem disputes Böhmer's claim that legal basis for excommunication comes from church discipline as set forth by the union of Christians (Pehem, §122). Similarly, he notes when Böhmer's conclusions do not apply to Catholic doctrines (Pehem, §116). Pehem bases many of his points on historical arguments, so his disputes with Böhmer, as well as with other scholars, are ones of historical

experience in church law proved fruitful to Catholic princes seeking to consolidate their authority over the church.[42] Given the Lutheran emphasis on the invisible church, it was also necessary to ensure that the religious core would be free from worldly pressure. Therefore, the distinction between the visible and the invisible church had to be strengthened to preserve the religious principle that the true church was incorruptible. Furthermore, the powers of the prince to shape the external form of the church had to be elaborated. From this constellation of ideas evolved the need to elaborate a "particular church (*ecclesia particularis*) in the sense of the constituted church in the territory (*verfassten Kirche des Landes*)."[43]

The Lutheran dogmatist Johann Gerhard (1582–1637) divided ecclesiastical authority (*potestam ecclesiam*) into external and internal powers. The Reformers had said that there were only two powers: civil and ecclesiastical; they could not affect each other. Now the ecclesiastical power itself was being split into exterior and interior aspects.[44] The concept of "internal church authority" was clearly derived from the Lutheran teaching of the inner Church and the ministry of the Word. Yet the expression of "external church authority" was new. It combined

---

interpretation, not dogma. The systematic introduction of history into Catholic church law was a major achievement of the Louvain jurist van Espen, who, at least as far as the Viennese jurists were concerned, had succeeded in making history an important source for the interpretation and explication of church law. But appeals to history by church lawyers meant that Protestant and Catholic jurists would need to confront the same sources, which is why Pehem's lectures are peppered with references to prominent Protestant writers. Böhmer taught at Halle from 1701 until he was named chancellor of the Duchy of Magdeburg in 1743. According to Peter Landau, his most important work was in his systemization of Evangelical Church law on the basis of canon law. His principle work in this matter was *Ius ecclesiasticum protestantium* (1714–1737). Although friendly to the State, he was also influenced by Pietism, leading him to emphasize that the state should not have influence over doctrine. See Peter Landau, "Böhmer, Justus Henning," in *Juristen. Ein biographisches Lexikon*, M. Stolleis, ed. (Munich: C. H. Beck, 1995) and Peter Landau, "Vom mitteralterlichen Recht zur neuzeitlichen Rechtswissenschaft," in *Rechts- und staatswissenschaftliche Veröffentlichung d. Görresgesellschaft*, neue Folge, 72 (1994), 317–33.

[42] On the development of Protestant territorial church law, see Martin Heckel, *Staat und Kirche nach den Lehren der evangelischen Juristen Deutschlands in der ersten Hälfte des 17. Jahrhunderts, Jus Ecclesiasticum*, vol. 6 (Munich: Claudius Verlag, 1968).

[43] Johannes Heckel, "*Cura religionis, ius in sacra, ius circa sacra*," in *Festschrift Ulrich Stutz* (Kirchenrechtliche Abhandlungen 117/118 (Stuttgart: F. Enke, 1938), 273.

[44] Heckel, 275. Heckel further argues that this is the first instance of separation of powers in German constitutional history. Whereas the concept of separation of powers is usually associated with English or French political theory, in Germany, it appears as a theological doctrine.

several of the older concepts that had been previously considered (at least conceptually) separate. Previously, the prince legitimated his powers over the church with different claims: as the preeminent member of society, as part of the secular authority's "custody" of the first table of the Ten Commandments, and as an authority over his subjects. This web of justifications had been constructed to ensure that the key evangelical doctrine of the incorruptible invisible church was preserved. The elegant distinction between internal and external authority combined these divergent concepts, yet the impetus to such an intellectual reorganization, Johannes Heckel notes, was not theological, but political.[45] Indeed, Gerhard had borrowed the idea from the Reformed Heidelberg theologian David Pareus (1548–1622), who had developed it as part of the polemical battle against Robert Bellarmine.[46] In short, the need for territorial princes to legitimate their increasing control over ecclesiastical affairs was a key development in the origins of the confessional state.

One of the most important concepts that Pehem borrowed from Protestant jurists in his defense of Josephine church policy was that of *ius circa sacra*. While it would seem that the term arises from natural law, it also has theological roots.[47] Indeed, Thomas Erastus (1524–1583) developed the concept in his treatise on Protestant excommunication.[48] He argued that the power to excommunicate rested with the state, since there was no way for a religious body with purely religious power to make the civil authority accept its decision. Otherwise, there would be two supreme authorities in the same community.[49] Of Erastus' contribution, Heckel states:

the distinction [he introduced] is extremely simple, and was for the student of nature quite evident. Human life, including social unions, play themselves out either in the spiritual or the sensual world. Accordingly, they can be considered either as *internal or external affairs. The criterion for this is sensual perception, corporality.*[50]

Once ecclesiastical affairs were assigned to either the inner or outer sphere, the door was open for the territorial lord to assert more control over

---

[45] Heckel, 276.

[46] Heckel, 276–9.

[47] Heckel, 284.

[48] Ruth Wesel-Roth, *Thomas Erastus. Ein Beitrag zur Geschichte der reformierten Kirche und zur Lehre von der Staatssouveränität.* Veröffentlichungen des Vereins für Kirchengeschichte in der evang. Landeskirche Badens, XV (Lahr/Baden: Moritz Schauenburg, 1954), 95f.

[49] Heckel, 290f.

[50] Heckel, 292.

ecclesiastical matters, such as administration, church property, and secular education, that could be defined as relating to the external or corporal sphere. Thus the Reformers' concept of the authority of the Christian Prince (*Obrigkeit*) had evolved to such a point where it could easily be absorbed into natural law definitions of secular authority.[51] The terminology of *jus circa sacra* was popularized by Hugo Grotius' *De imperio summarum potestatum circa sacra* (posthumously published in 1647).[52]

The arranged marriage of Protestant theology and natural law had been set up to benefit the territorial princes who sought to extend their control of ecclesiastical affairs. Yet by the early eighteenth century, it was natural law that was ultimately to provide Protestant theologians and jurists with the means of creating some free space for themselves from state control. They did this by elaborating a "collegial" interpretation of church law. As explained by Klaus Schlaich, collegialism owes its name to the *systema collegiale* in the writings of J. H. Boehmer in 1736. Boehmer in turn was influenced by the prominent theologians C. M. Pfaff (1686–1760) and J. L. von Mosheim (1694–1755).[53] The basic position of the collegialists arises from the view that the church at the time of the Apostles was a free association of equals. The *respublica christiana* had become an unequal society by the late Middle Ages, but was returned to its original equality by the Reformation.[54] "Equality" is here meant to refer to the relationship of the members of the church to the sacraments – the "priesthood of all believers" proclaimed by Luther. It is, in this sense, incompatible with traditional Catholicism, which maintained the validity of its hierarchy and saw the church as an objective repository of grace. Nevertheless, Catholic writers were able to draw significantly from the theory.

Protestant collegialism was, according to Schlaich, a particular response to fit, "the church and its law, which was theologically and transcendentally based, into the new, world-immanent, 'reasonable' [*vernunftmässigen*] legal system of the modern secular state."[55] Rooted in

---

[51] Heckel also notes that in providing solid legal and theological basis for the construction of a territorial "particular" church, the new theory of external ecclesiastical power allowed enabled an exit from the "naïve biblical political vision" that Christians should – ideally – be organized like the ancient Hebrew state. Heckel, 294–5.
[52] Heckel, 293.
[53] Schlaich, *Kollegialtheorie. Kirche, Recht und Staat in der Aufklärung. Jus Ecclesiasticum*, vol. 8 (Munich, 1969), 13–4.
[54] Schlaich, 14.
[55] Schlaich, 21.

the language of secular natural law, it was an attempt to come to terms with changing political realities.[56] Boehmer defined the Christian church as "a society of men, united by their Christian faith, gathered together in Christian religion.[57] "Religion" is not a particular property of the church; it is rather possessed completely by the individual, who brings it to the society.[58]

By defining the church as a society, collegialists were carving out a separate sphere for the church in which to act. They did not deny the territorial lord his rights in supervision of the church (*Kirchenaufsicht*), but they tried to delimit those areas in which the state did not have any interest. Thus it was important to differentiate authority over the church (*Kirchengewalt*) from supervision (*Kirchenaufsicht*), the latter still being the duty of the prince. The right to administer the church was known as the *iura circa sacra collegialia*, which implied that the church's rights were like those of any other "society" in the state. The rights reserved to the church included the right to order the liturgy, the means to the liturgy and preaching, and to decide religious conflicts on the grounds of official doctrine.[59] But collegial theory did not allow the church to claim exemption for its members from the authority of the state. That would destroy the unity of the state and create a *"status in statu* ... the State would become a two-headed monstrosity."[60]

Pehem was traveling along the same road as his Protestant colleagues, only he was coming from the opposite direction. Protestant jurists – at least those interested in the development of collegial theory – were trying to establish a separate sphere for the church in lands where the civil powers had, since the sixteenth century, asserted significant authority

---

[56] In terms of church law and its relation to the state, collegialism was a successor to the "episcopalism" of the seventeenth century. "Episcopalism" had underlain the claims of territorial rulers in the Religious Peace of Augsburg in 1555. The rights of the Catholic bishops in Protestant territories were declared suspended and handed over to the prince. This "episcopalism" gave way to a "territorialism," which was much bolder in claiming specific powers for the prince of the territory, putting more emphasis on the sovereignty of the ruler, and less in the middle-ground position that declared the bishop's power as "suspended." The ruler's powers as head of the church were now seen as permanent, not as a temporary response to a crisis in ecclesiastical authority. Collegialism represented a turn away from this tradition insofar as it did not start from a need to justify the princes' actions with regard to the church. Rather, it shifted to defining what the church actually *was*. See Schlaich, 18.

[57] Boehmer, *Principia Iuris Canonici* quoted in Schlaich, 49.

[58] Schlaich, 91.

[59] Schlaich, 227.

[60] Schlaich, 248.

over religious matters. Conversely, Pehem, like Riegger before him, was concerned with finding a legal basis for increasing state intervention in religious matters, while maintaining the fundamentals of Catholic doctrine. As in collegial theory, Pehem states that the Christian church arises from the body of Christians coming together to recognize the Christian religion.[61] The church is different from all other societies, though, because it was given its form by Christ, whereas even civil society was founded by human beings.[62] As noted above, Pehem cites the Protestant collegialists Mosheim and Boehmer, though he distances himself from them. The biggest difference between their legal writings and his, Pehem notes, derives from the fact that the Catholic church is an unequal society. Christ had given certain powers to people who are known as "Clerici, Pastores [or] Rectores." These dispense spiritual goods to *"laici, oves, subditi"* (lay, sheep, and subjects).[63]

In many ways, Pehem's notion of the "perfect" societies of the state and the church recall the language of Cardinal Bellarmine and his doctrine of the indirect temporal authority of the pope. But Pehem seems to have carried the issue a step further. Indeed, he inverted Bellarmine's claim that the pope may step into temporal affairs when questions of salvation are at stake. Pehem asserts, on the contrary, that the prince has the right to regulate religious practice when it threatens to disrupt or impede the progress of civil society. Pehem's achievement is to define religion in such a manner that state interference cannot affect its pure "ends." Both Bellarmine and Pehem were responding to new political realities where the authority of the church became more and more exclusively "moral." And both would resort to the language of natural law to justify their views. Pehem would also have at his disposal contract theories of the state which had made significant advances since the seventeenth century. Bellarmine sought to show how the pope could legitimately influence political affairs without trampling on the natural law basis of state sovereignty. Pehem was confronted with a doctrine of princely absolutism that aimed at coordinating political with economic forces. He sought to find a legitimate sphere for independent religious activity that did not interfere with the prince's duties and goals.

The state was now able to mobilize a variety of arguments to justify its intervention in the sacred by showing how religious affairs affected the political and economic sphere. The discussion of Josephine church law

[61] Pehem I, §46.
[62] Pehem I, §47.
[63] Pehem I, §125.

shows how those pushing for more state control over ecclesiastical affairs understood the role of the state with respect to religion and to the common good. The teaching of church law from the perspective of the secular law faculty fixed the distinction between canon law and church law. Canon law was now portrayed as the body of rules and regulations of a corporation within the state, relativizing it within the entire apparatus of state legislation regarding religion. By treating certain materials of canon law as "private law," the jurist necessarily defined canon law as that of a particular society within the state. Yet questions of jurisdiction were paramount, which is why the key sticking points were the definitions of *ius in sacra* and *ius circa sacra*.

FOM CANON LAW TO ECCLESIOLOGY

As important as the institutional and education realignment of canon law was the acceptance of Protestant natural law by a large cohort of Catholic thinkers. Catholic canonists had adopted principles of Protestant ecclesiastical law that had built on natural law contract theories of society. Yet these contract theories of society were not alien to Catholic thought. On the contrary, Protestants had at first rejected many of the tenets of natural law based on a theological anthropology that denigrated any innate human freedom before divine grace. It was the Spanish scholastics, in particular, who had revived a Thomist discourse of natural law. Their ideas were introduced into Protestant jurisprudence by Hugo Grotius.[64]

The acceptance of Protestant natural law was seen as problematic, to say the least, by some orthodox Catholics. Anselm Desing, the Benedictine monk who would later defend the wealth of the clergy against the policies of the Bavarian ecclesiastical council, worried that teaching natural law as found in the works of Pufendorf or Grotius to Catholic students was dangerous to Catholicism. Desing claimed to tear off the "mask" [*larva*] of natural law as taught in the works of Pufendorf and Wolff in his 1753 *Juris naturae larva detractata*.[65] For Desing, the problem was not with natural law *per se*, but with interpretations that did not allow that revelation completed natural law. The Protestant jurists were working to rehabilitate the natural law tradition for their own ends. Indeed, one of their major achievements was to transform a discipline as

---

[64] See in particular Quentin Skinner, *The Foundations of Modern Political Thought. Volume 2: The Age of Reformation* and John Neville Figgis, *From Gerson to Grotius: 1414–1625* (Cambridge: Cambridge University Press, 1907).

[65] *Larva* can also mean "ghost" or "evil spirit."

it had been elaborated by the Spanish scholastics in part as a refutation of Lutheran political thought.[66] The modern books of natural law [*neotericis juris naturae libris*] do not claim Scripture as proof, Desing says, because Scripture was not revealed to all peoples.[67] They include the works of pagans and poets, but not Moses, and write as if everyone between Christ and Grotius were ignorant of natural law.[68] Desing is particularly concerned that this natural law not be taught to Catholic youth because its goal is to overturn the Catholic church [*nihil alius intendunt, quam Catholicae rei eversienem*].[69]

Desing labels the proponents of modern natural law "socialists." He does so based on Pufendorf's use of man's natural "sociability" as the touchstone of his natural law theory.[70] Desing argues that to declare sociability as the fundamental fact and standard of natural law removes God as the highest goal and "head." For Desing, this attention to sociability alone would overturn society because religion would not be its basis. He accuses Pufendorf and the other proponents of natural law of adoring the absolutist prince, and of having replaced the love of God as the highest good with the love of the prince.[71]

While Desing was correct that modern Protestant natural law favored the growth of the secular state, he glossed over the principal reason why it did so without appealing to revelation. An essential feature of Protestant natural law was its aim to posit rules for civil society and secular ethics that would enable such systems to avoid the pitfalls and appeals to absolutes that its proponents saw as having led to the wars of religion.[72] It was not Thomist because it assumed a radical separation of religion and

---

[66] See Skinner, *The Foundations of Modern Political Thought. Volume 2: The Age of Reformation*.

[67] Anselm Desing, *Juris Naturae Larva Detracta compluribus libris sub titulo Juris Naturae Prodeuntibus* (Munich: 1753), 16.

[68] Ibid.

[69] Ibid., 17.

[70] On Desing, see Johann Baptist Schneyer, *Die Rechtsphilosophie Anselm Desings O. S. B. (1699–1772)* (Kallmünz: Michael Lassleben, 1932) and Manfred Knedlik and George Schrott, eds., *Anselm Desing (1699–1772). Ein benediktinischer Universalgelehrter im Zeitalter der Aufklärung* (Kallmünz: Michael Laßleben, 1999). On Desing as perhaps the first to use the term "socialist," see Hans Müller, *Ursprung und Geschichte des Wortes "Sozialismus"* (Hannover: J. H. W. Nietz Nachfolger, 1967) and Franco Venturi, *Utopia and Reform in the Enlightenment* (Cambridge: Cambridge University Press, 1971), 102.

[71] He says their axiom is "mihi placere principibus bonum est" (11, 27:8). Cited in Schneyer, *Die Rechtsphilosophie Anselm Desings O. S. B. (1699–1772)*, 42.

[72] Ian Hunter, *Rival Enlightenments: Civil and Metaphysical Philosophy in Early Modern Germany* (Cambridge: Cambridge University Press, 2001).

civic life. This is precisely why it was so productive and fruitful across Europe after 1648. Desing does not accept this separation, and therefore cannot accept the principles that would come to undergird collegialism (as he would also resist the economic and political rationale that led the state to encroach on the wealth of the church). His resistance shows how the philosophical, legal and moral understanding of the nature of the church and the role of religion in civil society were bound up with the political understanding of the church. The collegialists' discussion in a sense prepared the way for the acceptance – and even embrace – of the *de facto* elimination of the political and social constitution of the Catholic church as it existed in the Empire.

Many of those who were the most engaged in the public discussion of the nature and status of the Catholic church in Germany in the decades after 1763 also owed their material support to state positions. This is not to belittle their concerns or to cast doubt on their intentions. However, it should be noted that people who, a generation earlier, would have entered a monastery or joined the clergy without hesitation, were offered new opportunities in the expanding bureaucracy of the state. We also need to take seriously the idea that they were interested in religion and spirituality (even if there were a few cynical functionalists among them).[73]

The arrival of the absolutist state presented German Catholics with both dangers and opportunities. According to the older scholarly literature, the supporters of the German Catholic Enlightenment – and especially partisans of Joseph II – had shamelessly abandoned the church to the wiles of the state and its ministers.[74] A more sober perspective allows us to see the ways in which German Catholics acknowledged the dilemma that temporal authority posed to the church. The liberty of the church and state was the major concern of the German rethinking of the church. On the one hand, German Catholic thinkers wanted to secure the liberties of the German church against Rome (the goal of Hontheim's *de Statu Ecclesiae*), and on the other hand, they did not want the material and secular power of ecclesiastical institutions to impede either the church's

---

[73] See Peter Hersche, *Der Spätjansenismus in Österreich* (Veröffentlichungen der Kommission für Geschichte Oesterreichs, Oesterreichische Akademie der Wissenschaften, Bd. 7, 1977).

[74] This is particularly the case with regard to the discussion of Josephinism. The most prominent of the strident critics of Josephinism was the Jesuit Ferdinand Maas, who edited a five volume collection of documents about the Austrian church reform. He softened his views in later works. See Ferdinand Maass, ed., *Der Josephinismus, Quellen zu seiner Geschichte in Österreich 1760–1850. Amtliche Dokumente aus dem Wiener Haus-, Hof- und Staatsarchiv*, 5 vols. (Vienna: Verlag Herold, 1951–1961).

religious mission or the state's political and economic goals. Moreover, educated German Catholics saw the reform of the church as the best way to improve the morality of the people.

The legal principle behind collegialism was that the church needed to be recognized as a private society within the state. This was a transition from its – nominally, at least – dominant position in Old Regime politics and society, and specifically in its legal structures. The major characteristic of the new bourgeois legal order was the abolition of privilege (literally, private law), as codified in the legal system. In principle each individual – and by extension each moral and artificial person – stood in equal relation to the state. The system of estates (*Stände*), in which each privileged group had its own set of rights, was passing.[75] The most famous commentator on this transition was Hegel, who argued that the "general estate" – the universal class of educated, cosmopolitan bureaucrats – would sweep away the tyranny of local and private laws. This transition was no less true of the church. This move toward becoming a private society in law did not have to be taken as a sign of subjugation – it could also be a liberation. The church – as it would become increasingly in the nineteenth century – was becoming a private, voluntary association. To Catholic liberals, shedding claims and obligations of a public institution enabled it to exercise its moral authority with greater independence.[76]

A principle theme of the German canonists' movement was to "accommodate" the law of the church to the German nation. In a similar fashion, the principle motivation of collegialism was the desire to "accommodate" the law of the Church to the modern secular state – to absolutism, in other words. This desire to accommodate was multifaceted, and was done as much to defend the rights and liberty of the churches (Protestant and Catholic) as it was to benefit the state. One of the central tendencies of absolutism was its assault on corporate privileges – although

[75] This is of course a long-term process, and I am generalizing here. Frederick's *Allgemeines Landrecht* for the Prussian states in many ways preserved and codified social distinctions in the law. With wholesale introduction of the Napoleonic code in the west of Germany the principles of legal equality as embodied in the French system were brought to many parts of Germany. Nevertheless, the general point – that agitation against the old legal order had worked its way into the understanding to the place of privilege in the law – still holds.

[76] This is not to say that the church became a wholly "private" society in law overnight. Indeed, in Germany there was never a wholesale separation of church and state in the American sense. The state, for example, still collects church taxes and distributes them to the churches. Nevertheless the authority of canon law was completely transformed by the nineteenth century.

the distinct privileges of the nobility were often left intact as the price for political cooperation. Nevertheless, the overarching effect of the rise of the modern state was the leveling of mediating groups between the individual and the state. Or, as Ernst Troeltsch so dramatically put it, "absolutism pulveriz[ed] the peoples into individuals."[77] Collegialism, and the desire to define the church as a collection of individuals who come together to worship God, can therefore be seen as a proactive response to these social and political changes. The rise of the state gave Catholics a new task: what type of voluntary society would Christians now form? One possible response was that sketched out by the canonists, postulating as they did the church as a *perfect society*, complete in itself, where it could not be touched in its essential form by the state.[78] The Catholic hierarchy, however, was not entirely prepared for this solution, at least not in the eighteenth century. Only after the church's material and political base had been shaken by the French Revolution did it see the possibilities – spurred on, no doubt, by the lack of other choices – of living without its own source of power.[79] In Germany, at least, Catholics who found themselves almost universally a political minority in the nineteenth century did not have to look too far into the past to see how an autonomous Catholic church could understand itself.

As a "society," the church also needed to define how it was shaped and constituted. What was its relationship to the dominant culture? How did the social hierarchy shape its own constitution? How were elite and popular religious cultures to be reconciled within one "universal" church? How was a "German church" to be ultimately ruled from afar? In an age of nascent national feeling, how did the diverse nationalities of the international Catholic church accord with German linguistic and geographic peculiarities? These were questions that were posed in an age which later historians have recognized as the period of the "rise of the bourgeoisie," and therefore it must be asked about the effects of this rise on German Catholic self-understanding. The following section of this book will move from the legal connotation of the church as a society to the discussion of just how that "private society" (and sometimes "perfect society") was to be constituted. For in rethinking the church, German Catholics needed to rethink society as well.

---

[77] Ernst Troeltsch, *Religion in History* (Minneapolis: Fortress Press, 1991), 244.

[78] The terminology, significantly enough, was derived from the Investiture Struggle.

[79] Of course, this issue would not be resolved completely until the end of the Papal State in 1870.

PART TWO

THE UNIVERSAL CHURCH AND THE
UNIVERSAL CLASS

The Germans are still on the whole a very religious nation, and true religious formation and Enlightenment have attained a higher level among them than among any other nation. Just as it was among the Germans that the Reformation had its beginnings, so too among them in the eighteenth century there began a new revolution in religious knowledge and in the theological sciences, only this time without disturbance, violence, and war.

     – Karl Friedrich Stäudlin, 1804[1]

Religion should serve as a support for the state. It should enlighten the citizen about his duties. It should foster in him love of his calling, domestic order, industry, exactitude and fidelity toward his trade. It must provide a doctrine of felicity for society and for each of its members.

     – Johann Michael Bönicke, ca. 1780[2]

---

[1] K. F. Stäudlin, *Kirchliche Geographie und Statistik*, 2 vols. (Tübingen: 1804), 324.

[2] Johann Michael Bönicke, Consitorial Councillor (and chancellor) to the archbishop of Salzburg, cited in Hans Hollwerger, *Die Reform des Gottesdienstes zur Zeit des Josephinismus in Österreich* (Regensburg: 1976), 297.

6

Catholic Enlightenment and the Search
for a Bourgeois Catholicism

It is a shame that the German Catholic church did not have its own Sarpis and Richers! For it was exactly in this period [under Ferdninand II] that it received the oppressive yoke ... Their religion fell into the hands of the Jesuits, and, what is worse, in the hands of the worst of their order. ... What the Jesuits were able to achieve in other states only with violent cunning ... they were able to do in Germany practically unnoticed and for a much longer period of time than in other states, without great political revolutions.

– Peter Philip Wolf, *History of the Roman Catholic Church under Pius VI*[1]

CATHOLIC ENLIGHTENMENT AND REFORM CATHOLICISM

The reform program of educated German Catholics represented the culmination of several generations of pious renewal and religious reform. As such, it was part of a broader Catholic Enlightenment throughout Europe. But reform Catholicism in Germany had its own dynamic and set of problems that distinguished it from other such programs in the Catholic world. The most important of these were the political fragmentation of the Holy Roman Empire, the strength of Baroque Catholicism, and the biconfessional nature of German society. What the German reformers had in common with the Enlightened Catholic brethren was an animosity to the Jesuits that persisted even after the suppression of the Society in 1773.

[1] Peter Philipp Wolf, *Geschichte der römischkatholischen Kirche unter der Regierung Pius des Sechsten*, 4 vols. (Zürich, 1793–1802), 1:221.

125

This revolt against the Jesuit fathers, however, was only the tip of the iceberg. The rejection of the Jesuits reflected a more fundamental turning away from the very Baroque Catholicism that had formed middle-class Catholicism in Germany. That animosity was a symptom of the larger trend away from certain expressive forms of devotion and traditional piety on the part of educated, urban elite.[2] But this attitude cannot be understood as a rejection of Catholicism itself: the motives of this Catholic Enlightenment were as religious as were other major moments of reform and renewal in the history of Catholicism, for example in the late fifteenth century. German Catholic intellectuals rethought the church and its devotions in a language "intelligible to [their] generation," and in so doing sought to create a new form of religiosity that they saw as both appropriate to modern times and faithful to the traditions and doctrines of the church.[3] It was, in other words, a "bourgeois Catholicism" because in Germany, especially, the Catholicism imagined by these reformers appealed to the educated, city-dwelling intellectual elite and opposed the vital Baroque Catholicism of their rural compatriots. This situation provided the Catholic reform movement – as an effort to reform piety and practice throughout the German church – with its basic dynamic.

The strength of Baroque Catholicism in Germany was twofold. The nobility benefited from the structure of the *Reichskirche*, given the way that cathedral chapters and wealthy benefices were distributed. At the other end of the social spectrum, the practices and style of Baroque piety were firmly rooted in the countryside and enjoyed the persistent support of the Catholic peasantry.[4] The Catholic rethinking of the church was therefore aimed in two directions: first, against the structure of the *Reichskirche* and the ways that the predominance of the nobility threatened to make the church too worldly; and second, against the practices of the broad population which many reformers perceived as superstitious. The middle class was strengthened by, and supportive of, the absolutist state, to which it allied itself as a means of securing aid in its efforts to remake the church.

This chapter explores the creation of bourgeois Catholicism in light of the two factors that created it, namely the church and the state. The

[2] Rudolf Schlögl, *Glaube und Religion in der Säkularisierung: Die Katholische Stadt – Köln, Aachen, Münster – 1700–1840* (Munich: Oldenbourg, 1995).

[3] The quotation is from *Gaudium et Spes* (1965); see Chapter 1.

[4] Marc Forster, *Catholic Germany from the Reformation to the Enlightenment* (Palgrave Macmillan, 2008).

Enlightenment in Germany must be understood as the product of the growth of a literate, educated class of readers and writers, who more and more found themselves in the service of the state or the church. Service to the state was a marked feature of the German bourgeoisie in comparison to its European counterparts because the flowering of German territorial absolutism resulted in the creation of scores of courts and bureaucracies, whereas an economically independent bourgeoisie was relatively weak.[5] As Catholic and Protestant states alike grew more similar is function and ethos, the Catholic *Bürger* encountered an experience similar to that of his Protestant brethren. But in adapting religious life and practice to new times, the Protestant *bürger* enjoyed an advantage. In the words of Michael Maurer, "the Protestant territorial church was open to them."[6] The important point, however, is not that the Catholic hierarchy and papal primacy eventually won out in the wake of the French Revolution, but that in the eighteenth century, the Catholic bourgeoisie had sufficient grounds to believe that the church was open to it as well. This sense of opportunity and responsibility made the Catholic reform program imaginable, and provided its impetus and energy.[7]

The term "bourgeois" admittedly is a problematic one, loaded with multiple implications. Here, I use "bourgeois" in a cultural rather than a Marxist sense. One could of course employ exclusively the German term *bürger* and its cognates, but this does not solve any particular problems. Above all, it is the conceptualization of bourgeois culture and worldview that I seek to mobilize for my account. The bourgeoisie is the most difficult class to pin down: definitions are notoriously slippery, wavering as they do between legal, economic and cultural formulations. As Lothar Gall notes, early bourgeois society was not yet the society of classes that it would become in the nineteenth century. It was an open society that had

---

[5] Nicholas Boyle, *Who are We Now?: Christian Humanism and the Global Market from Hegel to Heaney* (Notre Dame: University of Notre Dame Press, 1998), 123–46.

[6] Michael Maurer, *Die Biographie des Bürgers. Lebensformen und Denkweisen in der formativen Phase des deutschen Bürgertums (1680–1815)* (Göttingen: 1996), 164.

[7] My analysis is indebted to ideas in Rudolf Schlögl, *Glaube und Religion in der Säkularisierung: Die Katholische Stadt – Köln, Aachen, Münster – 1700–1840* (Munich, 1995). One might object that Schlögl's book, as a social history, can only make its claims about the transformation of the religious ideas of the German Catholic bourgeoisie for the specific cities studied. Adopting his method for my subject would be a very different undertaking (perhaps a prosopographical study of Catholic Reform authors throughout Germany). However, while acknowledging that Schlögl's purpose is much different from mine, one can fruitfully mobilize his analysis to point to the different ways of understanding the shift in middle-class/*bürgerlich* Catholic attitude.

much to do with wealth and education.[8] While the nobility still retained its legal privileges (and wealthy bourgeois tried to have themselves ennobled to assure their status), the nobility and the middle classes were growing culturally together.[9] The topic of the German bourgeoisie and its "problems" has long been acknowledged as one of the key issues in modern German history and I hope with this book to contribute to the ways we see the position of the Catholic bourgeoisie – wedged between populist Ultramontanism and liberal Protestantism – in the nineteenth century by examining their attitudes and ideas in the previous century.[10] Debate about this term in other contexts shows that it is a key term in explorations of the relationship of the Enlightenment to modern culture, even if one ultimately questions the social reality behind the "myth" as Sarah Maza does for France (the German case is stronger).[11] On the balance, employing the concept of (or the search for) a bourgeois Catholicism enables us to link the Catholic reform debate to a much wider range of issues.

THE REVOLT AGAINST THE FATHERS

The assertion of intellectual and moral supremacy in the church on the part of educated German Catholics entailed a rejection of a particular aspect of their religious heritage. If there were a unifying feature of the Catholic Enlightenment, not only in Germany, but throughout Europe, it was in its anti-Jesuit impulse. In its turn away from the Jesuits, the *katholische Aufklärung* mirrored – albeit in less dramatic fashion – the assault on the Jesuits that was common to the European Enlightenment.

The Jesuits had played an important role in the formation of Catholic identity ever since the founding of the first colleges in Germany.[12]

---

[8] Lothar Gall, *Von der ständischen zur bürgerlichen Gesellschaft*, Enzyklopädie deutscher Geschichte 25 (Munich: Oldenbourg, 1993), 12.

[9] There is a good discussion of the problem in Robert Darnton's essay "A Bourgeois Puts his World in Order," in *The Great Cat Massacre* (New York: Vintage, 1984), 109–14.

[10] See David Blackbourn and Geoff Ely, *The Peculiarities of German History. Bourgeois Politics and Society in Nineteenth-Century Germany* (Oxford, New York: Oxford University Press, 1984).

[11] Sara Maza, *The Myth of the French Bourgeoisie* (Cambridge: Harvard University Press, 2003).

[12] Cologne, 1544; Vienna, 1552; and Ingolstadt, 1556. John O'Malley, *The First Jesuits* (Cambridge: Harvard University Press, 1993), 123f. For a comprehensive history of the role of the Society of Jesus in Germany see Bernhard Duhr, *Geschichte der Jesuiten in den Ländern deutscher Zunge*, 4 vols. (Freiburg: Herder, 1907–1913).

Through his preaching, teaching, and his three catechisms, Peter Canisius (1521–1597) shaped the Catholic response to the Reformation so much that Leo XIII would speak of him as "the second apostle of Germany after Boniface."[13] The Society's activities in Germany ranged from rural missions to school theaters, and eventually led to their monopoly on education. By the eighteenth century, every German Catholic university except Salzburg was run by the Society.[14] The Jesuits also established sodalities and Marian congregations that encouraged particular forms of devotion and communal religious practices. These congregations at first were intended for students at the colleges, but then grew to include large numbers of citizens and even rulers.[15] Finally, the Jesuits ran the German College in Rome, which was established in 1552 as a seminary for German priests.[16] As a Jesuit seminary, its goal was to educate pious, disciplined men, through rigorous spiritual practices. It was believed that only "athletes of faith" could save German Catholicism. However, as a papal seminar, the college was progressively formed into a tool of curial politics. For Germany, this meant recruiting sons of prominent noble families, who would subsequently be sent back to influential posts in cathedral chapters where they would be groomed for the episcopate. The need to educate powerful bishops – for in Germany they were princes as well as pastors – meant that as much attention was paid to canon law as to pastoral issues. Furthermore, the traditional Jesuit emphasis on reflection and spiritual exercises was watered down to appeal to more worldly aristocrats.[17]

In the decades before the suppression of the Society in 1773, there were tentative attempts to modify the curriculum in Jesuit schools. One notable example was the so-called Würzburg Theology, but these efforts did not go as far as anti-Jesuit reformers desired.[18] The main demands for

[13] Cathechism: 1555, 1556, and 1558; *Lexikon für Theologie und Kirche* 2: 915–8.

[14] Despite their later dominance in education, the Jesuits did not at first intend to become a teaching order. For a good account of the development of Jesuit educational institutions, see O'Malley, *The First Jesuits*, 200–42.

[15] On the role of the Marian congregations, see Louis Châtellier, *The Europe of the Devout: the Catholic Reformation and the Formation of a New Society*, trans. Jean Birrell (New York: Cambridge University Press, 1989).

[16] Peter Schmidt, *Das Collegium Germanicum in Rom und die Germaniker. Zur Funktion eines römischen Ausländerseminars (1552–1914)* (Tubingen: Max Niemeyer, 1984).

[17] W. Reinhard, "Einführung," in Ibid. See also Thomas A. Brady, Jr., *German Histories in the Age of Reformations, 1400–1650* (Cambridge: Cambridge University Press, 2008).

[18] Winfried Müller, *Universität und Orden. Die bayerische Landesuniversität Ingolstad zwischen der Aufhebung des Jesuitenordens und der Säkularisation, 1773–1803* (Berlin: Duncker & Humblot, 1986), 36–7.

Catholic university reform were in the fields of jurisprudence and history. These had become very dynamic fields in eighteenth-century Germany, starting in Halle, and then even more spectacularly in Göttingen.[19] The Jesuit *Plan of Studies* [*Ratio studiorum*] did not place much weight on legal education, nor, for that matter, on history. In contrast, the historical approach to the law animated and inspired some of the greatest German Protestant jurists of the day, such as Johann Jacob Moser and Johann Stephan Pütter.[20] As of the beginning of the eighteenth century, there was a growing need on the part of the state for more pragmatically educated ministers and servants, particularly those well-trained in law, natural sciences, and mathematics.[21]

The nature and purpose of education was at the center of the struggle. The Jesuits, committed as they were to traditional practices and devotions, did not see the need to modify the training of priests to accommodate the administrative needs of the state. In the period of their ascendancy, the Jesuits concentrated on the theological and philosophical faculties to the detriment of the "professional" faculties of medicine and law. This preference derived from their strongly religious motivation and their approach to knowledge. No less important than their role in university education and higher learning was Jesuit control of secondary schools. Perhaps even more significant than book learning was the religious and moral education these students received before the university. Indeed, it was at these schools – out of which grew such important cultural institutions as the confraternities and Jesuit drama – that the Fathers of the Society of Jesus tried to reshape society in the image of Christian piety.[22]

---

[19] For an overview of the problem, see Ibid; Notker Hammerstein, *Aufklärung und katholisches Reich. Untersuchungen zur Universtitätsreform und Politik katholischer Territorien des Heiligen Römischen Reichs deutscher Nation im 18. Jahrhundert* (Berlin: Dunker & Humblot, 1977). See also Charles E. McClelland, *State, Society, and University in Germany, 1700–1914* (Cambridge: Cambridge University Press, 1980).

[20] Hammerstein, *Aufklärung und katholisches Reich*, 27–30.

[21] Ibid., 42.

[22] It is worth noting that Jesuit "control" of German Catholic universities was not as monolithic as sometimes portrayed. As noted above, the Jesuits came to be the major figures in Catholic education almost haphazardly, and this was reflected in the variations in legal and administrative roles of the Society in the universities. Karl Hengst points out that one needs to distinguish among different levels of involvement by the Jesuits at the German universities. In some, they merely had members who occupied professorships. In others, they controlled either the philosophical or the theological faculty – and sometimes both. Only a few (Dillingen, Paderborn, Molsheim, Osnabrück, and Bamberg) can actually be labeled "Jesuit Universities" in the sense that the rector was a

While no one would doubt the influence of the Jesuits on German Catholicism, not everyone valued their service. Peter Philip Wolf (1761–1808), for one, thought that the Jesuits had wrought horrible damage to the German church.[23] In his four-volume *General History of the Jesuits*, which he began to publish in 1789, Wolf stated that the Jesuits "drove out the use of sound reason through their sensual religiosity, and implanted in the sensibilities of all Catholics an irresistible tendency toward enthusiasm and superstition [*unwiderstehlichen Hang zu Schwämerey und Aberglauben*]."[24] Wolf, who, as a youth, had escaped from his Jesuit teachers and later entered a seminary only to flee once more, was hardly unique in his strongly negative opinion of the Society of Jesus. His *History of the Jesuits* is consistently critical of the Society and its methods, yet acknowledges the talent and skill of its members.

Wolf admits that he overlooks the occasional "good" Jesuit in his account. As he explains, "even the useful things which individual members may have contributed cannot be compared to the unholiness of the entire body [*Heillose des ganzen Körpers*]." Accordingly, the

Jesuit, directly answering to the Superior General. Hengst also notes how in some older universities, like Trier, Mainz, and Würzburg, Jesuits took over the faculties without the statutes themselves being changed. Needless to say, the territorial lord had an easier time making changes and reforms when he controlled key administrative posts of the university. See Karl Hengst, *Jesuiten an Universitäten und Jesuitenuniversitäten. Zur Geschichte der Universitäten in der Oberdeutschen und Rheinischen Provinz der Gesellschaft Jesu im Zeitalter der konfessionellen Auseinandersetzung* (Paderborn: F. Schöningh, 1981), 295.

[23] Born in upper Bavaria, Wolf was educated in Munich partly by the Jesuits, until his attitudes toward religious matters caused him to flee. He wound up in Strasbourg, but soon had to return home for lack of resources. His parents placed him in the Alumnat of Weihenstephan so that he could be educated for the clergy, yet he soon fled this institution as well. After several rough years in Munich (including time in jail following an accusation of slander by a printer to whom he had been apprenticed), Wolf eventually wound up in Zurich, where he apprenticed with the publishing house of Orell, Geßner, and Füßli, learned the book trade, and began to have literary success. The Zurich Stadtbibliothek held a comprehensive collection of literature relating to the Jesuits given to the library by an Englishman. Wolf prints an extensive bibliography at the end of volume 4 of his *History of the Jesuits*. Wolf's other historical works include *Geschichte der römischkatholischen Kirche unter der Regierung Pius des Sechsten*, 4 vols.(Zürich, 1793–1802), and a history of Maximilian I of Bavaria. The latter work was commissioned in 1804 by Elector Max Joseph after Wolf's return to Munich, and was based on a plan by Montgelas, who eventually secured Wolf a pension from the Bavarian Academy of Sciences. He could only enjoy his newfound calm and security for a few years, however. In August of 1808 he was put into an asylum; his body was pulled from the Isar 4 days later. See *Allgemeine Deutsche Biographie* 43, 781–5.

[24] Peter Philipp Wolf, *Allgemeine Geschichte der Jesuiten. Von dem Ursprung ihres Ordens bis auf gegenwärtige Zeiten*, 4 vols. (Zürich, 1789–) Here, vol. 2, 173.

constitution, discipline, and effectiveness of the Society of Jesus are the true subjects of Wolf's history. Germany's political and religious fragmentation left it with few defenses against what Wolf portrays as a single-minded and disciplined group. In Wolf's account, the Jesuits exerted influence on all levels of society, from princely courts down to the common people. In Bavaria the Fathers found a particularly potent tool in "the practically pagan and idolatrous" Marian devotion, which they initiated under Elector Maximilian I. Jesuit success only augmented their standing among German Catholics, who were led even further into superstition by the Fathers:

One sees how the Catholics step-by-step were carried away by an extremely bigoted and superstitious devotionalism [*bigott-abergläubischen Andächtteley*] and how, during the Jesuit epoch, their religious practices became ever more tasteless and extravagant [*abgeschmackter und abentheuerlicher*]. It is therefore hardly surprising how, through such institutions, people were eventually led astray, forgot the simplicity of their religion, and slowly sank into the shadows of superstition. The enlightened Catholic, who had the misfortune to have been educated in Jesuit schools, will now shudder to look back on that path down which they led him during his schooling.[25]

Only recently, Wolf implies, has Catholicism escaped this dangerous path. The individual "enlightened Catholic" whom Wolf addresses stands for all German Catholics – or at least, so Wolf would desire. In this passage, Wolf expresses the expectation that German Catholics will soon look back at their own religious and devotional history and shake their heads in shame.

Part of Wolf's story is the denial of the importance of Jesuits to Catholic survival. He states:

it is nonsense to assert that Germany would not have become Catholic [after the Reformation] if they had not transformed all the monasteries into Jesuit colleges. One cannot deny the distinguished Benedictine Order – whose early members converted practically all of Germany to Christianity – its services to the church.[26]

Indeed, this Order continues to spread Christianity "without making as much noise as the Jesuits, who make themselves famous for the most insignificant things."[27] It is significant that he mentions them because the Order of Saint Benedict was very active in the Catholic Enlightenment, and represented an alternative vision of the German church, one that was

---

[25] Wolf, *Jesuiten*, vol. 2, 178–9.
[26] Wolf, *Jesuiten*, vol. 2, 145.
[27] Wolf, *Jesuiten*, vol. 2, 145.

stable and locally bound. While the Catholic Enlightenment, in its more radical expressions – and Wolf was certainly among its most radical exponents – was highly critical of monasticism, Wolf here argues that the enlightened Catholic

will ... be convinced that, by far and wide, the monks were nowhere nearly as harmful to the religion of the people as the Jesuits were. Just as the monks could not affect every class [*Stände*] in the same was as the Jesuits, so, too, were the monks not as experienced in the art of ... forcing their superstitious rubbish on people [*ihren abergläubischen Kram aufzudringen*].[28]

While certainly a backhanded compliment toward the traditional religious orders, Wolf's general point is that the most dangerous aspect of the Society of Jesus was not any particular belief or practice, but their very successful organization and centralized discipline.[29]

Wolf's persistent emphasis on popular superstition points to his work's central concern. For it was clear that the now-suppressed Society of Jesus no longer enjoyed the support of princely courts. Wolf's history is a contribution toward the general project of denying the role of Jesuit education and – more significantly, Jesuit devotional practices – in the formation of bourgeois German Catholic identity. While he was more radical than others, Wolf's writings illustrate attitudes toward the Jesuits among segments of the German Catholic population.[30] This is true on account of his background and education, but more importantly because of the intended audience of his writings, namely, educated German

---

[28] Wolf, *Jesuiten*, vol. 2, 178.

[29] When the Society was suppressed in 1773, reformers were jubilant and hopeful that victory was now assured against what they saw as the curialism and obscurantism represented by the Jesuits. Yet, as the prelate Franziskus Töpsl, an anti-Jesuit leader in the reformation of Bavarian education, feared, once the Jesuits were out of the way, monastic culture itself came under attack. See Richard van Dülmen, *Propst Franziskus Töpsl (1711–1796) und das Augustiner-Chorherrenstift Polling* (Kallmünz: Michael Lassleben, 1967), 208.

[30] Compare the comments of Michal Ignaz Schmidt:

[The Jesuits] united their ardor for religion with animosity and a spirit of persecution, and made this a general principle of their society. When such a society in principle draws everything to itself, and moreover is bound by oaths to foreign courts and superiors ... it makes no difference how learned and talented individual members may be. For such a society can hardly promise to represent the interests of a properly established national education.

Schmidt, *Neuere Geschichte der deutschen*, vol. 1, *Von dem Schmalkaldischen Krieg bis an des Ende der Regierung Karls V* (Vienna, 1785), 315.

Catholics and supporters of the reform program that was being progressively adopted by the absolutist state.

Almost 20 years after the suppression of the Society, Wolf felt that it still enjoyed residual affection and support in the German mind. Toward the end of his four-volume history, Wolf argues that Bavarian ex-Jesuits are seeking to reestablish their order.[31] More pernicious is their polemical literary activity. Wolf singles out the group of Augsburg ex-Jesuits (*Augsburger-Kriticker*) which was concentrated around the former Jesuit college of St. Salvator.[32] Wolf notes that their writings seem so unreasonable that one would think that any danger this group posed was illusory, a fairy tale. But to Wolf, their history shows that the Jesuits had always been unreasonable and had known how to use fanaticism and superstition to their advantage.[33]

Because, as Wolf had noted earlier, Germany's peculiar constitution rendered the society's traditional methods of seizing control of church and state from the top ineffective, they instead worked to gain influence over the popular mind:

Nevertheless, the Jesuits were never inactive in Germany. They had a far broader effect on the nation [*Nazion*] than was apparent. But the quieter their steps, the more dangerous they were. ... It was a risky business to overturn thrones, sacrifice secular rulers, and elevate themselves through revolution ... Much more feasible, profitable and secure [than these methods] was the enslavement of a people's understanding [*den Verstand eines Volkes zu unterjochen*] and the spreading of ignorance from the beggar's hut to the prince's palace ... It is undeniable that this plan – to base their power on the general ignorance of a people – was carried out with no greater care, profound political acumen, and with such great success, as in Germany.[34]

Wolf points to those innovations and institutions which the Jesuits had indeed employed to secure the place of Catholicism in Germany. Sodalities enabled them to reach different classes, and their "diligent" efforts to put themselves in charge of schools and seminaries demonstrate their desire "to educate the people and their shepherds according to the plan of their Order." It is therefore no mystery that the Jesuits, having succeeded

---

[31] Wolf, *Jesuiten*, vol. 4, 282.

[32] On this group and on the ex-Jesuits in general, see Michael Schaich, "'Religionis defensor acerrimus.' Joseph Anton Weissenbach und der Kreis der Augsburger Exjesuiten," in *Von "Obscuranten" und Eudämonisten: Gegenaufklärische, konservative und antirevolutionäre Publizisten im späten 18. Jahrhundert*, Christoph Weiß, ed. (St. Ingelbert: Röhrig Universitäts Verlag, 1997).

[33] Wolf, *Jesuiten*, vol. 4, 323.

[34] Wolf, *Jesuiten*, vol. 4, 2.

in leading the nation astray, should remain in such high regard in Germany, at least in comparison to other Catholic states.[35]

The search for influence over the common people explains the prominent focus on superstition in Wolf's account. The religious vision propagated by the ex-Jesuits, stressing as it did the sacramental and sensual aspects of Catholic devotion, appealed to the common people, and these writers maintained their convictions while losing middle class support. Typical Jesuit (and ex-Jesuit) writings were polemical and uncompromising, but that polemical appeal to the public was in itself a sign of their modernity.[36] They had been specialists in the Counter-Reformation art of polemic. Now that polemic was no longer aimed at Protestants, but at other Catholics.

At Augsburg, the controversial preacher Alois Merz and Joseph Anton Weissenbach led an active group of ex-Jesuits. From 1787–1796, Weissenbach edited a journal entitled *Critique of certain Critics, Reviewers and Pamphleteers* [*Kritik über gewisse Kritiker, Rezensenten und Broschürenmacher*].[37] One notable pamphleteer propounding traditional Catholicism was the ex-Jesuit Hermann Goldhagen. His *Religionsjournal*, published in Mainz from 1776 to 1792, vehemently opposed reformist theology, often attacking views advanced by his fellow Mainzers in the moderate *Mainz Journal of Ecclesiastical Affairs* [*Mainzer Monatsschrift von geistlichen Sachen*].[38]

Polemicists on both sides of the Catholic Enlightenment were equally vehement, ready to resort to conspiracy theories, and reluctant to give their opponents the benefit of the doubt.[39] Yet if we sift through the rhetorical bluster, the novelty of the situation emerges: namely, the

---

[35] Wolf, *Jesuiten*, vol. 4, 3.

[36] Cf. Darrin McMahon, *Enemies of Enlightenment: The French Counter-Enlightenment and the Making of Modernity* (New York: Oxford University Press, 2001).

[37] Schaich, "Religionis defensor acerrimus." Schaich also notes that Augsburg was an important center for the printing of anti-*Aufklärung* literature. This was commented on by the *Aufklärer* Lorenz Hübner, the editor of the Salzburg *Oberdeutsche allgemeine Litteraturzeitung* with a certain amount of dismay: "weite Kreise der Bevölkerung 'von den neuen litterarischen Producten nichts kennen [lernen], als was ihnen die Mäckler der Augsburgischen Buchhändler auf dem Rücken zutragen.' " Citation from *Oberdeutsche allgemeine Litteraturzeitung* 1 (1788), np. Schaich, 87.

[38] Franz Dumont, "Hermann Goldhagen und seine '*Religionsjournal*,'" in *Von "Obscuranten" und Eudämonisten*, Christoph Weiß, ed. and Blanning, *Reform and Revolution in Mainz*, 206.

[39] Wolf, for example, accuses the Jesuits or their agents of poisoning Clement XIV. He also admonished his readers to be on the lookout: "Gefährlicher, als das Proselytenmachen, ist die Verbindung der Jesuiten mit den Rosenkreuzern und andern geheimen Gesellschaften und Logen," Wolf, Jesuiten, vol. 4, 327.

politicization of the Catholic public around issues of reform and traditional religion. The intensity of that discussion arose in part from a real conflict of visions about the nature of religious authority over the common people.

Anti-Jesuitism in Germany was not just a mask for anticlericalism; it provided a unified front for a variety of Catholic reformers, many of whom were clergymen.[40] It is true that some of the animosity can be viewed as a holdover from the conflict with the Jansenists in France. But where there were bona fide Jansenists in Germany, they often worked *with* the absolutist state, not *against* it as in France.[41] The moralizing Augustinian rigorism of the Jansenists was put at the service of the centralizing, bureaucratic state, especially in Austria. Once educational reformers met resistance on the part of an entrenched Society of Jesus, their antipathy grew. The imagined alternative to Jesuit education, however, was not lay teachers but the involvement of the other major religious orders. In Bavaria, for example, the Benedictines and Augustinian Canon-Regulars were strongly represented in world of Catholic learning; indeed they experienced a revival in the eighteenth century.[42]

In addition to differences in educational philosophies, there were also structural differences between the Jesuits and the pre-Reformation orders. For example, a Benedictine monk was bound to his house and his abbot. He could serve elsewhere, but needed permission from his superior. In Bavaria, the heads of these houses were part of the territorial estates [*Landstand*], and while there was little real power left in that body by the eighteenth century, there was an important psychological and cultural sense in which the monasteries could be seen as part of the national treasury of wealth and intellect. The monastic settlements were part of the *Germania Sacra*, some having their origins as far back as Carolingian times. The great Benedictine abbeys that were being rebuilt in baroque splendor had served as centers of culture and devotion for centuries. Significantly, their contributions to Christianity long preceded the

---

[40] Richard van Dülmen, "Antijesuitismus und katholische Aufklärung in Deutschland," *Historisches Jahrbuch* 89:1 (1969), 52–80.

[41] See especially Peter Hersche, *Der Spätjansenismus in Österreich*. Hersche provides an important corrective to the charge that Theresian-Josephine church policy was motivated by a purely instrumental and materialist Enlightenment. He focuses on the pious "Jansenist" motivations of several important advisors, notably Maria Theresa's doctor, van Swieten. An important route of Jansenist thought into Austria was via the Austrian Netherlands.

[42] Dülmen, *Polling*, 201.

Reformation. Defenders of monastic wealth argued that ecclesiastical foundations and lands could serve as financial reserves for the state constituting a bulwark of the national wealth.[43] In his *History of the Black Forest,* the abbot Martin Gerbert of St. Blasien emphasized how the monastic settlements of the Benedictines had tamed the land and made it arable.[44] The Jesuits could make no such claim, for they left traces not in the physical transformation of the land, but in language and practice.[45]

Jesuit educational activities became so successful and popular because they filled a real need in providing the Catholic world with an educated bulwark of loyal, devout Catholics. By the middle of the eighteenth century, they had in a sense become victims of their own success. The very middle classes that they had formed were now rejecting a key element of the Jesuit ethos – its universalism. For Jesuit universalism – with its spiritual heart in Rome – was the foundation of its strength in the era of confessional conflict. But in the age of Immanuel Kant's "world citizen," the Jesuit was the true *doppelgänger* of the Enlightenment cosmopolitan. In the Jesuit, the bourgeois Catholic encountered the "social reality" that a large portion of his countrymen adhered to a different form of ecclesiastical life than he did.[46] The peculiarity of German Catholicism was that there existed strong enough rival structures in the other orders and the state that the bourgeois did not feel compelled to reject the institutions of the church altogether, but could realistically hope to reshape the church after his own fashion. This attitude partly explains the popularity of Hontheim's *de Statu,* and why it created such a stir in the literate Catholic world. In hindsight, Hontheim's program was not realistic, but it was by definition *imaginable*. The German Catholic revolt against their

---

[43] Anselm Desing, *Staatsfrage: Sind die Güter und Einkünfte der Geistlichkeit dem Staate schädlich oder nicht? Beantwortet und Lochstein und Neubergern entgegen gesetzt* (Munich, 1768).

[44] Martin Gerbert, *Historia Nigrae Silvae Ordinis Sancti Benedicti Coloniae* (St. Blasien, 1783) and *Geschichte des Schwarzwaldes,* 2 vols., translated into German by Adalbert Weh (Freiburg, 1993, 1996), 12f.

[45] Though Jesuit churches did have a major impact. Il Gesu in Rome was the first important baroque church, whose distinctive style fostered imitations throughout Europe. For the classic statement see Heinrich Wölfflin, *Renaissance und Barock. Eine Untersuchung über Wesen und entstehung des Barockstils in Italien,* fourth edition (Munich, 1926). For Bavaria, see Benno Hubensteiner, *Vom Geist des Barock. Kultur und Frömmigkeit im alten Bayern* (Munich: Süddeutscher Verlag, 1967). See also Jeffrey Chipps Smith, *Sensuous Worship: Jesuits and the Art of the Early Catholic Reformation in Germany* (Princeton, NJ: Princeton University Press, 2002).

[46] For the terminology employed here, see Bernhard Groethuysen, *Die Entstehung der bürgerlichen Welt- und Lebensanschaung in Frankreich* (Halle: Max Niemeyer, 1927), 4.

Jesuit Fathers was not a Voltairian rejection of the institutional church or a Catholic past. Instead, educated German Catholics perceived the church as a constitutive element of society, but were frustrated in their efforts to make the church reflect their values, particularly when confronted with popular religious sentiments.

CATHOLIC REFORMERS BETWEEN CHURCH AND STATE

While many reformers enthusiastically, if overoptimistically, proclaimed that absolutist princes could change religious practices and sensibilities through edicts and laws, some contemporaries realized that economic conditions played a far more significant role in the social constitution of the church.[47] For example, one commentator argued that laws aimed at limiting monasticism – in this case in Joseph II's Austria – did not cause the decline of new religious vocations. Instead, the main factor was an increase of alternatives for the laity, as Augustin Schelle observed in a pamphlet:

It is true that, in recent times, the cloisters, especially in Austria, do not have as many aspirants as before. But the cause of this is not the aforementioned [Josephine] restrictions. Rather, in addition to a change in the ways of thinking – which has its roots in a change in the education in the public, and especially Latin, schools – there are more opportunities to find an occupation in the secular estates. For a few years now, many more people than before can earn their bread in the expanded military, in newly-created factories, in expanded trade, or in toll service, etc. They prefer to enjoy more freedom and nurture the hope of becoming the head of a family than to live as celibate clergymen. The restrictions therefore did not lead to the decline [in candidates]. The opportunities to make a living outside of the clerical estate contributed the most toward this phenomenon.[48]

The lay Catholic bourgeois in the 1780s, therefore, was someone who, had he been born a generation earlier, would have entered a cloister or joined the secular clergy. The shifting economic conditions that Schelle outlined enabled space for a reconsideration of the social constitution of the

---

[47] Luise Schorn-Schütte notes that, contrary to representations in earlier literature the Catholic clergy in the Holy Roman Empire were by and large from the urban bourgeoisie, not the peasantry. Luise Schorn-Schütte, "Priest, Preacher, Pastor: Research on Clerical Office in Early Modern Europe," *Central European History* (2000), 9–11.

[48] [Augustin Schelle], *Ueber den Cölibat der Geistlichen und die Bevölkerung in katholischen Staaten, aus Gründen der politischen Rechenkunst. Voran gehen Geburts- Trauungs- und Sterbelisten von der Reischstadt Augsburg und Betrachtungen darüber* (Salzburg, 1784), 66f.

church. This social reality underlay the development of bourgeois Catholic consciousness.

As is commonly observed, there was an intimate connection between the rise of the bourgeoisie and the modern bureaucratic state. Nicholas Boyle writes that

the German eighteenth-century intellectual was confined within a one-dimensional system – wherever he turned he found the State. Neither the University nor the Church offered him the possibility of [economic] independence, even if he wanted it, and Germany's economic structure made it unlikely that he would be a man of private means.[49]

Boyle further notes how the state needed the universities to supply its officials – which in Protestant countries also meant ecclesiastical officials. Theology was still the best-funded university discipline, and most states demanded at least nominal confessional loyalty of its servants. The state produced university-educated youths whose opportunities for employment outside the state or the church were limited, which meant that conformity to official religious doctrine and behavior was required for material survival.[50] Moreover, it was in the absolutist state's interest to undermine traditional associations and corporate privileges. The autonomy of traditional associations was weakened in the creation of new positions for educated non-nobles – particularly those trained in law – as officials and ministers.[51]

The church and the state were the two great incubators – to borrow Mack Walker's term – of the German bourgeoisie.[52] This assertion holds for both Catholic and Protestant Germany, which raises the question of how the different paths of the churches shaped the bourgeoisie in the respective confessions. The states, it can be argued, developed more or less in tandem, though they could never claim to be completely sovereign

---

[49] Nicholas Boyle, *Goethe: the Poet and the Age. Vol. 1: The Poetry of Desire (1749–1790)* (Oxford: Oxford University Press, 1992), 19. See also the essay "Understanding Germany" in Boyle, *Who are We Now?: Christian Humanism and the Global Market from Hegel to Heaney.*

[50] Boyle, *Goethe: the Poet and the Age. Vol. 1: The poetry of desire (1749–1790)* 24.

[51] James Sheehan, *German History, 1770–1866* (Oxford, New York: Oxford University Press, 1989), 135.

[52] Mack Walker, *German Home Towns: Community, State, and General Estate, 1648–1871* (Ithaca: Cornell University Press, 1998). Walker uses the term "incubator" to refer to the way in which the Empire's structure protected the weak against the strong and provided a leveling element that was essential to the development of the German hometown.

because of the emperor's nominal authority.[53] The great states could build armies and bureaucracies to rival fully sovereign states in every physical sense. However, sovereignty as a legitimating concept was not available to the princes of the Empire. This peculiarity had been characterized as a flaw by nineteenth-century Borussian scholarship but is now acknowledged to have been fruitful for the emergence of an "imperial patriotism." This patriotism did not necessarily lead to rabid nationalism, but instead fostered solidarity among weak states and hindered the development of a large centralized state.[54] Germans could owe their allegiance to an abstract concept of the nation, because there was no viable entity that could claim full sovereignty over it. Indeed, the nation was deposited in both the state and the church, but wholly in neither.

Unique to the Empire was the fact that it was constituted not only by many states but also by several churches. Following the peace of Westphalia, German states had grown more similar in their basic form and function, but in terms of religious culture, the churches had grown farther apart. The question of religious culture is an important one because of what it tells us about the ethos – and, more concretely, the schooling – of the bourgeoisie. The accepted historical narrative of the German bourgeoisie has been written with Protestant culture in mind. There is the historiographical tradition in which Protestantism in its various guises is seen as nurturing middle-class culture and consciousness. The most obvious example of this is the way in which Pietism has long been acknowledged as a key factor in the emergence of Protestant (Lutheran) consciousness. Therefore our ideas about the German bourgeoisie are largely shaped by Protestant self-understanding. Yet this is not necessarily false. Both Catholic and Protestant self-understanding was predicated on an image of the other side.[55] Toward the end of the eighteenth century, Catholics were attempting to come to terms with a growing sense that they had fallen behind their Protestant brethren. This dilemma is not unrelated to the growth of German vernacular culture. While statistics of book production show that secular works were outstripping theological

---

[53] The crowned heads of the Empire were those who had their kingdoms outside its borders. The Elector of Brandenburg was king only in Prussia.

[54] See Maiken Umbach, *Federalism and Enlightenment in Germany, 1740–1806* (London: Hambeldon Press, 2000).

[55] This would become even sharper for German liberalism in the nineteenth century. See Michael Gross, *The War Against Catholicism: Liberal Identity and the Anti-Catholic Imagination in Nineteenth-Century Germany* (Ann Arbor: University of Michigan Press, 2004).

themes in German book printing, it is nevertheless an important point that the modern German language and scholarship are deeply indebted to Luther.[56] The other half of this story is that German Catholics who continued to write in Latin still inhabited the world of universal learning. Moreover, their cultural universe was potentially as broad as the Catholic world itself. German Catholic use of Latin was not a sign of weakness or backwardness, but was an indication of the universalism of its intellectual aspirations.[57]

If, as noted above, the state and the church were the incubators of the bourgeoisie, it is important to consider the role of educational institutions in the formation of bourgeois identity. The universities, which in polemical attacks by outsiders were pilloried for their adherence to outworn models of scholarship, were key institutions in the intellectual life of the established churches. For this reason, thorough disparagement of whole systems of learning must be seen as part of a larger political and institutional struggle not just against certain ideas (i.e., those particular to scholastic metaphysics and method), but against a competing vision for the organization of religious and intellectual life.[58]

---

[56] Sheehan, *German History*, 153. It should be pointed out these statistics, as in Albert Ward's *Book Production, Fiction, and the German Reading Public, 1740–1800* (Oxford: Clarendon Press, 1974), are drawn mainly from the Leipzig book fair, and would not necessarily include works that circulated outside of this world, for example, the devotional tracts printed in monastic institutions and sold at pilgrimage sites. On the importance of Catholic printing houses based in Augsburg, see Michael Schaich, "Religionis defensor acerrimus," 87. The continued importance of religious matters in the public sphere is discussed in H. C. Erik Midelfort, *Exorcism and Enlightenment. Johann Joseph Gassner and the Demons of Eighteenth-Century Germany* (New Haven: Yale University Press, 2005).

[57] See Blackall, *Emergence of German as a Literary Language.*

[58] From the very beginning, universities had a religious purpose, chartered as they were by bishops. The Reformation resulted in the founding of several new universities in Germany, as well as the re-organization of several older institutions such as Wittenberg and Tübingen. The founding of the University of Halle under Pietist auspices in 1694 represented a significant new development, and is commonly taken as the birth of the modern university. At Halle, the Pietists had achieved the zenith of their institutional strength. Their aim was to improve the world by first converting individuals – individuals who were destined to occupy important places in the state and in society. Both Halle, and, later, Göttingen (1734), were the creation of ambitious dynastic powers. Similarly, learned academies, like the Prussian Royal Academy of Sciences (*königliche Akadamie der Wissenschaften*), and later the Bavarian academy were at least in part created as responses to perceived insularity and independence (financial and political as well as intellectual) of the universities. See Notker Hammerstein, "Zur Geschichte der deutschen Universität im Zeitalter der Aufklärung," in *Res publica litteraria. Ausgewählte Aufsätze zur frühneuzeitlichen Bildungs-, Wissenschafts- und Universitätsgeschichte* (Berlin: Dunker & Humblot, 2000), 11.

Over the course of the eighteenth century, educated middle-class Catholics would progressively try to model themselves on their Protestant counterparts.[59] As long as it was largely under control of the Jesuits in Germany (with the exception of the Benedictine University of Salzburg), Catholic education retained its international and Latin character. Until the establishment of state academies, the only alternative centers of learning were the monasteries. This diverging educational history of Protestant and Catholic Germany reflects the different institutional configurations of the Protestant and Catholic bourgeoisie. The power struggle over educational reform lies at the core of the German Catholic Enlightenment in the eighteenth century. The Catholic bourgeoisie found itself in the center of a struggle for legitimacy between the absolutist secular state and an international, centralizing church. The dilemma facing the bourgeois Catholic was that both the church and the state could lay valid claim to his parentage.

Eighty years ago, Bernard Groethuysen tried to trace the origins of the bourgeois spirit by examining conditions in France. He posited a growing assertion of moral and intellectual independence from the church in pre-Revolutionary France. He suggested that the bourgeois were not unaware that they had separated themselves from a vast portion of their countrymen, and that this social awareness was therefore among their key concerns. His formulation bears repeating:

In order to understand the development of bourgeois consciousness in its relation and opposition to the church, we must not proceed from particular views of the church which allow themselves to be presented and formulated, but rather from the shape of ecclesiastical life itself [*kirchliche Leben*]. In the eighteenth century, the Catholic church remains "reality." In large measure it still determines the thoughts and feelings of an entire segment of the population: it is a social reality ... Millions of people continue to go to church, to confess, to follow processions. They continue to live in the ecclesiastical community: indeed, most of them could not even imagine life outside this community. It is this social-historical reality that the bourgeois must confront.[60]

Groethuysen's work reflected the prevailing assumption that the French Enlightenment and Revolution could stand in for the general story of western modernity. His assertion of an absolute opposition of bourgeois

---

[59] More directly, some families would send their sons to Protestant universities. Kaunitz, the future Austrian chancellor, studied at Göttingen.

[60] Bernhard Groethuysen, *Die Entstehung der bürgerlichen Welt- und Lebensanschaung in Frankreich* (Halle: Max Niemeyer, 1927), 4.

thinkers and the Catholic church bears revision.[61] We also need to revise his monolithic characterization of the church and acknowledge the motivations of religiously minded reformers.[62] These caveats to Groethuysen's formulation are all the more necessary for German Catholicism, because of the fundamentally different role of the state, and because of the constitutional role of the Catholic church in the Empire. Nevertheless, his remarks bear fruit if we focus on his observation that bourgeois Catholics were forced to confront their growing sense of alienation from the beliefs and practices of a large segment of the population. In Germany, the bourgeoisie did not respond by abandoning the church, but instead – as Karl Marx observed in a different context – sought to remake it in its own image.

[61] See John McManners, *Church and Society in eighteenth-century France*, 2 vols. (Oxford: Oxford University Press, 1998).

[62] See, for example, Dale K. Van Kley, *The Religious Origins of the French Revolution: from Calvin to the Civil Constitution, 1560–1791* (New Haven: Yale University Press, 1996).

7

A Program for Reform

THE CHURCH AND THE PUBLIC

In rethinking the church, educated German Catholics "scrutinize[ed] the signs of the times" and imagined a Catholicism that, they felt, would do away with outworn accretion and would be suited to the world in which they lived.[1] While the diversity of visions prevents a monolithic account, a sample of the pamphlet literature can at least lend insight into the shape of the religious world of German Catholic Enlightenment thinkers. This pamphlet literature constituted a Catholic subculture of the public sphere, and reflected the conditions of the literary world of *Publizistik*, the typically German discourse on public affairs.[2] The educated German Catholics who participated in this forum considered the church in some form to be subject to public discussion and debate.[3] This was a specifically German Catholic public sphere, but it was not hermetically sealed from the influence of Protestant German vernacular works. Benedikt Werkmeister, for one,

---

[1] *Gaudium et Spes*, 1965, §4.
[2] For a brief account and further references, see James J. Sheehan, *German History, 1770–1866* (Oxford, New York: Oxford University Press, 1989), 190ff. On reading and writing publics, see James Van Horn Melton, *The Rise of the Public in Enlightenment Europe* (New York: Cambridge University Press, 2001), 79–160.
[3] This can be related to Dale van Kley's argument in *The Religious Origins of the French Revolution: from Calvin to the Civil Constitution, 1560–1791* (New Haven: Yale University Press, 1996). He maintains that the underground *Nouvelles Ecclesiastiques* – written by Jansenists disaffected with civil and ecclesiastical governance – played a significant part in the rise of the political public sphere in France. In Germany, the difference is not only that those clamoring for change were not excluded from political power, but also that there were several different public forums. The Jansenist case in France is therefore illuminating, but the German situation deserves evaluation in its own right.

contended that the Enlightenment was spread in Catholic parts of Germany through contact with Protestants. This contact was made possible by the spread of Freemasonry among the Catholic laity and the reading of Protestant literature, particularly the works of C. F. Gellert (1715–1769) and J. G. H. Feder (1740–1821).[4] Furthermore, Werkmeister noted, the alliance of the houses of Saxony and Bavaria during the Seven Years' War, and especially the Saxon presence in Munich during the war, introduced Catholics to new ideas:

> I can still remember how the party of bigots complained bitterly about the decline of religion in Bavaria, and they blamed the Saxons for an entirely new and unheard of freedom of thought. Soon thereafter followed the establishment of the Bavarian Academy of Sciences.[5]

The German Catholic literary discourse was not separate from the international Catholic public sphere, which was nourished by works in Latin, Italian, and French.[6] The relatively recent emergence of a vernacular German Catholic discourse was grafted onto not only the long-standing Latin culture of international learning, but also the official Latin culture of orthodox Roman Catholicism. New in the second half of the eighteenth century was the emergence of a self-conscious vernacular German Catholic literary scene. Not all contributions to the German Catholic discussion were original works, however, as translations and reeditions could appear at important times. An out-of-print work was essentially not available at all, unless one had access to a princely or monastic library. But an inexpensive pamphlet reprint of, say, Paolo Sarpi could be very influential. These translations were an important constituent of the public discourse of reform Catholicism.

German Catholics were concerned principally with the public good, and in their writings on religion, they attempted to connect their visions of religious reform to the general welfare of society.[7] The Italian scholar Ludovico Muratori (1672–1750) was admired, his works were frequently

---

[4] [Werkmeister, Benedikt Maria], *Freykirch Thomas, oder freymüthige Untersuchungen über die Unfehlbarkeit der katholischen Kirche,* vol. 1 (Frankfurt and Leipzig, 1792), viii.

[5] Werkmeister, vi–vii.

[6] Spanish works do not seem to have been reviewed much in German Catholic journals, except when translated into Latin. Critics of the Jesuits would point out that the Society did a poor job of teaching modern languages.

[7] For an exhaustive discussion of reform literature, see Klaus-Peter Burkarth, *"Raisonable" Katholiken. Volksaufklärung im katholischen Deutschland um 1800,* Unpublished dissertation, University of Essen, 1994.

translated, and his opinions were often cited.[8] Muratori had written that, while church and religious processions are good, an excess of them turns people away from work.[9] He also argued that the rights of secular princes had to be respected for the good of both the church and the state. Previous centuries, Muratori wrote, had witnessed conflict between princes of church and state, because they had tried to take each other's authority, and this was held to be to the disadvantage of public welfare. Muratori argued that sovereigns who tried to influence matters of faith and dogma often usurped the rights of clergy. For the public good, one needs to let the respective powers have their separate spheres for the spiritual and temporal happiness of the people.[10] Although Muratori admired the Ancients, he encouraged princes to educate their subjects in modern moral philosophy, because the moderns have thoroughly analyzed the "ways, inclinations, and passions of man, in small actions as well as in great ones."[11] Muratori frequently emphasized the central importance of the virtue of charity, arguing that it was the true mark of the Christian – and that charity was better exercised in favor of the poor than toward the house of God.[12]

This emphasis on the virtue of charity constituted the most pronounced element of reform Catholicism's educational program: the moral instruction of the common people. In its extreme forms, Jesus was more often spoken of as a "teacher of virtue" than as a savior. This Enlightenment interest in a moral religion can be contrasted to the rise of the popular devotion to the Sacred Heart, or to Alphonse of Liguori's founding, in 1732, of a congregation dedicated to the Redeemer. In his lectures on pastoral theology, which were officially prescribed for Habsburg lands, Franz Giftschütz (1748–1788) stated that Jesus "taught true, practical philosophy and purified moral doctrine."[13] The dangers of teaching casuistry to the common man were stated, and pastors were

---

[8] See Fabio Marri and Maria Lieber, eds., *Die Glückseligkeit des Gemeinen Wesens. Wege der Ideen zwischen Italien und Deutschland im Zeitalter des Aufklärung* (Frankfurt: Peter Lang, 1999). See also Fabio Marri, Maria Lieber, and Christian Weyers, *Lodovico Antonio Muratori und Deutschland: Studien zur Kultur- und Geistesgeschichte der Frühaufklärung*, Italien in Geschichte und Gegenwart Bd. 8 (Frankfurt am Main, New York: Peter Lang, 1997).

[9] Ludovico Muratori, *Traité sur le Bonheur Public* [orig. 1749], French tr. 1772, 361.

[10] Muratori, *Traité sur le Bonheur Public*, 363.

[11] Muratori, *Traité sur le Bonheur Public*, 397.

[12] Muratori, *Charité chretienne envers le prochaine*, 1745.

[13] Franz Giftschütz, *Leitfaden für die in den k.-k. Erbländen vorgeschriebenen Vorlesung über die Pastoraltheologie* (Vienna, 1785), 2.

encouraged to emphasize the duties of the citizen.[14] The *Aufklärer* were particularly aware of problems of communication and education, and they incorporated modern conceptions of psychology and epistemology into their suggestions for reform. Yet they also assumed that their own variety of religious experience was the most authentic. They were concerned, of course, with eliminating superstition, which they frequently saw as fostered by certain obscurities in the church's own teachings. Giftschütz saw in the teaching of miracles a chance to attack superstition: one should teach how seldom, indeed, God performed miracles.[15]

Notable is the way in which the *Aufklärer* tried to incorporate their reform program into the teaching of traditional doctrines. Abbot Johann Ignaz Felbiger (1724–1788) of Sagan, an influential educational reformer in Silesia and, later, at Vienna, wrote that the "art" of catechizing needed to take into account the faculty of understanding.[16] It must also emphasize the duties of a Christian instead of dwelling on sin and punishment, which only served to distract the catechumen without actually telling him or her what should be done.[17] "Religion," Felbiger proclaimed:

is not a work of memory or pure reason, but rather a work of the will ... One should not present religion only as the means to eternal salvation, but also show how the observance of every duty also promotes our temporal happiness.[18]

Giftschütz noted that "proofs by reason" (i.e., in the manner of rationalist philosophers such as Wolff) are useless and possibly dangerous in religious education, because they attempt "to show the common man that the founder of our religion did not teach anything contrary to reason," yet he may very well be turned against the duties of his religion when he cannot "base them in his own experience and consciousness."[19] Felix Blau and Anton Dorsch in Mainz – later members of the Mainz Jacobin club during the French occupation – insisted that reforming efforts must distinguish between "internal" and "external" service to God. They

---

[14] Giftschütz, 67–8.

[15] Giftschütz, 56.

[16] On school reform, see James Van Horn Melton, *Absolutism and the eighteenth-century Origins of Compulsory Schooling in Prussia and Austria* (Cambridge, New York: Cambridge University Press, 1988).

[17] Felbiger, *Vorlesungen über die Kunst zu katechisierung, die er seinen jungen geistlichen zu halten pflege. Von ihm selbst entworfen, und zum erstenmal vorgetragen im Monat Merz 177* (Vienna, 1774), 9; 42.

[18] Felbiger, 60.

[19] Giftschütz, 39.

acknowledged that "transcendental ideas lose all their power when they are not connected to sensory signs ... The concepts of God's qualities and influence on the universe are symbolized through pictures and the institutions of external devotion."[20] However, the external service [*äussere Gottesdienst*] is a means and not an end, which they identify as true, inward devotion.[21] The authors recommended that the Latin mass should be abolished in favor of the vernacular, since it could not arouse the proper feelings among those who did not know the language.[22]

Heinrich Braun's *Introduction to Clerical Eloquence* [*Anleitung zur geistlichen Beredsamkeit*] was widely praised.[23] Braun (1732–1792) extolled simplicity in speaking and sought to instruct preachers that the best way to communicate religious truths was to have a proper understanding of the aesthetic dimensions of their homilies. This effort to simplify the art of the sermon, it has been suggested, was part of a broader rhetorical shift that included the visual arts as well, particularly evident in the decline of rococo ornamentation in church decoration.[24] Frank Büttner argues that the Enlightenment critique that the rococo style played lightly with the truth was in fact an attack on its rhetorical strategy, which sought to work by creating the proper "affect" for the reception of religious and moral truths.[25] Büttner suggests that this *Stilwandel* was a sign of the crisis of courtly society in wake of absolutism, as the court lost many of its traditional forms of representative power, and as the idea of the public becomes the main focus of legitimacy.[26] However one interprets the nature of this shift, Büttner has raised an important point about the relationship between style and its social ramifications.

---

[20] [F. Blau and A. Dorsch] *Beyträge zur Verbesserung des äussern Gottesdienstes in der katholischen Kirche* (Frankfurt, 1789), 12.

[21] Blau and Dorsch, 15.

[22] Blau and Dorsch, 22.

[23] Heinrich Braun, *Anleitung zer geistlichen Beredsamkeit* (Munich, 1776).

[24] Frank Büttner "Abschied von Pracht und Rhetorik. Überlegungen zu den geistesgeschichtlichen Voraussetzungen des Stilwandels in der Sakraldekoration des ausgehenden 18. Jahrhunderts in Süddeutschland," in *Herbst des Barock. Studien zum Stilwandel*, Andreas Tacke, ed. (Munich and Berlin: Deutscher Kunstverlag, 1998), 165–73.

[25] Büttner notes that Braun had a predecessor in Fenélon (*Dialogue sur l'eloquence*, 1718) and Muratori (*Contra sublime loquentes in cathedra seu Dignitas Eloquentiae popularis* (1757), [orig. Italian, 1750]). Muratori argued that rhetorical ornaments only serve the vanity of the preacher. Instead, style must be clear, easy, and understandable.

[26] Büttner, 171. Büttner argues that while an important factor in the decline of rococo church buildings in Bavaria was financial, one cannot ignore the social and political elements, since in earlier ages princes and prelates had gone into debt to pay for large building projects. Büttner, 165.

The Catholic *Aufklärer* who praised simplicity in spoken and written style held that by "purifying" religious practices and buildings of their scholastic and sensual excess one could better communicate fundamental religious truths. Yet they were speaking to a religious sensibility that suited their own – mostly urban – educated tastes. Significantly, Catholic reformers had come to share this religious sensibility with the majority of the nobility as well – in other words, as far as taste and intellectual aspirations went, there was not much of a gap between the bourgeois and noble German Catholic. Together, they set their sights on the reformation of the practices and beliefs of the common people.

Frustrated by their inability to carry out their vision for changing Catholic practice, the authors of many of the reform pamphlets and books laid blame on the institutional makeup of the church. The most outright challenge to the ecclesiastical hierarchy was Hontheim's *de Statu*. Many reformers, however, would go farther than Hontheim: it was not just the legal centralization of the church and the political activities of the Curia that were harmful, but also the church's very acceptance of wealth and worldly power. Such arguments resembled the views of Paolo Sarpi, who had written that the danger of corruption went back to the origins of the church: Judas was put in charge of the purse to buy necessary things for the community and to distribute the surplus to the poor. Yet his contact with money fostered avarice and led him to sell Jesus to the authorities.[27] In this historical view, it was only the superior virtue of the early Fathers that preserved the church against corruption. In Sarpi's version, the government of the church was originally communal in form, yet it grew to proportions where not everyone could participate, and governance was placed in the hands of ministers.[28]

Similar criticisms were also applied to the institution of monasticism. The Louvain jurist van Espen wrote on the "vice of property" among monastic orders. He stated that religious who retain large rents must examine their consciences to assure that they are not infected with the vice of possessiveness, and that they should strive toward reestablishing the monastic ideal of poverty and communal possession of what goods they do have.[29] Van Espen quoted St. Basil to the effect that the monastic life

[27] Paolo Sarpi, *Traité des Bénéfice* (French Translation, 1767). This argument could be stretched back to the Franciscan poverty dispute.
[28] Sarpi, 90.
[29] Van Espen, *Dissertation canonique sur la vice de la Proprieté des Religieux et des Religieuses* [translated from Latin] (Lyon, 1693), 33–7.

strives toward a vision of a "perfect society" by abolishing personal possession of goods – a requirement that must exist in spirit and not just in law.[30] The implication is that wealthy monasteries, even where individual property was not allowed, could not but foster possessiveness among their monks.

The monastic orders came in for the harshest – and at times the most palpably unfair – criticism, especially after the Jesuits had been suppressed.[31] To the regular clergy were imputed many, if not all, of the failures and transgressions of the church in the past. Except for a few extremists, the cry was not to destroy the influence of the institutional Church but to abolish the monastic spirit. In an anonymously published pamphlet, M. A. Wittola voiced the not uncommon opinion that the mendicant orders were responsible for the spirit of intolerance that arose with their attacks on heretics: "one must admit that the spirit of persecution [*Verfolgunsgeist*] among us Catholics is of the same epoch as the reign of the monks, especially the mendicants."[32] It is not the church itself that it at fault, Wittola insists:

O not at all! Voltaire and other shallow heads ascribe this horrible outrage [the persecuting spirit] to the church. But we do not need to believe him and should instead listen to Bossuet, Noailles, Colbert ... and other great bishops of recent times. ... It was only bad prelates and priests, seduced by monks, who were the persecutors of heretics.[33]

With his *On the Civil and Spiritual Improvement of Monasticism*, Peter Adolf Winkopp (1759–1813) nodded to C. W. Dohm's famous book on Jewish emancipation.[34] Winkopp emphasized the need for priests to be moral instructors, and indicated that contemplative monks were not suited to such an important task.

The mendicant orders were accused of corrupting the morality of the people through their preaching and educational missions.[35] A review in the Salzburg *Oberdeutsche Allgemeine Literaturzeitung* criticizes a set of published speeches for its use of the "unphilosophical term 'monastic

---

[30] Van Espen, 328.
[31] See Winfried Müller, *Im Vorfeld der Säkularisation* (Cologne: Böhlau, 1989).
[32] [Marx Anton Wittola], *Schreiben eine österreichischen Pfarrers über die Tolerance nach der Grundsätzen der katholischen Kirche*, 1781, 14.
[33] Wittola, 21.
[34] Peter Adolf Winkopp, *Uber die bürgerlich und geistliche Verbesserung des Monchwesens* (Gera, 1783) and C. W. Dohm, *Uber die bürgerliche Verbesserung der Juden* (Berlin and Stettin: 1781).
[35] Anon., *Freymüthige Bemerkungen über die Klosteraufhebung in Baiern*, 1802, 5–6.

virtue' [*unphilosophische Begriffe Mönchentugend*]," and concludes than an enlightened prince should reform the monasteries.[36] For their part, reform-minded monks were aware of the dangers of the rising tide of anti-monastic feeling. As Beda Aschenbrenner, the abbot of Oberalteich, put it in his *Aufklärungs Almanach für Abbte und Vorsteher katholischer Kloster* [*Enlightenment Almanach for abbots and superiors of Catholic Cloisters*]: "Reform yourselves – and you will be treated mildly! Otherwise you are wishing upon yourself and your pupils your collapse – your suppression."[37]

The most virulent critics were indiscriminate in their attacks on monasticism, attempting to impute the supposed vices of a few orders or their representatives to the very nature of monasticism. This naturally disturbed many of the Catholic *Aufklärer* who were themselves monks, as well as moderate laymen who not only appreciated the historical importance of monasticism for German Catholicism, but also thought that it still had a vital part to play in the preservation of culture and learning. Behind the vigorous attack on monasticism lurked a deeper antipathy toward the semi-monastic nature of the secular clergy of the Latin church.[38]

THE VIEW FROM THE CLOISTER: THE "CATHOLIC PATRIOTS" OF BANZ

Although the appeal – and in many ways the driving force – of the Catholic reform program was rooted in the lay piety of educated, urban Catholics, monastic institutions remained vital centers of learning and education. Especially given the semi-monopoly that Jesuits enjoyed over the universities, monastic academies – such as the famous Bavarian foundation of Augustinian Canons Regular at Polling – served as important alternative sources of scholarship, and also places where many middle-class Catholics could secure a career in the church. Monasticism, therefore, had a particular role in the Catholic Enlightenment in

---

[36] *Oberdeutsche Allgemeine Literaturzeitung*, 1. Vierteljahr, January–March, 1788, 14.
[37] Beda Aschenbrenner, *Aufklärungs Almanach für Abbte und Vorsteher katholischer Kloster* (1784), 112. Cited in Anton Hoffmann, *Beda Aschenbrenner (1756–1817). Lezter Abte von Oberalteich: Leben und Werk* (Passau, 1964).
[38] The situation of the Latin clergy, where parish priests and bishops alike lived – at least in principle – in a semi-monastic state, can be contrasted to the structure of the Orthodox church, where only prelates were required to take vows of chastity.

Germany, and made for a substantially different type of clerical contribution in comparison with the role of the clergy in the Protestant Enlightenment.

A synoptic view of the moderate – and clerical – *katholische Aufklärung* can be gleaned by surveying a journal dedicated to the review of the public literature. In 1775 Placidius Sprenger (1735–1806), a Benedictine monk of Banz in Franconia, began publishing a new journal entitled *Literature from Catholic Germany. For its Honor and Use. Published by Catholic Patriots.*[39] The editor writes that this new journal is proud to look beyond the borders of its Franconian home and serve as a "general library" of Catholic Germany, an *"allgemeine Bibliothek des katholischen Deutschlands.*[40] The reference is to Friedrich Nicolai's *Allgemeine deutsche Bibliothek*, the most important source of reviews and a major organ of the Berlin *Aufklärung*.[41] Sprenger complains that while "on the one side, Protestant Germany is almost suffocated by the number of its learned journals and newspapers, we, on the other side," have almost nothing.[42] Sprenger announces that his journal will contain reviews of books by German Catholics, news from Catholic universities and academies and from Catholic states outside of Germany, excerpts from recent Protestant journals as well as refutations of errors in Protestant journals concerning Catholic literature.[43] He continues: "it cannot escape those of our coreligionists who spend time reading Protestant

---

[39] *Litteratur des katholischen Deutschlands, zu dessen Ehre und Nutzen, herausgegeben von katholischen Patrioten* (Koburg, 1775–). The journal was offered as a continuation of the short-lived *Fränkische Zuschauer*. For a history of the journal in the context of the intellectual life of the abbey, see Wilhelm Forster, "Die kirchliche Aufklärung bei den Benediktinern der Abtei Banz," *Studien und Mitteilungen zur Geschichte des Benediktinerordens und seiner Zweige* 63 (1951): 172–233 and 64 (1952): 110–233.

[40] *Litteratur des katholischen Deutschlands*, "Vorrede," np.

[41] On Nicolai, see Pamela Eve Selwyn, *Everyday Life in the German Book Trade: Friedrich Nicolai as Bookseller and Publisher in the Age of Enlightenment, 1750–1810* (University Park: Pennsylvania State University Press, 2000) and Horst Möller, *Aufklärung in Preussen: der Verleger, Publizist und Geschichtsschreiber Friedrich Nicolai* (Berlin: Colloquium Verlag, 1974). On German periodicals in this period, see Joachim Kirchner, *Das Deutsche Zeitschriftenwesen. Seine Geschichte und seine Probleme. Teil 1. Von den Anfängen bi zum Zeitalter der Romantik. 2.* neubearbeitete und erweiterte Auflage (Wisbaden, 1958). For Catholic periodicals, see especially 121f.

[42] *Litteratur*, I, 1, 1775, "Vorrede," np. [5].

[43] In a later issue, the editors rescind this request by giving nod to the growing volume of Catholic writings: "Die Herrn Mitarbeiter weden ersucht, künftighin keine Recensionen von protestantischen Schriften mehr einzusenden, indem der Raum für die täglich mehr anwachsenden katholischen Schriftsteller zu enge werden will," *Litteratur*, III, iv, 1780, 598.

journals that one not seldom finds false representations of our literature, as well as hardly fair judgments about our writers."[44] The editor promises to scatter such errors and prejudicial reports "out of patriotic love." Yet, while Sprenger vows to avoid polemic, he also announces that he will brook no unjustified attacks:

the spiteful ones are in the end the hereticators [*Ketzermacher*]. Under the pretty cloak of religious zeal they sharpen their wolf's fangs on their prey, rip sentences out of context and spin [the prey] around until they have the appearance of heretics ... We will not allow such fiends [*Unholden*] to condemn our writings without even having read them. If they try, however, to engage us, we promise ahead of time that we will defend ourselves against them without mercy. For to go leniently around this loveless rabble [*liebelosen Gesinde*] would be as foolish as to oppose the club of Hercules with a foxtail.[45]

This appeal to limit polemic is characteristic of the moderate Catholic Enlightenment, which adopted the language of accommodation and reform. The past was not to be rejected whole cloth.

A survey of the journal reveals several key concerns of the moderate Catholic Enlightenment as expressed in the literature reviewed, as well as the comments of the editor and contributors (the articles are unsigned, so it is difficult to distinguish between the editor and corresponding contributors). First, there is concern for the influence of religious practice on the common people. In a long review of a collection sermons, the reviewer expresses disappointment that the work is not "by a German imitator of Bourdaloue or Massillon," as had been originally expected.[46] The reviewer criticizes the style and method of the sermons:

are the truths of salvation, the duties toward God and fellow man, the most basic sacred doctrines of the holy Fathers so preached out [*durchgepredigt*] and so exhausted, that one is forced to take refuge in devotional fantasies that reek of the pulpit barbarity [*Kanzelbarbarey*] of the fifteenth century?[47]

Furthermore, the continued use of unclear and abstruse examples should

not cause us to wonder that among the common people, there is greater weight on external devotions, and that his inclination is toward the veneration of and

---

[44] *Litteratur*, I, 1, 1775, "Vorrede," np. [5].
[45] *Litteratur*, I, 1, 1775, "Vorrede," np. [5].
[46] Litteratur, I, ii, 1776, 8f. Review of Benignus Reiß, OP, *Geistreiche Predigen an denen gewöhnlichen Monatsonntagen des heiligen Rosenkranzes vorgetragen*. 2 Bände (Augsburg, 1773). Louis Bourdaloue (1632–1704) and Jean-Baptiste Massillon (1663–1742) were renown for their preaching and sermons.
[47] *Litteratur*, I, ii, 1776, 20.

reliance on the saints, more than toward belief in the omnipotence, prudence, mercy and justice of the Most Holy?

It is clear that these problems will persist "as long as one does not use more restraint with this tone from the pulpits." The reviewer reminds that one must always assure that sermons and examples are clear to the "common mass [*gemeinen Haufen*]" because "it is the largest."[48] Other reviews in the journal comment on several new school curricula (here, the prince-bishopric of Münster), appreciating the emphasis on virtue and the avoidance of dry lectures. "The love of religion and virtue must become passion [*Leidenschaft*] in the student's heart, so it can counterbalance his other passions."[49]

The journal's reviewers particularly appreciated works that emphasized the importance of the pastor as the preceptor of the people. One book, it was noted, reminded that the

secular priest who spreads the Gospel is the general instructor of the people [*Allgemeine Volkslehrer*] and therefore should live in the middle of his parish so that he can be ... the light to the confused and a staff for the wavering.

It is further noted that this book "should be in the cabinet of every prince and ecclesiastical councilor."[50] Another book referred to is the *Practical Catholic Handbook of Religion for Thinking Christians*, by a Salzburg Benedictine. The idea is that common people need a basic book that explains their faith and distinguishes between civil tolerance, which has to do with the state, and theological tolerance, which is a matter of conscience.[51]

Despite its enthusiasm for such attempts at popular enlightenment, the journal also expresses reservations that these efforts will not always succeed if pursued too fast. A new periodical entitled *Der katholische Volckslehrer eine periodische Schrift für das unstudierte Publikum* [*The Catholic People's Instructor: A periodical for the uneducated public*] is judged as perhaps too ambitious: "there are indeed regions where the uneducated public, the *Bürgerstand*, is more insightful than the estate of Latin-educated scholars." Special attention is paid to the church in the

---

[48] *Litteratur*, I, ii, 1776, 21.

[49] *Litteratur*, II, ii, 1777, 384f.

[50] *Litteratur*, V, ii, 1785, 187. Review of Philipp Jacob von Huth, *Bildung des Priesters*, 1784. Huth was himself a Bavarian ecclesiastical councilor.

[51] *Litteratur*, V, iii, 1785, 335. Review of Simpert Schwarzhuber, OSB, *Praktisch katholisches Religionshandbuch für nachdenkende Christen. Auf höchsten Befehl des Hochwürdigestn R. Fürsten und Erzbischofs zu Salzburg*, 1784/1785.

early centuries – drawing from the work of Muratori, Fleury, and Mabillon, with the implication that the early church had been a model of piety, whereas in later centuries it became lax by allowing false devotion and false saints. The reviewer implies that, while these attitudes may be common enough among educated Catholics, "our author certainly would not wish that the people should carry out reform, as once did the crowd in London [*so etwa wie der Pöbel ehedem in London*]."[52] He warns that reform writings may be easily misunderstood by the common people, comparing these works to the political writings of Rousseau and Montesquieu, which, if excerpted, could be misconstrued and might lead to misbehavior. Similarly, it is implied, if one acts too quickly against "superstition," the people will only be strengthened in their beliefs, much in the same way that Protestant attacks on the pope only make his support among the people stronger.[53]

The reviewers of *Litteratur des katholischen Deutschland* also address strictly theological and philosophical texts. A review of the ex-Jesuit Benedict Stattler's (1728–1797) *Ethica Christiana universalis* [*Universal Christian Ethics*] reveals their distrust of theological and philosophical "systems" in favor of simple Christian morality based on revelation. The reviewer states the common view that the "science of morality" had languished under scholasticism, and that Stattler is now attempting to build a new system. He purports to take on freethinkers with theological morality, proving his points with "geometric rigor." The reviewer notes that the exaggerated need for numbered paragraphs (marked with §§) has gone too far. Of course, one needs thoroughness and clarity, but one should not have to refer back 10 pages to see what is being proved. It is, the reviewer says, like eating one's meals while on stilts, rather than seated.[54] The review proclaims the limits of philosophy to properly clarify morality; instead, the theologian must point out how revelation shows the proper way:

We have noticed that the author appears to have adopted the principle that one can philosophically prove theological truths. How easily a philosopher steps towards enthusiasm! Heuz, Hirnhaym and Malebranche devalue reason so much that they deny any certainty in knowledge in order to elevate holy revelation. Herr Stattler has the opposite intention: in order to prove theological truths with philosophy, he mis-uses faith.[55]

---

[52] *Litteratur*, V, iv, 1785, 577.
[53] *Litteratur*, V, iv, 1785, 577.
[54] *Litteratur*, I, iii, 1776, 25f.
[55] *Litteratur*, I, iii, 1776, 27.

The key point is the connection the reviewer makes between an overreliance on "philosophy" and the dangers of "enthusiasm." The moderate Catholic Enlighteners here represented by the journal held that matters of doctrine and belief needed to be simplified and stripped of their worldly accretions and modifications. This is how they justified their animosity toward the religious teachings of the Jesuits. Stattler, an influential ex-Jesuit, had indeed rejected the traditional scholastic style of the Society, but had replaced it with a similar reliance on worldly philosophy, it was alleged. This, the reformers feared, still threatened to place human reasoning and institutions at the center of religious life, whereas they wanted to assure the central role of biblical Christianity. They felt that false belief led to false behavior, which is why much energy of the Catholic Enlighteners was spent in attacks on the "superstition" they felt lay at the root of immorality. On the other hand, no less than their orthodox opponents, they saw Christianity as holding society together. This meant that to reform society, one needed to reform Catholic practice. But to do so required a certain level of authority and power that was not forthcoming from the Roman hierarchy.

A final important issue which can be gleaned from a survey of the journal *Litteratur des katholischen Deutschlands* is the editors' and reviewers' sense of the shape of German Catholicism. The church was much more than its institutions and doctrines, and it is was impossible for reformers to conceive of their culture as divorced from its religious context. There persisted the belief in the possibility of a harmony between the civil and religious authority – the *concordia sacerdotii et imperii* – in which the sum was greater than its parts. This is evident, first of all, in the reformer's interest in ecclesiastical and religious history. Yet there was also a growing sense of disillusionment and anxiety after the 1780s, particularly in regard to anti-monasticism. This was undoubtedly fostered by Joseph II's ecclesiastical policies, particularly his suppression of some 600 cloisters.[56] Even in *stiftische* Germany – that is, the Germany of the small ecclesiastical states – where the Austrian monarch had no such power to suppress religious foundations, Josephine policies and its attendant propaganda served to polarize discussions of Catholic reform. Joseph's actions emboldened critics of monasticism. One notable satire was Ignaz von Born's (1742–1791) *Monachologia, or Handbook of the*

---

[56] See Beales, *Prosperity and Plunder: European Catholic Monasteries in the Age of Revolution, 1650–1815* and Winfried Müller, *Im Vorfeld der Säkularisation. Briefe aus bayerischen Klöstern 1794–1803* (Cologne: Böhlau, 1989), 2.

Natural History of Monks, arranged according to the Linnaean System.[57] The editors of the journal advise that, rather than responding polemically and in anger, as had one author in a sloppy reply, one should just laugh off works that are only written to make money.[58]

Despite this apparent nonchalance, however, there is an increasing note of disappointment over the rancorous antimonastic tone of reform pamphlets. Care is taken to highlight works that point to the historical and present contributions of monasticism to state and society, such as Abbot Martin Gerbert's (1720–1793) *History of the Black Forest*:

One notes how from the beginning monks did not only practice silent contemplation – or, as several scribblers of our enlightened century would have it, laziness – but that they mainly occupied themselves with preaching and pastoral work and with projects that proved very useful for our fatherland.[59]

The same Gerbert had also published studies of early Germanic liturgies and early church music; the reviewer was careful to point to differences between the early German and the Roman liturgy.[60] Anti-Jesuitism was in part sustained and made possible by the vision of a German Catholicism that predated the Reformation and was constituted in its monastic culture. Yet, as the anxieties of the writers in *Litteratur des katholischen Deutschlands* show, the historical contributions of these old orders were being dismissed, despite the rather active efforts of moderate and learned religious.

Accompanying this sense of rising disrespect was a growing skepticism on the part of moderates towards the state. Aside from outright suppression, one method civil authorities used to limit the growth of monasteries and cloisters was to raise age limits for professing vows.

---

[57] *Joa. Physiophili Specimen Monachologiae Methodo Linnaeana*, 1783. An English version was printed in 1852, with significant additions and illustrations, including a section on the Jesuits. The author/translator notes:

When the present work was composed, they [the Jesuits] did not exist either in Austria or and other part of Western Europe. The Austrian naturalist, considering them on that account an extinct species, made no mention of them in this work.

Monachologia, 77.

[58] *Litteratur*, V, i, 1784, 78–84.

[59] *Litteratur*, V, ii, 1785, 234. See similar comments in *Litteratur* VI, iv, 1786, 582. See Martin Gerbert, *Historia Nigrae Silvae Ordinis Sancti Benedicti Coloniae*, 2 Volumes (St. Blasien, 1783).

[60] *Litteratur*, III, iv, 1780, 535. See Martin Gerbert, *Vetus liturgia alemannica*, 2 vols. (St. Blasien, 1776), as well as *De veteri liturgia Alemannica* (St. Blasien, 1770), and *Monumenta veteris liturgiae alemannicae* (St. Blasien, 1777).

Sometimes these laws could be quite absurd, such as when women were forbidden to take any vows until sometime in their 40s – thus assuring that female cloisters would die out, or at least be populated solely by widows. These vows were socially and legally significant, because they were accepted as binding for life by both the church and the state, and they altered the juridical and civil status of the juror. Critics of any state involvement argued that the state thereby acquired authority over a purely religious matter. In 1776 review, *Litteratur des katholischen Deutschlands* accepts the position that the civil authority should have some say over vows, since the privileges associated with the vows were originally granted by the prince. It follows from basic principles of contracts that no one can remove himself from the authority of the prince without his permission. The juring individual agrees to forgo rights of inheritance, the ability to hold office, and so forth, the reviewer reasons, and in return the state will not draft him into the army and will allow him to be tried in ecclesiastical courts. The author concludes that such requirements can in fact be beneficial to monastic culture, since they prevent young people from taking binding vows before they are ready. Indeed, the point is that the territorial lord is not ignoring the rights of the church but in fact works on behalf of the church and is the "protector" of the canons.[61] Yet, into the 1780s, the editor begins to show wariness toward such state-sponsored attempts at reform: he complains that Joseph's new rules for monasticism aim to return monks not to the rule of St. Benedict but to that of eastern (Orthodox) monks, where monastic orders did not develop as separate institutions as they did in the West.[62]

Similar skepticism on the part of moderate Catholic reformers is shown toward theoretical schemes, as a long review of a German translation of *Scienza della Legislazione* [*The Science of Legislation*] by the Neapolitan political theorist and legal reformer Gaetano Filangieri (1752–1788) demonstrates.[63] While generally positive – the reviewer thinks that Filangieri outshines Montesquieu, Justi, and Fenelon – questions

---

[61] *Litteratur*, I, iii, 1776, 49–57. Review of Stephen Rauttenstrauch, OSB, *de Jure Principis praefigendi maturiorem Professione monasticae solemni aetatem Diatriba* (Prague, 1773).

[62] *Litteratur*, IV, iii, 1782, 443. Comment *on Sieben Kapiteln von Klosterleuten* (Wien, 1782) and "Monasticism, Byzantine," *Dictionary of the Middle Ages* 8, 456–9.

[63] On Filangieri, see Marcello Maestro, *Gaetano Filangieri and His Science of Legislation*. Transactions of the American Philosophical Society. New Series, vol. 66, part 6, 1976.

are raised as to the dependability of the state's ministers who would oversee the church:

This bird sings a new song on page 335. The whole state is supposed to assure the maintenance of the clergy. Who is this state? Presumably the administrators of the state: the minister, the head of the treasury – in short, the *Messieurs* Officials [*Beamten*]. The fox over the eggs. Is this some kind of Neapolitan knight's trick? How would these goods be administered? Whoever knows anything about the world and about civil servants can see what would happen.[64]

Similar sentiments are expressed in a review of a work which is announced as a "handbook" for priests and state officials.[65] The author speaks of the "revolutions" of the last 20 years, and notes that individual reforms alone will not suffice without a recognition of deeper problems: namely, one must finally determine the boundaries of authority between church and state. This was a common enough assertion – and indeed a problem stretching back at least to Marsilius of Padua. The eighteenth century did not lack for new treatments of this theme by Catholic authors in Italy, Germany, and France, and it would appear that the current work was largely derivative from larger treatises.[66] The review is interesting, however, for the reviewer's comments. He wishes that the author had asserted that the right of self-preservation belongs to the church as well as to the state. For it flows "from the apostolic mission" that has been so often resisted:

Certainly the religious society that Jesus founded has, like any other corporation, the basic law, the fundamental duty, and the original right to preserve and to perfect itself [*sich selbst zu erhalten, sich selbst zu vervollkommenen*]. It can and must apply any means for preservation and perfection. It is allowed for it to accumulate heritable property, to missionize, incorporate and exclude, and everything else that is linked to the right of missionary activity and congregating. Whosoever exercises these rights can only do so insofar as they are ecclesiastical laws that are applied according to the principles of the church.[67]

---

[64] *Litteratur*, V, iv, 1785, 567f.

[65] Anon., *Grundsätze zur Feststellung der Eintracht zwischen der politischen und kirchlichen Macht in katholischen Staates. Ein Handbuch für Priester und Staatsmänner*, 1785. Reviewed in *Litteratur*, VI, i, 1786.

[66] The reviewer notes that better treatments are to be found in *Commentario de Limitibus utriusque potestatis* (Regensburg, 1781) (Anon., but it is noted that it is by a Benedictine); the pamphlet *Was ist der Kaiser* (1783); and [J. Pey] *De l'Autorité des deux Puissances* (Strasbourg, 1780). It is alleged that the author has copied many passages from the French work without attribution.

[67] *Litteratur*, VI, i, 1786, 110.

This passage is notable because it comes from a journal that usually supported reform efforts. Yet it was becoming clearer by the 1780s that something was bound to give in the efforts to reconceptualize the relative roles of the church and the state. The journal acknowledges that autonomy is of singular importance to the church. Whereas in earlier opinions, comments in the journal had indicated that the state was the protector of its mission – and therefore could be trusted – the increasing and successful attacks on church property gave pause to those moderate reformers who worried for the liberty of the church. For educated churchmen – who were immersed in a culture of clerical learning – the terms of this struggle reached back to the slogans of the Investiture Controversy, when the "liberty of the church" had been at stake.

The dilemma faced by these reforming Catholics was that they envisioned a continuing role for themselves as the moral and intellectual leaders of the Catholic church in Germany. They sought to derive their authority from an institution – the church – that had historically mediated between state and society. Their allegiance to the Catholic church was a fundamental aspect of their identity, yet they found themselves at odds with elements of the international church's mission. Regardless of whether they accepted or rejected moves for legal and canonical distance from Rome (as advocated by Hontheim), they did at least tacitly embrace a form of cultural autonomy – hence the interest in historical forms of the German liturgy and local church history. They sought to be "reasonable" Catholics, and assumed that they should naturally be the educators and leaders of the Catholic people. And this was where the movement for Roman centralization had the upper hand, because the papacy and the burgeoning culture of ultramontanism was better equipped to retain the sympathies of the common people. From the ultramontane perspective, this popular support would prove to be more enduring than the assurances of the state's ministers and the wealth left to the church by the nobility.

THE LIMITS OF ENLIGHTENMENT

From its origins in the early eighteenth century, the Catholic Enlightenment developed in various, sometimes contradictory, directions.[68] Early in the eighteenth century, important Catholic theologians embraced a

---

[68] For a recent overview, though with a different emphasis, see Dale K. Van Kley, "Catholic Conciliar Reform in an Age of Anti-Catholic Revolution. France, Italy, and the Netherlands, 1758–180," in *Religion and Politics in Enlightenment Europe*, James Bradley and Dale K. Van Kley, eds. (Notre Dame: University of Notre Dame Press, 2001), 46–118.

certain kind of moral optimism that enabled the church to overcome the difficulties of rigorist Augustinian theology.[69] In this, the Catholic Enlightenment in Germany bore some resemblances to what J. G. A. Pocock has identified as an "Arminian Enlightenment" in the Cavinist cultures of Europe.[70] The early Catholic Enlightenment held that the vision of religious and social reform could be united. Yet as religious sensibilities became increasingly differentiated among Catholics, social differences began to become real obstacles to common visions. The history of *German* Catholicism is never wholly a German story, just as it cannot be told from the perspective of the church's hierarchy alone. Like other aspects of Catholic church history, the problematic of bourgeois consciousness had national, as well as international, dimensions. It is possible to speak of the evolution of a bourgeois Catholic self-understanding within the church – critics and "reformers" who never quite left the church, yet were frequently at odds (at least intellectually) with official teachings.[71] This Catholic bourgeois view can be characterized as a type of "ecclesiastical republicanism." In the modern era of the church, this tradition goes back as far as Paolo Sarpi's *History of the Council of Trent.*[72] William Bouwsma has noted that Sarpi's history treats the church as an (originally) spiritual republic, and thus asks the classic "republican" questions of Renaissance historiography. Namely, how does a republic degenerate into a monarchy, and can the process be reversed?[73] The implication of Sarpi's history (as in his *Treatise on*

---

[69] I have developed this argument elsewhere. See Michael Printy, "The Intellectual Origins of Popular Catholicism: Catholic Moral Theology in the Age of Enlightenment," *Catholic Historical Review* 91, no. 3 (2005).

[70] J. G. A. Pocock, *Barbarism and Religion. Volume I: The Enlightenments of Edward Gibbon* (Cambridge: Cambridge University Press, 1999), 50–71.

[71] An interesting comparison can be made using Reinhart Koselleck's classic account of the "self image of Enlightenment thinkers," in which he describes the process by which bourgeois thinkers set themselves up in (loyal) opposition to the state. Koselleck argues that as a response to religious civil war, absolutism was conditioned on the banishing of morality from politics. A supposedly free space for criticism was thereby created. Because they lacked real political power, and claimed to accept the authority of the state, critics could argue that they presented no physical threat and should therefore be left to their own devices. See Reinhart Koselleck, *Critique and Crisis: Enlightenment and the Pathogenesis of Modern Society* (Cambridge: MIT Press, 1988).

[72] See William Bouwsma, *Venice and the Defense of Republican Liberty: Renaissance Values in the Age of the Counter-Reformation* (Berkeley and Los Angeles: University of California Press, 1968) and David Wootton, *Paolo Sarpi: Between Renaissance and Enlightenment* (Cambridge: Cambridge University Press, 1983).

[73] Bouwsma, 608. David Wootton (in *Paolo Sarpi*) has argued that Sarpi was actually an atheist, and that he maintained a religious façade only in his public writings and in his

Benefices) was that the human and material element in the church constantly threatened to corrupt its spiritual mission – a common theme that runs through medieval and early modern reform literature.

Whereas the Protestant answer to this threat of corruptibility was to spiritualize the church, Catholic historiography, if it were to maintain the Catholic insistence on the sacramentality of the church, needed to allow for human weakness. Partisans of the "republican" view of the church sought to come to terms with the fragility of ecclesiastical virtue.[74] Yet critics of this view – that is, Catholics strictly loyal to the hierarchy – might well ask what the spiritualizers of the church would offer in the stead of a strong central (i.e., papal) church with significant worldly resources.[75] It should be clear that the eighteenth-century debate between "republican" (episcopalist) and "monarchical" (papalist) visions of the church – notwithstanding the multitude of visions in between – were echoes of long-standing disputes within Catholicism, most obviously those around the Conciliar movement of the fifteenth century.[76] Ecclesiastical politics are framed within a very long time horizon, and were understood on multiple levels by the participants. What was novel about the eighteenth-century dispute – and indeed what is most particular about the *German* Catholic experience – was the emergence of a bourgeois self-understanding and religious sensibility that tried to lay claim to moral leadership within the church. New in the eighteenth century was the view that the state was now strong enough – and willing – to act on long-standing threats to seize and administer church property and to diminish the rule of canon law. A significant factor in the state's new power was that it had a large portion of the bourgeoisie on its side.

position as official theologian to the Republic of Venice. Whatever the status of Sarpi's personal views, it is his public personality and the influence of his works on subsequent generations of Catholics that is of interest here.

[74] Here I borrow a concept from J. G. A. Pocock, *The Machiavellian Moment. Florentine Political Thought and the Atlantic Republican Tradition* (Princeton: Princeton University Press, 1975).

[75] The portrait of Sarpi (reproduced in Wootton, *Paolo Sarpi*) in the Bodleian library depicts Sarpi as the "eviscerator" of the Council of Trent – perhaps this was the case in the eyes of scholars, but Trent had succeeded by pastoral and papal standards.

[76] Not all ecclesiastical republicans were necessarily supporters of the episcopalist position. As Peter Philip Wolf put it "die Kirche kann und darf keine Monarchie, sie muss eine Republik seyn. Ihre natürlichen Repräsentanten sind nicht bloss der Klerus als Stand, sondern jeder Katholik kann als Mitglied, seine Kirche repräsentieren." Peter Philipp Wolf, *Vorschlag zu einer Reformation der katholischen Kirche* (Leipzig und Luzern, 1800), 48.

The logical extreme of the tradition of critique that originated in Sarpi's history of the council of Trent appears in Felix Blau's *Kritische Geschichte der kirchlichen Unfehlbarkeit* [*Critical History of Ecclesiastical Infallibility*, 1791].[77] Like Sarpi before him, Blau (1754–1798), a professor of theology at Mainz, and later a supporter of the French during their occupation of that city, applies historical principles to show how contingent actions of the church's ministers can and have led the church astray. Blau does not attack *papal* infallibility, but *ecclesiastical* infallibility, a far more radical step.[78] For he goes beyond the conciliar tradition, which held that a general Council was superior to the pope and was the final arbiter of matters of faith and morals. Blau denies that there could be any final arbiter, in essence rejecting the notion of the church's *magesterium*. He portrays the doctrine of infallibility historically, implying that it was an aspect of the faith that Catholics have now outgrown. Blau argued that the transformation of Protestant theology in the eighteenth century was also a challenge to received Catholic positions about the supposedly immutable nature of its doctrine.[79] In Blau's view, the movement away from the authority of the symbolic books corrects a vital flaw that had arisen in the Protestant churches, and which had rendered Catholicism more advantageous. Now that the Protestants have rejected the declaration that the symbolic books are permanent articles of faith, the Catholic position no longer has the upper hand.[80] In being coerced to swear allegiance to specific doctrines, Blau implies, Protestants had been forced to accept positions that may have been false, whereas Catholics could place their allegiance in the institution itself. Despite his positive comments about this relatively new Protestant position, he criticizes the discrepancy between official teaching and the practices of the Protestant churches. He states that

---

[77] Felix Anton Blau, *Kritische Geschichte der kirchlichen Unfehlbarkeit, zur Beförderung einer freieren Prüfung des katholizismus* (Frankfurt, 1791). Blau (1754–1798) quotes and refers to Sarpi and his French translator Le Courayer often throughout the work. For biographical information, see H. Mathy, "Felix Anton Blau (1754–1798). Ein mainzer Lebensbild aus der Zeit der Aufklärung und französischen Revolution, zugleich ein Beitrag zur radikalen Aufklärungstheologie am Mittelrhein," in *Mainzer Zeitschrift* 67/68 (1972/1973), 1–29. On Blau's ideas in relation to the conciliar tradition, see Herman-Josef Sieben, *Die katholischen Konzilsidee von der Reformation bis zur Aufklärung* (Paderborn: Schönigh, 1988).

[78] On papal infallibility, see Brian Tierney, *Origins of Papal Infallibility, 1150–1350. A Study of Concepts of Infallibility, Sovereignty and Tradition in the Middle Ages* (Leiden: E. J. Brill, 1988 [1972]).

[79] Blau, vii.

[80] Blau, xf.

Protestants have the right to examine for themselves the tenants of belief but can still be told by the (Protestant) church that they are wrong.[81] He claims that the Protestant church denies its infallibility, "and yet binds and persecutes as if it were infallible," and its instructors are required to teach specific doctrines.[82]

An important part of Blau's argument is that every era has its own religious truths, and one cannot expect them to remain the same over generations.[83] Infallibility had served its purpose in earlier times, when it was sufficient to trust in the authority and correctness of the church – that it would determine the correct doctrine for the faithful, and more importantly, would not lead them down false paths. Blau pleads for the autonomy of the theologian, arguing that because doctrine can be shown to have substantially changed over the centuries, only the right to freely investigate scripture and doctrines of faith will allow believers to follow their conscience. While Blau was not singular in his critique of infallibility – Benedikt Maria Werkmeister (1745–1823) penned an anonymous work on the same theme – his approach seems the most serious and most considered.[84] He avoids polemical language, and though in hindsight his program never had much chance to be accepted, his optimism about the possibilities of reasoned reform is a testament to the wide range of possibilities open to the *katholische Aufklärung*, especially from his perspective in Mainz.[85] The University of Mainz attracted an interesting array of scholars from across Germany. Furthermore, as a prince-bishopric, the state did not loom as large at Mainz as it did in Bavaria and Austria. In these latter two cases, the *katholische Aufklärung* could not be freed from suspicions of supporting the notion of a state church (*Staatskirchentum*).

Blau was not naively optimistic about the role of the state, at least in his later writings. His treatise on infallibility can thus be read not only as

---

[81] Blau, *Unfehlbarkeit*, 513.

[82] Blau, *Unfehlbarkeit*, 517.

[83] He does not go so far as Lessing, however, in arguing that God revealed himself progressively throughout history according to the capabilities of human beings to understand him.

[84] [Benedikt Maria Werkmeister], *Freykirch Thomas, oder ferymüthige Untersuchungen über die Unfehlbarkeit der katholischen Kirche*, vol. 1 (Frankfurt und Leipzig, 1792). Werkmeister's treatise openly relies on Enlightenment Protestant theology, employs essentially polemical language, and is unqualified in its praise for Josephine policies. Blau, on the other hand, seems to be more seriously attempting to win over theologians (at least those on the fence or already leaning in his direction). Werkmeister was a Benedictine monk from 1765 to 1791. For more on Werkmeister, see August Hagen, *Die kirchliche Aufklärung in der Diözese Rottenburg* (Stuttgart, 1953).

[85] See Blanning, *Reform and Revolution*.

the culmination of a tradition within the Catholic *Aufklärung*, but also as a precursor to the views of many nineteenth-century liberal Catholics. Indeed, while Blau would support the French during the occupation of Mainz, and would work as a judge in the French administration of the annexed German territories, he was critical of the Civil Constitution of the Clergy in those aspects where it asserted authority over matters of faith. Blau's *Critique of the Religious Laws in France since the Revolution* was indebted to Kant as well as to the Abbé Gregoire.[86] The thrust of Blau's argument is that not only should the church restrict itself to purely spiritual matters, but also that the state should not try to influence these issues. "The state does not have the right of reformation [*Reformationsrecht*]," Blau argues, nor should it make citizens swear oaths, which are matters of conscience.[87] However, the state does have the right to create institutions of moral education, as that falls within the bounds of the protection of civil society.[88] Blau writes that

according to a law of reason, every person is a member of the general church [*allgemeine Kirche*]. He is obliged to the visible or particular church only insofar as he sees it as a means and a tool to work for the goals of the general church.[89]

What Blau has in mind is something like a religion of humanity, yet he leaves room for particular and historical religions within it. Judaism and Christianity teach the same moral doctrine in essence – it is only when these religious societies attain worldly powers that they stray down false paths. At least nominally, Blau expresses as much concern for the liberation of the church from the state as vice versa. He is thus aware of the dangers of the statist bias of the *katholische Aufklärung*, and, more importantly, he heralds several important themes of nineteenth-century liberal Catholicism.[90] Blau's theology and philosophy represented the logical – which is not the same as the polemical – extreme of the Catholic Enlightenment.

---

[86] Felix Anton Blau, *Kritik der seit der Revolution in Frankreich gemachten Religionsverordnungen, auf reine Prinzipien des Staats- und Kirchenrechts gegründet* (Strasbourg: F. G. Levrault, 1797). The copy in the Bibliothèque Nationale de France is hand-inscribed "an Citoyen Gregoire" and bears the stamp "Leges Gregoire." According to Mathy ("Blau," 23), Blau knew Gregiore personally and respected him, yet criticized him for still accepting infallibility. Blau was imprisoned by the Prussians at Königstein from 1793 to 1795. Upon release, he went to Paris and worked in the ministry of justice and also wrote for the organ of German revolutionaries. He returned to Mainz when the French retook it, and worked as a criminal judge. See Sieben, 485.

[87] Blau, *Kritik*, 137.

[88] Blau, *Kritik*, 122.

[89] Blau, *Kritik*, 66.

[90] See, in particular, the thought of Henri Lacordaire (1802–1861).

8

Pastors of Enlightenment: Reforming the Secular Clergy

Dissenting from a popular and strongly held opinion, I venture to suggest that when a nation deprives the Catholic clergy of the ownership of real estate and replaces the income drawn from it by fixed salaries, the nation is furthering the interests of the Holy See and the temporal power and these alone, and is also suppressing one of the chief elements of freedom within its borders. For a man who in respect of all that counts most in his spiritual life is subject to a foreign authority and is not allowed to have a family has only one possible link with the soil of the country in which he lives. Cut this link and he belongs nowhere in particular ... though an excellent member of the Christian *civitas*, he is but an imperfect citizen in the mundane sense.

   – Tocqueville, *The Old Regime and the French Revolution*[1]

REFORMING THE CLERGY

The secular clergy was at the nexus of the rethinking of the church. Ideas and plans for the reformation of the clergy touched the heart of relations between the church and state. They were inseparable from questions of the structure of church hierarchy and were the canvas onto which reformers projected their visions of social reform.[2]

Competing visions of the clergy and the type of religious practices, they should be supporting lurked behind the contest over the institutional

---

[1] Alexis de Tocqueville, *The Old Regime and the French Revolution*, trans. Stuart Gilbert (New York: Anchor, 1955), 28.

[2] For a useful overview, with interesting observations about the implications of clerical reform for political thought, see Luise Schorn-Schütte, "Priest, Preacher, Pastor: Research on Clerical Office in Early Modern Europe," *Central European History* (2000).

apparatus of the church. Joseph II's efforts to exert centralized authority over the training of priests were met with howls of protest that clergy would thereby become salaried servants of the state. Recent literature on Josephine reforms emphasizes that, while control and rationalization were certainly important aspects of these reforms, such desires did not preclude a genuine religious concern with improving the secular clergy and religious practice in general.[3]

Focusing on the state alone also overlooks a more significant process regarding the social standing of the pastor. Immediately apparent, of course, is the fact that priests would become dependent on the state, which has seized other church lands – especially of suppressed monasteries – and, after 1773, those of the Jesuits. But just as significant is that once the priest receives his income from a centralized fund, he is no longer supported by a benefice that is situated in the community he serves. Instead, his position has become implicated in a money economy. While a clergymen was not necessarily a "farmer" in any direct sense – he could hire someone to work the land, after all – once his income was not tied to a particular benefice, he was henceforth separated from the agricultural life of his parish. It is illuminating to consider that in the nineteenth century, after the Empire and the *Reichskirche* were dismantled, the newly constituted German Catholic church would carry out essentially these very types of reforms. The point is that both the state and subsequently the German church were trying to form the clergy into a professional class.[4] The debate over benefices was therefore a struggle over the power of bishops and the independence and loyalty of the clergy.[5]

An important part of this story is the benefice system itself, which had originated in the Middle Ages. The secular clergy was under a bishop, whereas the centralized mendicant orders (Franciscan, Dominican, Augustinian Hermits, and Carmelites) as well as the Cistercians and Premonstratensians were exempt from the local bishop's authority. They lived apart, and while the secular clergy was still tied into social

---

[3] Derek Beales, *Joseph II: In the Shadow of Maria Theresa, 1741–1780* (Cambridge: Cambridge University Press, 1987). On the seminary reforms, see William Bowman, *Priest and Parish in Vienna, 1780–1880* (Boston: Humanities Press, 1999).

[4] On the terminology, see Joseph Bergin, "Between Estate and Profession: The Catholic Parish Clergy of Early Modern Western Europe," in *Social Orders and Social Classes in Europe since 1500: Studies in Social Stratification*, M. L. Bush, ed. (New York: Longman, 1992).

[5] For a comparison with the Protestant clergy, see C. Scott Dixon and Luise Schorn-Schütte, eds., *The Protestant Clergy in Early Modern Europe* (London: Palgrave, 2003).

hierarchies, the vows of the regular clergy in principle leveled social distinctions.[6] The cathedral chapters were composed mainly of nobles, though exceptions were made for bourgeois with academic titles.[7] These positions were usually endowed with comfortable incomes. In order to be ordained, a candidate had to prove that he had a benefice to support him. The ecclesiastical hierarchy wanted to ensure the social and economic independence of the priest so that he could exercise his sacramental office and would not be tempted to sell sacraments to support himself. Benefices often had to be accumulated, since some were too small.[8] Wealthy patrons often would set up small chapels with an endowment for priests to say mass – perhaps in memory of a loved one or in thanks for a particular event. These smaller positions served as stepping-stones for an ecclesiastical career, but the priest was not always successful in landing more positions.[9] The social and economic differences separating the lower and higher clergy could be quite dramatic. Often, those possessing high ecclesiastical offices – and incomes – would delegate pastoral responsibilities to the lower clergy. Gatz states that "at the furthest end of the scale there was even an ecclesiastical proletariat, with insecure or insufficient resources." He concludes that

there existed a confusing spectrum of clerics with widely varying social and educational status and lifestyle ... from the well-off *Stiftkleriker* ... to the poor country priest, far from the city, who partook in the lifeworld of the village and had to rely on agriculture and hospitality for income.[10]

Fixing these structural problems was among the major goals of the fathers at the council of Trent. By the eighteenth century, Tridentine reforms could be shown to be taking root among the rural clergy, especially in ending concubinage and in lessening the influence of the patron of a benefice. For as long as a patron had significant say over who was appointed to his parish, the bishops were restricted in their reforming efforts. Among the reforms was the establishment of diocesan

---

[6] Erwin Gatz, ed., *Geschichte des kirchlichen Lebens in den deutschprachigen Ländern seit dem Ende des 18. Jahrhunderts. Die katholische Kirche.* Vol. 4: *Der Diözesanklerus* (Freiburg: Herder, 1995), 25.

[7] The exact composition of the chapters varied with some being more inclusive than others. The social makeup of the cathedral chapters is extensively analyzed in Peter Hersche, *Die deutsche Domkapital*, 3 vols. (Bern: 1984).

[8] Gatz, ed., *Geschichte des kirchlichen Lebens in den deutschprachigen Ländern seit dem Ende des 18. Jahrhunderts. Die katholische Kirche.* Vol. 4: *Der Diözesanklerus.*

[9] Ibid., 28.

[10] Ibid.

commissions that would first test the candidate, who would then be passed on to the patron.[11] Still, bishops had problems in shaping the clergy according to their demands when they did not have access to the necessary resources. Extrapolating from Eduard Hegel's work on Cologne, Gatz notes that until the eighteenth century, a lack of priests or pastoral workers was not always the main problem. Instead, the difficulty was in training and education, which itself was related to the fact that there was not always effective diocesan control over pastoral work. "The root of the failure," Gatz notes, "lay in both cases in the medieval structure of the church, especially in the benefice system of the ecclesiastical office and the thereby handicapped administrative power of the bishop." For example, of a thousand or so parishes in his diocese, the archbishop of Cologne could freely fill only about 40 parishes, the rest being restricted by patronage rights of nobles, incorporated into monasteries, or otherwise subjected to restrictions.[12] Among the principle complaints of the German bishops was that they did not have enough control over the collation of benefices. Feller noted this too, yet expressed skepticism that worldly German prince-bishops would necessarily distribute these resources in a more pious way than the current system.[13] In any case, it was clear to all sides of the conflict that structural reform of some type was needed. The question was who would take the lead in this reform: the bishops, the pope, or lay princes?

The Tridentine ideal of reforming the clergy often stumbled on such practical and entrenched issues as those of the benefice system. The most successful reforming impulses came from new orders and institutions, which were more quickly able to meet demands for change because they did not have the same legal and institutional barriers. The most notable of these new orders was, of course, the Society of Jesus, whose seminaries trained the large majority of priests in Germany and in other Catholic countries. Yet there were among the orders differences that could have long-lasting effects, such as the Oratory of Cardinal Bérulle (founded in 1613 as the *Oratoire de Jésus-Christ*).[14] The Oratory had as its particular mission the sanctification – that is, the moral and spiritual improvement – of the secular clergy, and established seminaries with the goal of fulfilling Tridentine prescriptions. The priests of the Oratory took special vows to

[11] Gatz, Ibid., 35.
[12] Gatz, Ibid., 37.
[13] On Feller, see Chapter 4.
[14] Bérulle's Oratory was modeled on that of Philip Neri (1515–1595).

their bishops (renewals of the vows of obedience made at consecration), whereas the Jesuits were bound closely to the pope in their vow concerning "missions," giving them a certain mobility that was not available to those bound to a particular diocese.[15] The ethos of the Oratory embodied a distinctively French dedication to the notion that the office of the bishop represented what Louis Thomassin (himself an Oratorian) would call the "plenitude" of the sacramental ministry [*sacerdoce*].[16] It is difficult to imagine such an ethos taking hold in German Catholicism, where the bishops were also princes.[17] Indeed, it is precisely this incongruity that François Feller mocked in his comments on the German episcopal movement. Yet without a certain moral authority – an ecclesiastical legitimacy independent from temporal powers – an episcopal-centered reformation of the clergy would be an uphill struggle in Germany until after the Empire itself had come apart.

Perhaps the best way to grasp the issues concerning the secular clergy in the latter half of the eighteenth century is to sketch the different paths one could imagine at the time. One path consisted of a concerted reform effort by each bishop in his diocese: more visitations, and especially better seminaries and secular education for candidates. The bishops would need more control over benefices to ensure that their legal authority over priests was bolstered by a real control over the compensation and remuneration of their clergy. A second route to reform would be that the secular prince would strengthen educational institutions (even if leaving the strictly theological examinations to the bishops). The prince would finance these efforts by suppressing monasteries and using the confiscated funds of the Jesuit order. A major obstacle lay in the fact that the prince – whose territory was rarely contiguous – would have to deal with several different bishops. His plans would also come into conflict with exempt monastic institutions which not only had the patronage for many parishes, but often supplied the priests from their own orders as well. A third

---

[15] Charles E. Williams, *The French Oratorians and Absolutism, 1611–1641*, American University Studies, Series IX, vol. 47 (New York: Peter Lang, 1989), 82. On the "fourth vow" as a "vow of mobility," see John O'Malley, *The First Jesuits* (Cambridge: Harvard University Press, 1993), 299.

[16] Louis Thomassin, *Ancienne et Nouvelle Discipline de l'Eglise, Touchant les Benefices et les Beneficiers* (Nouvelle edition revue, corigée & rangée suivant l'ordre de L'Edition Latine avec ses augmentations) (Paris: Chez Francois Montalant, 1725), 1.

[17] Bartholomew Holzhauser (1613–1658) founded an order similar to that of the Oratorians (*Institutum clericorum saecularium in communi viventium* also known as the Bartholomites) in 1640, but the movement never reached the level of importance of the Jesuits and did not survive the Secularization of 1803.

path therefore involved these monastic institutions, which had the economic and human resources to meet demands for parish priests. While abbots were quite willing to send out members of their community to serve in parishes, they were reluctant to relinquish legal authority over their charges. Any comprehensive solution involving monasteries would need the collaboration of Rome, for it held in many cases the only authority over these institutions. Given that tensions between the papacy and the episcopate ran high, such harmonious cooperation seemed unlikely, even if in principle the resources and institutions existed to meet demand. Complicating – if not dominating – matters was that underneath these inter-church and church–state conflicts lay significantly different visions of how religious practice was to be reformed and taught.

That reform projects necessarily involved an attack on entrenched interests is clear from the history of Joseph II's plans to create new parishes in the Habsburg lands. Joseph II linked the suppression of cloisters – a desideratum of the Catholic Enlighteners on ideological grounds – with the practical goal of creating a more efficient parish system.[18] Plans for the creation of more parishes went back to the reign of Maria Theresa, who was particularly shocked at the discovery of secret Protestantism in her territory. It was realized that the only effective method of ensuring Catholicism in these areas was to strengthen the education of the clergy, and to make unwieldy parishes more manageable.[19] A Religion Commission was set up for this purpose. The biggest obstacle proved to be financial. A first attempt at creating a Religion Fund – which was to be financed by willing contributions of bishops, abbies and wealthy parishes, but which also envisioned centralized state control of the wealth of cloisters so that the state might administer the surplus – failed once Pope Benedict XIV rejected the plan. The pope also rejected a more modest plan on the grounds that even a fund whose contributions were all voluntary would nevertheless still be completely under state supervision. A different obstacle, as Johann Joseph Cardinal von Trautson, archbishop of Vienna noted, was that the consistorial councilors enjoyed the income of large and rich parishes. Papal disapproval and war with Prussia brought the Religion Commission to an end, but the principle was established that parishioners

[18] Johann Weißensteiner, "Die josephinische Pfarregulierung," in Gatz, Erwin, ed, *Geschichte des kirchlichen Lebens in den deutschprachigen Ländern seit dem Ende des 18. Jahrhunderts. Vol. 1 Die Bisthümer und ihre Pfarreien* (Freiburg: Herder, 1991), 62.
[19] Weißensteiner, 52.

should not live more than an hour's travel from their parish church.[20] Joseph's personal and energetic involvement got things moving again after 1780. A survey of all ecclesiastical goods and personnel was undertaken, which determined that of 33,737 ecclesiastical persons, fewer than half were serving as pastors.[21] In 1782 the first Cloister Suppression patent ordered the closure of all cloisters of the contemplative orders, and eventually it was determined that the income from these institutions was to go to a Religion Fund. It was also ordered that the (ex) regular clergy were to be examined to see who was capable of serving in the parishes.[22] While the new parishes themselves lasted, most of Joseph's other reforms did not – and indeed sparked revolt in the Austrian Netherlands. Leopold II repealed most of his brother's legislation.[23]

The Secularization left, for the most part, property and goods devoted to parishes intact and mainly affected the land and wealth of the cloisters and the collegiate foundations (*Stifte*). Since the Secularization allowed, but did not require, the territorial princes to suppress abbies and other institutions, the process unfolded differently in each state. And while the parishes themselves were not materially reduced, the *Patronat* was kept intact – transferred from the abbot or prince-bishop to the territorial lord.[24] While after 1803 the bishops no longer had to contend with monastic institutions as competitors in their diocese, they had lost much of the material independence that they had enjoyed as territorial princes. There was also a great effort made to reform the clergy and particularly to ensure that priests served as moral exemplars. The seminary of Michael Sailer and the clerical conferences of Ignaz von Wessenberg represented two of the most important strides in this direction. The strength of

---

[20] Weißensteiner, 52–3.

[21] The report concludes:

19, 116 für Staat und Religion unnütze und schädliche Glieder schwälgten in Trägheit und Müssiggang, verzehrten die reichen Einkünfte ihrer Pfründe oder den Schweiß der arbeitenden Klasse von Bürgern, welche sie anbei zur Belohnung mit Aberglauben und Unwissenheit zu verwirren suchten.

HHStA, Kaiser-Franz-Akten 75 (alt 75e) fol 17v, cited in Weißensteiner, 55.

[22] Weißensteiner, 55–6.

[23] Weißensteiner, 62. On the revolt see most recently Derek Beales, *Prosperity and Plunder: European Catholic Monasteries in the Age of Revolution, 1650–1815* (Cambridge: Cambridge University Press, 2003), 210–28.

[24] Erwin Gatz, ed., "Die Pfarrei von der Säkularisation bis zum Beginn der großen Binnenwanderungen," in *Geschichte des kirchlichen Lebens in den deutschprachigen Ländern seit dem Ende des 18. Jahrhunderts*, vol. 1, *Die Bisthümer und ihre Pfarreien* (Freiburg: Herder, 1991), 73.

popular Catholicism drew in large part on the special status of the parish clergy. As Emmet Larkin has argued for Ireland, the loyalty of the common people toward their priests could only be assured if the priests themselves upheld certain standards. Hence episcopal control of the clergy was a key tool in consolidating popular support for the church hierarchy.[25] The struggle between the bishops and the papacy was not mere posturing, but part of a crisis of legitimacy over *who* would reform the German church.

PASTORS OF ENLIGHTENMENT

Commentators who otherwise were radically opposed in their opinions of the nature of the clergy and the means to reform it could agree at least on the problem: the secular clergy was in dire straits toward the end of the eighteenth century. Matthäus Fingerlos (1748–1817), an advocate of teaching Kantian philosophy to seminarians and regent of the seminary in Salzburg, observed in 1800:

The signs of the time are not favorable. Some thirty years ago even old men were respectful toward priests; now not even children are. Then, young students were drawn toward this estate in droves, whereas nowadays it is practically supposed in some places that one needs to press young men [into service] like English sailors. Earlier, one spoke the word "Priest" with respect, now it is used here and there as an insult. Those are the signs of the time, and they are getting more visible from year to year.[26]

While it had not yet come to press-gangs, those on the other side of the theological divide could agree that the secular clergy was in need of a major overhaul. The ex-Jesuit Benedict Stattler noted that

the demands for a reformation of the church among us Catholics are becoming almost as loud, and perhaps even more brusque, than in the times of the Councils of Constance and Basel, yes even at the time of Luther's revolt.[27]

---

[25] Emmet Larkin, "The Devotional Revolution in Ireland," *American Historical Review* 77:3 (June, 1972), 625–52. It is also important, as Margaret Anderson points out in her important essay, not to simplify the relationship between the hierarchy and the motivations of the majority of believers. See Margaret Lavinia Anderson, "Piety and Politics: Recent Work on German Catholicism," *Journal of Modern History* December (1991): 681–716.

[26] Fingerlos, *Wozu sind geistliche da?* (Salzburg, 1800), vol. 2, 311–2.

[27] Benedikt Stattler, *Wahre und allein hinreichende Reformationsart des katholischen gesammten Priesterstandes, nach der ursprünglichen Idee seines göttlichen Stifters* (Ulm, 1791), iii.

However, he continued, calls for radical reforms of doctrine and clerical practice missed the point:

It is sad that one does not arrive at the only obviously true and sufficient means, and instead always wants to pursue side issues. Many writings in recent years have recommended the abolition of priestly celibacy as the principle means to improve the state of the clergy – a means that would certainly denigrate and ruin it completely. Others think that all would be improved if only the papal see were brought down and the metropolitans and bishops raised up, provincial councils re-introduced and the old church discipline once again used as an example. However, I firmly believe that the only way towards a successful reformation is by taking steps to assure that we have worthy bishops, priests, pastors and teachers – that is, good clerical shepherds from all classes.[28]

Even when Stattler dismisses as "side issues" core parts of the Catholic Reform program, he does acknowledge the pressing need for institutional reform.

The title of Matthaus Fingerlos' handbook on clerical education gets right to the point: *What are Priests For?* In determining the "main purpose" (*Hauptzweck*) of the priesthood, Fingerlos quickly dismisses the idea that the principle function of the priesthood is to be found in its ceremonial role, in reading the mass or praying, and much less in the perfection of the individual priest. These are all important elements of the office, of course, but they do not constitute the *raison d'être* of the priesthood. Rather, Fingerlos proclaims, "the highest purpose of the clerical estate is in the promotion of good morals though the education of the people."[29] Fingerlos emphasizes the social significance of the clergy, pointing out that it forms a weighty proportion of the population of the Catholic countries. He estimates the number of male clergy at 300,000 in all of Europe. In Switzerland, Holland, Poland, Russia, England, and Germany, the number is 134,000.[30] He also calculates the cost of maintaining them. He does not imply that the clergy are necessarily wasteful, as so many ardent anticlerical tracts do. Rather, he uses these numbers to reinforce the seriousness of the question, as well as the benefits of a successful reformation. The second volume of his handbook is dedicated to the methods that would enable the clergy to best fulfill their purpose as moral educators. These fall into two categories: proper education of seminarians, and fostering of good morals among priests (*Wissenschaft und Sitten*).

---

[28] Stattler, *Priesterstands*, iv.
[29] Fingerlos, *Geistliche*, 50.
[30] Fingerlos, *Geistliche*, 11. Fingerlos does not tell us the source of this information.

As would be expected from the director of a seminary, Fingerlos places high hopes on the beneficial effects of a solid education. Striking is the importance he puts on through philosophical education. Indeed, he sees this as the foundation of effective pastoral work. "Yet," he notes:

one could object that the secular clergy are mostly going to be priests in the countryside, and will serve as pastors to peasants [*Bauern*]. For what purpose would they need among these people such a grand philosophy? ... Even peasants have understanding, and some a significant amount of cleverness [*einen beträchtlichen scharfsinnigen*]. Often they encounter different dogmatic, moral or legal doubts, and they come to the priest for help. If the priest is to help settle his cares, then he must have a fundamental philosophical education.[31]

Peasants, Fingerlos notes, are exposed to so many maxims and ideas from their contact with government officials or through books and pamphlets that have arrived "even in distant valleys."[32] Unexamined ideas could lead to unfortunate actions, but as a representative of education and civilization in the countryside, the local priest can keep his flock on the straight and narrow as long as he has all the intellectual tools needed for modern life. Fingerlos emphasizes that philosophical eclecticism will not serve this purpose, and he insists that a system must be chosen. He quickly dismisses all other philosophical "systems" (i.e., those of Locke, Spinoza, or Epicurus, etc.) in favor of "critical philosophy,"[33] because it best meets the rule that one should choose the system that fosters morals: "if there ever was a philosophical system that encouraged good morals and religion, that even reinforced the purpose of states and religion, that in this manner was a beneficial gift for mankind ... it is critical philosophy."[34]

In addition to his philosophical education, the priest, Fingerlos believed, must also be learned in several ecclesiastical disciplines, as well as in assorted areas ranging from the law to agriculture and from botany to architecture. Fingerlos devotes the major portion of his handbook to these issues of education. He stresses, however, that the priest can only be effective as an instructor of morals if he himself lives virtuously. Not only

---

[31] Fingerlos, *Geistliche*, vol. 2, 28.
[32] Fingerlos, *Geistliche*, vol. 2, 29.
[33] Fingerlos, *Geistliche*, vol. 2, 30.
[34] Fingerlos, *Geistliche*, vol. 2, 60. Controversy over the use of Kant in Catholic theology would explode in the nineteenth century. See Christoph Weber, *Aufklärung und Orthodoxie am Mittelrhein, 1829–1859* (Munich, Paderborn, and Vienna: Ferdinand Schöningh, 1973) and Norbert Fischer, ed., *Kant und der Katholizismus. Stationen einer wechselhaften Geschichte* (Freiburg: Herder, 2005).

is he obliged to live morally like everyone else, he also has a contractual obligation to do so: "one can even say that he is paid to behave virtuously."[35] Fingerlos then discusses several key vices that the clergy need to particularly avoid, such as greed, pride (in particular, *Pfaffenstolz* – priestly pride),[36] and gluttony.

In discussing lust, Fingerlos addresses the question of celibacy. He notes that many arguments have been made for and against the institution, and all one can say is that celibacy has not improved knowledge and morals. However, he continues, "marriage among the priests of other faiths has also not ennobled their own and their people's knowledge and morals." Jewish and Muslim "priests," he notes, are married, yet they have no advantage over Catholic priests. Rehearsing an unexamined misogyny charateristic of the age, Fingerlos declares: "it seems to me that the motor for improving the moral education of the people must be found somewhere else than with women." In other words, ending celibacy – which Fingerlos sees as something that may happen soon anyway because of changing times – will not automatically lead to the desired improvements among the clergy.[37] Toward the end of his handbook, Fingerlos proclaims "It is better to have no priest at all in an area than to have a bad one. For a bad priest rots the community, whereas where there is none, there is no one to spoil anything."[38]

---

[35] Fingerlos, *Geistliche*, vol. 2, 245.

[36] Fingerlos, *Geistliche*, vol. 2, 260.

[37] Fingerlos, *Geistliche*, vol. 2, 273. While he does not explicitly argue that celibacy allows the vice of lust to fester, he does recount at length an example of how a priest who indulges his lust with a "prostitute" [*Dirne*] is then lead to all sorts of other vices – lying to cover it up, bribing the woman to keep silent, adopting false airs of piety to keep suspicions away, and so forth. For an engaging discussion of German Enlightenment attitudes toward women and sexuality that would have informed Fingerlos' attitudes, see Isabel V. Hull, *Sexuality, State, and Civil Society in Germany, 1700–1815* (Ithaca: Cornell University Press, 1996).

[38] Fingerlos, *Geistliche*, vol. 2, 308. It would seem that Fingerlos sets aside the question of salvation, and would thus have a hard time maintaining that he was Catholic. Yet he *was* the director of the Salzburg seminary. We should keep in mind what Karl Barth observed of many eighteenth-century Protestant theologians: even where they seem in hindsight to be rationalizing away core elements of religious doctrine, all we can do is accept their claim to represent religious truth as they saw it. (See Karl Barth, *Protestant Theology in the Nineteenth Century. Its Background and History*, trans. Brian Cozens and John Bowden (Grand Rapids , MI: Eerdmans, 2001 [orig. 1947]). It is in the interest of historical understanding to adopt the broadest possible definition of Catholicism, so as to avoid the need to question the motives of the actors. Whether or not Fingerlos was a "good" Catholic is obviously not a question that can or should be posed by the historian. What can be established was that it was practically unthinkable for Fingerlos that the moral and philosophical education of the common people could take place

In the same year that Fingerlos' handbook was published, Peter Philip Wolf penned a tract that agreed with the main points of the Salzburg seminary director, yet went much farther in its arguments. Wolf also states that a secular or civic education was very important for the priest's daily interactions, and that he should also be taught basic medicine for emergencies.[39] However, he blames the institution of celibacy for the poor morals of the clergy:

If indeed celibacy was introduced [i.e. at the time of Gregory the VII] because of the poor behavior of the clergy, then it needs to be abolished for the same reasons. On account of the fact that the clergy do not have wives their morals have not improved, on the contrary they have become much worse. Concubinage is practically common practice among Catholic clergy, and certainly they would not happily accept the duty to marry because they would thereby be robbed of the pleasure [*Reize*] of forbidden interaction with the female sex.[40]

Wolf continues by praising the benefits of married clergy, not only for the priest himself, but also for the entire parish:

The suppression of celibacy would undoubtedly improve the morals of the clergy. Moreover, such an action would carry with it important consequences. Without a doubt, a married pastor [*beweibte Pfarrer*] would be much more skillful than an unmarried one in ministering to the parish. He often finds himself in situations where it is of extreme importance to understand household relations. As head of a family, his example influences all other family heads. His wife is the model for all the wives of the community. Through his children he raises the children of the village.[41]

Wolf goes significantly farther than those who merely advocated ending celibacy as a requirement for the priesthood.[42] It is not simply a question

without the Catholic priest. Given the lack of any evidence that Fingerlos was being outrightly cynical, it is best for us to take his profession of loyalty to the Catholic religion at face value rather than impute present views of religion to him.

[39] Peter Philipp Wolf, *Vorschlag zu einer Reformation der katholischen Kirche* (Leipzig und Luzern, 1800), 25; 55.

[40] Wolf, *Reformation*, 29. It should be born in mind that Wolf relished polemic and that his assertions should not always be taken at face value.

[41] Wolf, *Reformation*, 31–2.

[42] For a full overview, see Paul Picard, *Zölibatsdiskussion im katholischen Deutschland der Aufklärungszeit*. Moraltheologische Studien, Historische Abteiung, vol. 3, J. G. Ziegler, ed. (Düsseldorf, 1975); Kenan Osborne, O. F. M., *Priesthood. A History of the Ordained Ministry in the Roman Catholic Church* (Mahwah, NJ: Paulist Press, 1988); Henry C. Lea, *History of Sacerdotal Celibacy in the Christian Church*, 2 vols. (London: Williams and Norgate, 1907); Winfried Leinweber, *Der Streit um den Zölibat im 19, Jahrhundert* (Münster: Aschendorff, 1978); and Richard G. Cunningham, *The Tridentine Concept of Sacerdotal Celibacy* (Rome: Pontifical Lateran University, 1972).

here of allowing priests to marry so that they are not led astray by lust – that it is "better to marry than to burn" in Paul's words. Rather, Wolf is suggesting that the priest has a *duty* to marry, to create the ideal bourgeois family within the village.

It may, of course, be argued that Wolf could not claim to represent Catholicism in any meaningful way. After all, he suggested that the best way to solve the problem of unbelief was to reduce the number of dogmas one was required to believe.[43] He recommended more individual reading of Scripture and praised Protestants for their biblical scholarship. Indeed, he proclaimed, "one has no reason to be mistrustful of Protestants. For it is to them alone that we should be thankful that Christianity is still certain in those things which the Roman priesthood has shaken to its foundations."[44] He lays the blame squarely at the feet of the papacy, which, in its single-minded pursuit of power, was happy to foster

the religion of the crowd [*Pöbel*], and never to protect the religion of reason. Religion is made an object of passion, when instead it should be an object of reason. In this, how much closer do the Protestants come to the goal![45]

Wolf sees the recent death of Pius VI as the chance to restructure the church. Dogma will no longer be the concern of theologians, and instead will be treated by historians.[46] Wolf claims that even priests no longer believe in the doctrine of transubstantiation – indeed they are "secretly ashamed of it" – so it should not be taught anymore.[47] Wolf's proposals were unrealistic, yet they were only extreme versions of the *Aufklärer's* conviction that errors of belief and dogma had dangerous consequences for the behavior of the people. "Some ask for gentleness with respect to the errors of the crowd," Wolf states, "but how is this possible when these errors are the source of moral decay?"[48] Superstition and fanaticism render practical religion impotent and destroy civil society. Wolf's fears, as well as the associations of superstition with immorality, are typical enough. The significance of his tract for the present argument is not to be found in his rather unrealistic hope that the entire dogmatic and sacramental apparatus of the Catholic church would be changed. Rather, his

---

[43] Wolf, *Reformation*, 50. "Das zu viele Glauben schadet der Religion weit mehr, als man denkt. Es giebt nur deswegen so viele Ungläubige, weil man zu vielen Glauben fordern."
[44] Wolf, *Reformation*, 51.
[45] Wolf, *Reformation*, 52.
[46] Wolf, *Reformation*, 54.
[47] Wolf, *Reformation*, 61.
[48] Wolf, *Reformation*, 72.

concerns reflect an awareness of the "social-historical reality" of ecclesiastical life in which the vast majority of the population continued to live. Whatever Wolf's personal beliefs, the church could not be simply rejected because it no longer served *him*. Instead, it needed to be remade so that his values could become truly *catholic*.

There were those who defended the institution of celibacy. While predating the attacks of Wolf and the criticisms of Fingerlos, a pamplet by Augustin Schelle (1742–1805), a Benedictine monk and professor of ethics, law, and history at the University at Salzburg, reflects the views of some church thinkers in the last few decades of the eighteenth century. Against the argument of cameralists that clerical celibacy was responsible for economic backwardness, Schelle pointed out that the institution served as a social safety valve. There are many unmarried in Catholic states who are *not* bound by oaths of celibacy, Schelle argued, mostly because they do not have sufficient income to support a household. That agricultural laborers have no problem finding employment and armies have enough recruits show that there is no lack of population, but rather a lack of work. [49] Schelle notes that "in order to care for his people, many a benevolent prince creates new offices. He does not look for people for positions, but rather tries to find positions for people." [50] Limiting or abolishing celibacy would only make things worse, unless economic conditions improved. Furthermore, Schelle argued, morals would actually worsen without the institution of celibacy:

When, if in such conditions a numerous and heretofore unmarried clergy now would enter into the state of matrimony, what would happen? The clergy would recruit itself, and would take no more children from the other estates [*Stände*], and would even have a surplus that would need to find its sustenance outside of the clergy. .... There would necessarily be an increase in the numbers of poor, the lazy, thieves, and robbers. [51]

Schelle's comments here raise two points. First, he suggests that a married clergy would create a self-replicating clerical class, a familiar phenomenon in German Lutheranism. Second, his arguments assume a static economic model: while increased population is generally desired,

[49] [Augustin Schelle], *Ueber den Cölibat der Geistlichen und die Bevölkerung un katholischen Staaten, aus Gründen der politischen Rechenkunst. Voran gehen Geburts – Trauungs – und Sterbelisten von der Reischstadt Augsburg und Betrachtungen darüber* (Salzburg, 1784), 66f.

[50] Schelle, 70.

[51] Schelle, 70.

there need to be safety valves. It is not assumed that the economy will grow to accommodate an expanding population. Schelle's treatise does not provide a vigorous defense of clerical celibacy, but it does meet economic and pragmatic objections on their own ground.

A more principled and ultimately more trenchant defense of clerical celibacy was presented by the ex-Jesuit Benedict Stattler.[52] Stattler argues two main points: first, celibacy is essential for the priesthood to serve its purpose; and second, only a significant social and constitutional change in the German Catholic church would allow for the proper reformation of the clergy. While Stattler does not ignore traditional orthodox arguments in favor of celibacy, his treatise is interesting for his nondogmatic analysis of effective clerical organization. Like other critics, Stattler emphasizes the importance of clerical education. He particularly stresses that "in order to consistently withstand the impudence of those who mock religion," bishops should be competent and well-trained, and that the apostolic office must be filled with practiced, experienced men who have been rigorously educated from early youth. As he argues later on in the text, the aristocratic nature of the German episcopate does not help: "nobility is certainly not an essential ingredient of the idea of a divine plan of Jesus' apostolate."[53] His treatise is important for its argument that the reformation of the clergy was not possible under the conditions of the current aristocratic church, and in its concern to create an elite corps of clergy that would command general respect. He is obviously basing his ideas on the model of the Society of Jesus. However, Stattler does not want to create a new order of independent priests, but instead a priesthood within clear, rational diocesan borders and episcopal authority.

In the first section of the treatise, which deals with the "necessity" of clerical celibacy for the Catholic clergy, Stattler argues that society requires a division of labor, both for agricultural and physical work, as well as for the higher arts. From this he concludes that often peasants and handworkers are not in a position to morally educate their children:

therefore, for the general good is required a class of people who devote themselves exclusively to spiritual service, and who are necessary to teach Christian duty to the ignorant, to those brought up without morals, and, as always, to

---

[52] Benedikt Stattler, *Wahre und allein hinreichende Reformationsart des katholischen gesammten Priesterstandes, nach der ursprünglichen Idee seines göttlichen Stifters* (Ulm, 1791).

[53] Stattler, vii.

those already corrupted by vice. They must motivate their hearts through loving admonition and suggestion.[54]

In response to those who suggest that married priests would serve as good examples to the populace, Stattler points to the social disruptions that a married pastor would present. Instead of living on his modest income as he should, the priest would have to provide "appropriate support" [*standmäßige Unterhalt*] for his wife and children. Moreover, because the priest holds a position of honor within the community, he would necessarily need to establish a respectable household, which could entail hiring servants and supporting them.[55] More blatant in its misogyny is Stattler's assertion that "the priest's wife [*Priesterfrau*] ... would certainly be proud of her position, and would want herself and her children to be maintained more splendidly than the common bourgeois wife."[56] Though he reserves his harshest words for wives from wealthy families, Stattler is unabashed in stating that the association of women with the priesthood can only introduce vanity into the ministry. Clerical benefices, which Stattler elsewhere urges need to be restricted and rationalized, would not provide sufficient income for such social expenses. One solution would be to increase the income, but this would only lay new debts on the "sheep." One could also only allow wealthy men – or men with wealthy wives – into the ministry, a step which would hinder any real efforts toward creating a disciplined and educated clergy. It is also unlikely that the wealthy would choose to work in a poor parish, as they are rarely inclined to "take up the cross" and live among the poor.[57] Finally, one could allow priests to take up an occupation alongside their ministry, an option that Stattler notes would obviously conflict with their spiritual mission.

---

[54] Stattler, 18.

[55] One might suggest that Stattler was only turning his head away from the problem of clerical concubinage. Indeed, it had always been a strong argument on the part of the opponents of clerical celibacy that the secular clergy was by and large incapable of living continently, and that it was better to allow marriage than to force priests to live illicitly – for this would only sully the authority of the Church. This opinion was not necessarily positive about marriage or contact with women, proposing, in effect, a decriminalization of concubinage rather than a valorization of marriage. On the other hand, one of the greatest successes of nineteenth century bishops was the effective enforcement of moral standard of the clergy. Certainly there were complaints and backsliders, but compared to earlier ages, the clergy was better disciplined than it ever had been before. See for example, Emmet Larkin, "The Devotional Revolution in Ireland, 1850–75," *The American Historical Review*, vol. 77, no. 3 (June, 1972), 625–52.

[56] Stattler, 73f.

[57] Stattler, 75–6.

Stattler envisions structural changes that would be necessary to improve the image of the Catholic clergy. There are, he states, too many priests; in particular, one needs to limit the number of benefices that are used only for "good living." The priesthood must be reserved for pastoral care.[58] (He elsewhere remarks that God is not more honored by 10 masses with no participants than by one large mass with real devotion.)[59] Stattler's principle concern is that the clergy needs to be respected, and he argues that the history of the "decline of the secular clergy" should serve as an example. He traces this decline to the ending of the practice of communal living among bishops and their priests and in the creation of free-standing parish benefices. Given their own income, priests were overcome by the luxury.

Once people lost confidence in them [the secular clergy], they tried first to take the tithe, and then along with this they tried to transfer all the priestly dignity to the monks. Eventually, people even attempted to reassign the ministry of a group of parishes to religious priests. Finally, the mendicants came and established their own institutions of ministry supported by papal privileges, interfered with the parishes, and drew the people to themselves.[60]

Stattler's account, while undoubtedly too schematic to recount accurately the fortunes of the secular clergy, serves to illustrate his general point:

a thousand years of experience show us that the Christian people have always, without comparison, had more trust in the ministry and spiritual activities of religious priests, who are bought up in and accustomed to the communal life of evangelical perfection, than they have shown toward individual priests who differ from the former in that other than the duty of celibacy, they are not obliged to strive for evangelical perfection.[61]

Stattler acknowledges that the prevalence of the regular clergy in the ministry is not ideal. Indeed, it seems like "a patchwork and sloppy" solution to problems that would best be solved within the normal "God-ordained hierarchy and order." The solution is to transform the cloisters [*Prälatenklöster*] into institutes for priestly education, which would simultaneously end complaints about the uselessness of the cloister *and* improve the secular clergy.[62]

[58] Stattler, 97.
[59] Stattler, 107.
[60] Stattler, 117.
[61] Stattler, 117–8.
[62] Statter, 118.

Stattler is not naïve about the social and political difficulties involved in making these changes. He does not shy away from laying blame: clearly, the aristocratic nature of the German episcopate keeps true reform at bay.[63] He doubts that the German church will reform itself without major papal intervention.[64] In some ways, he hopes for what Napoleon would later accomplish – the end of the German aristocratic church, and particularly the system of election by cathedral chapter:

Given the constitution [of the German church], the urgently-needed reforms for our priesthood cannot be hoped for, indeed are not possible. For these must come from bishops and canons who themselves need to be reformed but certainly will not reform themselves. We must first have canons who are well-studied and experienced in all ecclesiastical disciplines, who are practiced in the ministry and all priestly duties, and who are not lazy and given over to the pleasant life. They must themselves show the way in priestly duties, preach, hear confessions and read masses ... Only then can a nation count on them [the canons] to elect a competent bishop out of their midst.[65]

Stattler certainly could not predict that in little over a decade, the temporal constitution of the German church, along with the rest of the Empire, would cease to exist.[66] What his comments do reveal, however, is an awareness that the social and legal organization of the Old Regime church was not longer able to serve the church's goals. In this, Stattler, the hardened orthodox polemicist and opponent of most Catholic reform ideas, shared a key concern with the other reformers of the age: only the

---

[63] Stattler, 153.

Noch eine traurige Frage: Ist es bey der jezigen Art Bischöfe zu wählen möglich, daß wir würdige Bischöfe jemals bekommen? *Nur von Domherren, und nur aus Domherren,* dörfen für und alle deutsche Bischöfe erwählet worden!!! Ist nicht das was schreckbares für die ganze deutsche Kirche? Alter Adel ist also das ordinäre Haupterfoderniß zur Wahlfähigkeit oder Apostolatfähigkeit des Christenthums bey allen unsern Bisthümern!! Ich bin überzeugt, daß aus allen Erziehungen verschiedener Standesleute keine unschicklicher zum Bischofsamte sey als jene unserer Edelleute; und unter diesen ist noch gemeiniglich die schlechteste jene der Kadetten vom Hause. Und nun eben diese werden schier allein zu Domstellen hergelassen.

[64] Stattler, 154.

Muß immerfort das ewige Heil vieler tausend Seelen, und der Wohlstand des ganzen Religion dem Hochmuth und dem Geize so eines Theiles des Adels aufgeopfert werden? ... Ich wünsche es so sehr, als ich das Heil des deutschen Kirche liebe. Hoffe es aber noch nicht.

[65] Stattler, 177.
[66] Stattler's comments are also a brief against the claims of the German bishops that they need more freedom from the pope to institute reform.

restructuring of the secular clergy would solve the problems of the German church.

What was at stake in the debate over how to restructure the priesthood was the image of society the clergy was supposed to reflect. The bourgeois *Aufklärer* saw the clergy as the mirror of the enlightened philosopher – not the radical anticlerical *philosophe* of the French, but the reasonable, enlightened Christian that was, in many ways, an ideal they projected onto German Protestantism.[67] Celibacy, while not the only issue, was a key point of contention, because beneath it lay questions of values and their sources. Stattler represented the view that the ideal society was to be found not in the natural order of civil society, but in the evangelical counsels. Yet he made his points not by relying on biblical citations or theological subtleties. The interest of his argument instead lies in his functional analysis of the efficacy of priestly organization. It is no mistake that Stattler's priestly institutes resemble Jesuit seminaries, yet Stattler envisions a situation where the old "patchwork" solution is no longer necessary, and diocesan secular clergy will embody the ideal of ministry:

The accusation that [these institutes] would lead to a re-establishment of the Jesuit order is laughable ... Who does not see the difference between our new priestly institute and the Order of the Jesuits? He who dreams of such a thing does not understand the true institute. What's more, these seminaries would make the re-creation of the Jesuit order unnecessary and redundant.[68]

This was indeed the point: the new class of priests – better disciplined, well-educated, and fully integrated into the normal ecclesiastical hierarchy – embodied a notion of a universal class that represented a standing challenge to the values of bourgeois life.[69]

---

[67] On the development of the "pastoral family" in German Protestantism, see Susan C. Karant-Nunn, "The Emergence of the Pastoral Family in the German Reformation: The Parsonage as a Site of Socio-religious Change," in *The Protestant Clergy in Early Modern Europe*, C. Scott Dixon and Luise Schorn-Schütte, eds. (London: Palgrave, 2003).

[68] Stattler, 245.

[69] The debates over the reformation of the secular clergy, while shaped in the eighteenth century, took concrete form in the reconstruction of the German church in the nineteenth century. The two great German champions – which here can serve only as shorthand – of the moderate *Aufklärung* position and the more orthodox, Rome-centered perspective were Heinrich Ignaz Wessenberg and Johann Michael Sailer respectively. See Franz Schnabel, *Deutsche Geschichte im neunzhenten Jahrhundert*, vol. 4: *Die religiösen Kräfte*, third edition (Freiburg: Herder, 1951).

9

Gallican Longings: Nation and Religion in the German Enlightenment

As discussed in an earlier chapter, the intense interest in pre-Reformation canon law and the idealization of the fifteenth century as failed moment for a German national church played a central role in the arguments of the German canon lawyers intent on establishing jurisdictional autonomy from Rome. This Gallican idea, as it evolved into the eighteenth century, assumed that the church played a central role in politics and society. The Catholic reform program assumed a sense of responsibility and leadership for the German church. Formed as it was by the church, the German Catholic bourgeoisie felt an obligation to tie the Catholic past with a Catholic future. Because the German church had not succeeded in securing the rights and liberties that its French counterpart had (as early as the fifteenth century), German Catholics could pin their hopes for moral and intellectual leadership of the church on an imagined future legal autonomy in ways that French Catholics did not.[1]

This process of rethinking took place within a larger debate about the German nation that intensified with the Seven Years' War and its

---

[1] David Bell argues that, with respect to the invention of nationalism in France, the legal autonomy of the Gallican church was not "construed ... in cultural terms," and that far more important was Jansenism and its "radically new ways of imagining the relationship between the heavenly and terrestrial cities." Because the legal autonomy of the French church was long a settled issue – albeit with significant flair-ups – and because the monarchy had so successfully asserted its position, the legal redefinition of the church was not as important for French as it was for German Catholics. See David Avrom Bell, *The Cult of the Nation in France: Inventing Nationalism, 1680–1800* (Cambridge: Harvard University Press, 2001), 17.

aftermath.[2] This debate was pushed further along by the Carl Friedrich von Moser's pamphlet on the "German National Spirit," published in 1765, which argued that Germans needed to cultivate a sense of nationhood to overcome their weaknesses and divisions.[3] This does not mean, however, that the Catholic reform debate was merely an add-on to a larger discussion, because Protestants, too, rethought their churches and the meaning of the Reformation in response to shifting notions of authority, the self, and society.[4] In trying to reform the church, German Catholics questioned not only what it meant to be Catholic, but also what it meant to be German. To rethink the church was also to rethink the nation, and to transform the meaning of these concepts one had to confront their history.

FROM BARBARISM TO RELIGION: CHURCH HISTORY AND THE ENLIGHTENED NARRATIVE

As part of their program of religious and social reform, reformist Catholics mobilized historical arguments about issues ranging from canon law, to rituals and devotional practices, to the economic and political power of ecclesiastical institutions. I will focus here on one attempt to create a comprehensive narrative of the Germans and their church, namely the *History of the Germans* [*Geschichte der Deutschen*] by Michael Ignaz Schmidt (1736–1794), a Catholic priest and educational reformer from Arnstein (Lower Franconia) in the diocese of Würzburg.[5] As a school reformer and contributor to the periodical

---

[2] Hans-Martin Bilitz, *Aus Liebe zum Vaterland. Die deutsche Nation im 18. Jahrhundert* (Hamburg: Humburger Edition, 2000), 145.

[3] Nicholas Vazsonyi notes that Moser emphasized that the German national spirit had to be "learned" and not simply discovered (although, as Vazsonyi further points out, Moser muddled this idea in the pamphlet, giving rise to misunderstanding by his contemporaries). In other words, Moser did not assume a pre-existing, or lost, German spirit. Rather, it was a something that needed to be created in response to the conditions in which Germans found themselves. See Nicholas Vazsonyi, "Montesquieu, Friedrich Carl von Moser, and the "National Spirit Debate" in Germany, 1765–67," *German Studies Review* 22, no. 2 (1999).

[4] For a brief account of the ways in which Protestants redefined the Reformation in this period see Michael Printy, "The Reformation of the Enlightenment: German Histories in the Eighteenth Century," in *Politics and Reformations: Histories and Reformations. Essays in Honor of Thomas A. Brady, Jr.*, Christopher Ocker et al., eds. (Leiden: Brill, 2007).

[5] On Schmidt's role in educational reform in Würzburg, see Sebastian Merkle, "Würzburg im Zeitalter der Aufklärung," in *Ausgewählte Reden und Aufsätze*, Theobald Freudenberger, ed. (Würzburg: Ferdinand Schöningh, 1965 [1912]). For a full biography see the work of his colleague Franz Oberthür, *Michael Ignaz Schmidt's des Geschichtschreibers der Deutschen Lebens-Geschichte. Ein so wichtiger als reichhaltiger Beytrag*

The Franconian Observer [*Fränkischer Zuschauer*] Schmidt embodied the pedagogically oriented and publicly engaged Enlightenment in Germany. On the strength of the first volumes of his *History*, he was invited to Vienna and ultimately accepted a position as director of the House and State Archives (as it was then known) in 1780.

Schmidt's significance lay not in his innovations of method or theory, but in his intention to write a history of the Germans for the wider educated public.[6] In this intention, his greatest interlocutors were not the famed ecclesiastical historians of previous generations but his contemporaries writing "Enlightenment" historical narratives in France, Italy, and Great Britain.[7] Schmidt's *History of the Germans* partook of a broad interest in history on the part of the general German reading public.[8]

As a historian in the tradition of the "Enlightened narrative," Schmidt ranks among the most significant writers of narrative history in the eighteenth century. In his recent work on Edward Gibbon, J. G. A. Pocock has offered a compelling definition of the "Enlightened narrative" animating the historical work of vanguard eighteenth-century authors:

The history of civil society and its morality underlay the history of the system of states through which Europeans had recaptured control of their civil affairs after

zur Kulturgeschichte der Deutschen (Hannover: 1802), 286. Before turning to history, Schmidt had written a treatise on the "history of self-awareness" indebted to English epistemology, and an important work on the proper method of catechizing. Schmidt's role as archivist is briefly discussed in Walter Pillich, "Staatskanzler Kaunitz und die Archivforschung (1762–1794)," in *Festschrift zur Feier des Zweihundertjährigen Bestandes des Haus-, Hof- und Staatsarchivs*, Leo Santifaller, ed. (Vienna: Druck- und Kommissions-Verlag der österreichischen Staatsdruckerei, 1949), 109f. Schmidt's other work included: *Geschichte des Selbstgefühls* (1772), and *Der Katechist nach seinen Eigenschaften und Pflichten, oder die rechte Weise die ersten Gründe der Religion zu lehren*. Aus dem Lateinischen übersetzt durch Benedictum Strauch, mit einer Vorrede des Saganischen Prälaten Johann Ignaz von Felbiger (Bamberg and Würzburg, 1772) [orig. Latin edition, 1769].

[6] Hans-Wolfgang Bergerhausen, "Michael Ignaz Schmidt in der historiographischen Tradition der Aufklärung," in *Michael Ignaz Schmidt (1736–1794) in seiner Zeit. Der aufgeklärte Theologe, Bildungsreformer und "Historiker der Deutschen" aus Franken in neuer Sicht*, Peter Baumgart, ed. *Quellen und Beiträge zur geschichte der Universität Würzburg 9* (Neustadt/ a.d. Aisch: 1996), 64.

[7] Karen O'Brien, *Narratives of Enlightenment: Cosmopolitan History from Voltaire to Gibbon* (Cambridge: Cambridge University Press, 1997) and J. G. A. Pocock, *Barbarism and Religion, Volume II: Narratives of Civil Government* (Cambridge: Cambridge University Press, 1999).

[8] Otto Dann, "Das historische Interese in der deutschen Gesellschaft des 18. Jahrhunderts. Geschichte und historische Forschung in den zeitgenössichen Zeitschriften," in *Historische Forschung im 18. Jahrhundert. Organisation-Zielsetzung-Ergebnisse*, Karl Hammer and Jürgen Voss, eds. (Pariser Historischen Studien, 13) (Bonn, 1976), 407–12.

the long night of "barbarism and religion," a phrase as old as the renaissance of letters and used to denote the "Christian millennium" of feudal and ecclesiastical control of a submerged civilisation, which could be dated from Constantine to Charles V or from Charlemagne to Louis XIV. ["Modern" critical scholarship] joined with the techniques of historical understanding developed by the great jurists of the age – German, French, and Scottish – to form a systemized civil morality meant to enable Europeans to live in their own world, if not without religion then without ecclesiastical disturbance or domination. Enlightened historiography is, almost without exception, the execution of this purpose. The Enlightened historians – Voltaire, Hume, Robertson – are concerned with the exit from the Christian millennium into a Europe of state power and civil society.[9]

This new, and modern, view of history was made possible by the emergence of powerful centralized states. The creators of these histories projected their secular views of politics back onto the sixteenth and seventeenth centuries to find the origins of the modern enlightened state in the emergence of the European state system or, in the case of Voltaire, in Louis XIV's monarchy, which became the model for all great monarchies. In all the cases cited by Pocock, the reemergence of state and civil society was predicated upon the thesis that the Catholic church had overstepped its bounds (even if it had, willy nilly, enabled the preservation of civilization).

Compared to the likes of Voltaire or the Neapolitan Pietro Gianonne, Schmidt comes off as a moderate, who saw a much more positive role for religion and even the clergy in the formation of modern Europe. Indeed, Schmidt's work most readily invites comparison with William Robertson, whose *History of Scotland* (1759) saw the Scottish church as a pillar of the nation, and from whose *History of the Reign of Charles V* (1769) Schmidt drew for his own account of the Reformation era.[10] A consideration of Schmidt's *History* as part of the broader family of "Enlightened narrative," moreover, should also modify our understanding of the nature of that project. The "Enlightened narrative" greeted the reassertion of authority by the secular state – which occurred by most accounts around

---

[9] J. G. A. Pocock, *Barbarism and Religion. Volume I: The Enlightenments of Edward Gibbon*, 4.

[10] While one could certainly find other eighteenth-century historians beside Robertson who were not as anti-clerical as Voltaire or Gianonne, Robertson's involvement in Scottish church politics, as a leader of the Moderate party, further invites comparison with Schmidt's support for the Catholic reform movement. According to Peter Baumgart, Pütter and Gatterer compared Schmidt favorably to Robertson. See Peter Baumgart, "Michael Ignaz Schmidt (1736–1794), Leben und Werk," in *Michael Ignaz Schmidt (1736–1794) in seiner Zeit*, 121. See also Richard B. Sher, *Church and University in the Scottish Enlightenment: the Moderate Literati of Edinburgh* (Princeton: Princeton University Press, 1985).

the time of the Reformation, or, in Voltaire's case, with Louis XIV –
against the "encroachments" of the church.[11] What Schmidt's account of
the history of the German people brings to this discussion is that Germany's unique constitution did not result in the emergence of a single
strong state, but in a series of territorial states that were capable or
reasserting their authority in secular affairs. As a religious "nation,"
however, the Germans could still lay claim to an ecclesiastical and religious organization that could bind them together beyond territorial
boundaries.

Schmidt's significance must also be assessed in the context of German
biconfessionalism. Schmidt, after all, was accorded the title "the first
historian of the Germans," and even if there is good reason to question
the propriety of these types of claims to primacy in general, it must
nevertheless be acknowledged that his narrative history did represent
something new in German historical practice. While his account of Luther
caused consternation among a fair number of otherwise sympathetic
Protestant compatriots, the fact of their disappointment must be taken
into account – they had, after all, been led to expect "better" by the
quality of his earlier work. Schmidt's account of the Reformation, and,
more importantly, of the history of the pre-Reformation German national
church, stood out in the prominence it was assigned as part of the history
of the development of German manners. Schmidt's narrative history
embodied the Gallican longings of Enlightened German Catholics, and
represented the moderate position of these reformers. On the one hand,
they needed to assert their version of Catholicism against the Roman
hierarchy and its partisans at home, while on the other, they needed to
establish German Catholicism's valid claim to its share of Enlightenment
without breaking entirely from its past.

The two central themes of Schmidt's history – the progress of
enlightenment and political development of the German nation – are
linked in his portrayal of the moral and religious history of the people.
Indeed, as Schmidt states in the preface, the purpose of history is not
merely to portray the continual shift of rulers and dynasties, for "in the
end, a nation as a whole was virtuous or vice-ridden, happy or unhappy,
according to the ways its religion, government, and laws were constituted."[12] In order to show the ways in which the German people has

---

[11] Pocock, *Barbarism and Religion, Volume II: Narratives of Civil Government.*
[12] Michael Ignaz Schmidt, *Geschichte der Deutschen*, second edition, 11 vols. (Ulm: 1778–
1793), I, ix.

progressed, Schmidt starts from the earliest known times, and chronicles the effects of the interactions of the Germanic tribes with the Roman Empire.

Once the Germans conquered the Roman Empire, the stage was set for a great social and cultural transformation of their nation. The Romans, who had grown soft and lost their warrior abilities – partly on account of "Asiatic riches" – succumbed to the Germans.[13] Yet soon it was the Germans who were to succumb, at least in part, to the influence of civilization and a settled lifestyle, as Schmidt notes in a chapter entitled "Manners and Character of the Germans in their new quarters." Theodoric has just killed Odoacer (493) and laid claim to Italy, and the German tribes have settled there for good:

These peoples were all of a sudden planted in a new world: Other manners, other language, other concepts, other laws, other clothing, and other style of life. In short, everything was different with them than it had been before. In such conditions, people regard each other, and both despise and emulate them at the same time without being aware of what is happening. Because each people lost of bit of its own nature, a third type of character appeared that was wholly representative of neither of the other two ... In the conquered lands the barbarians created a republic for themselves, and the Romans did the same. Each had its own laws, manners, and customs, only that the latter had to obey the former.[14]

But for all of their political and military success, the new situation of the German nation did not lead to immediate improvements in their lifestyle. They became accustomed to luxury, and lost touch with their old ways. Thus Schmidt concludes the first book of his history, which had narrated the story of the Germans from their nomadic warrior days to the fall of the Roman Empire:

Things, the names of which they hardly knew before, now became real needs, and had much more negative effects on their morals because their passions were as strong and lively as before – only now these passions had been multiplied by an endless supply of goods. For this reason one finds in their subsequent history so many instances where gruesomeness, superstition, faithlessness, and weakness

---

[13] Ibid., 120–34. Cf. William Robertson, *History of the Reign of Charles V*, 3 vols. (Philadelphia: 1871 [1769]), vol. 1, 9.

[14] Schmidt, *Geschichte der Deutschen*, I, 180. Schmidt's understanding of the cultural progression of a nation motivates an aside about the early laws (such as the Salic law and the *Sachsenspiegel*) of the Germans. Grotius, he notes praises them, whereas Leibniz argues that it would be a mistake to reintroduce them. It would, Schmidt states, be like putting the fruit back in the seed. The laws were good for the conditions in which they were made. In the same way, a man cannot wear the clothes he had on as a child. Schmidt, *Geschichte der Deutschen*, I, 199.

are woven together that one does not know whether to feel pity or indignation. I do not want to say that in their old homeland [the Germans] were more virtuous; but certainly they were not so depraved as they were now. In general, it seems that in all ways, the period of time between the cultivated and uncultivated condition is the worst. One cannot say exactly when the cultured state begins to be fully realized. Once refinement outweighs barbarism, it would appear that hopes for better times arise, and one no longer has reason to wish for a return to the state of savagery.[15]

In the second book of the history, which runs from the establishment of the Frankish kingdom to the advent of Charlemagne, Schmidt shows how the German people were able to overcome the difficulties of this rough transition from the stage of nomadic barbarism to civilization. The two most important factors in this transformation were the creation of a strong centralized kingdom, and the widespread introduction of Catholic – as opposed to Arian – Christianity. Ever since the baptism of Clovis, the Frankish kings had realized the power of embracing Catholicism. Schmidt notes that the church did not naively suppose that Clovis was motivated by purely religious factors: "One can easily imagine that the examination of [the King's] morals [in preparation for baptism] was not as strict as could be. The booty was too great. One needed to act quickly, so that the opportunity would not disappear."[16] Naturally, even after his christening, the king found many opportunities to transgress the laws of his new religion. Nevertheless, the precedent had been established for the German rulers' connections with Rome, a tradition which would later be strengthened by Charlemagne.

The greatest role in the early refinement of German manners was played by Boniface and the Irish and Scottish missionaries to Germany.[17] Schmidt acknowledges that under the Christian (Roman) emperors, the Christian religion was planted in the cities on the Rhine. But the cities were destroyed by the barbarian invasions. And while in the "middle ages it was fashionable for every respectable church to claim an apostle's disciple as its founder," these myths have been disproved, and these "first bishops" disappeared again.[18] Boniface exerted considerable energy in

---

[15] Schmidt, *Geschichte der Deutschen*, I, 209–10.

[16] Ibid., 221.

[17] He refers to "Irland und Schottland," commonly called "Hibernia," as breeding-grounds for important missionaries. Specifically, Schmidt lists Killian (d. 687) in Franconia; Emmeram (d 635) and Rupertus (d. 718) in Bavaria; and Willibrodus (d. 739) in Friesland. Ibid, 402–4.

[18] Schmidt, *Geschichte der Deutschen*, I, 402–3.

attacking "heathen superstitions." Schmidt admits that Boniface's "pious eye may have seen double" and exaggerated the vices of the Germans, but nonetheless, the situation of the Frankish church was quite poor.[19] The Germans, who had shown "solid judgment in their political constitution," were like enraged "lions" when it came to matters of religion and feeling. Schmidt does not refrain from airing the misogynist aside that the German tendency toward superstition was only natural, given the prominence of women in matters of religion.[20] Boniface's services did not stop at matters of ritual and doctrine: he also made strides to get the Germans to stop eating horseflesh, and was worried about their appetite for beaver, stork, crow, and rabbit. (He also solicited the help of the pope, who told Boniface that if the Germans must eat fat bacon [*Speck*], they should smoke and boil it first, or at least wait until after Easter to eat it.)[21]

While Boniface's personal commitment and example were significant, even more important were the lasting changes he introduced into the German church:

Saint Boniface knew no better means to improve morals and restore church discipline than by reinstating councils. But because this was a work that required more strength than he possessed by himself, he sought the aid of two different authorities, namely the secular and the papal.[22]

For Schmidt, it is quite obvious that a lay prince would have the duty and power to help reform church discipline. He disputes the assessment made by the Bollandist Daniel Papebroche (1628–1714), who, Schmidt claims, saw Boniface's appeal to secular authority as an unfortunate tarnishing of ecclesiastical dignity. Schmidt, for his part, describes Boniface's accomplishment as a "masterpiece of wisdom," for Boniface was able to

involve the secular prince with the interests of religion. What else could Boniface have done, as a foreign priest, given that powerful laymen were in possession of bishoprics and abbeys, or with such bishops that wielded the crosier in one hand and the sword in other.

Moreover, Boniface's reforms threatened the "raw and ignorant" with the loss of not only their offices but also their incomes. Boniface compared himself to a guard dog, who cannot do anything without helpers.[23]

[19] Ibid., 410.
[20] Ibid., 45.
[21] Ibid., 6, footnote q.
[22] Ibid., 411.
[23] Ibid., 413.

In addition to the institution of national church councils, Boniface was also instrumental in the formation of an institution that still existed in the form of the Imperial Diet (*Reichstag*). It was common for the early Germans to discuss important affairs at assemblies of the people. Schmidt states that the bishops were present at the extraordinary meetings of the people [*außerordentliche Versammlungen des Volkes*]. When the laws needed to be improved, bishops were indispensable, because the matter at hand mainly involved bringing the laws in accord with Christianity. Bishops were also active when the people had complaints against the king.[24] Carloman (son of Charles Martel) invited Boniface and the bishops to come to the annual gathering of the nation. Boniface saw the benefit of having the support of the powerful, and Carloman saw this as a way of improving the morals of the people. Edicts were issued in the name of the lay authority because it was an assembly of the people and the powerful at which the bishops were present, not vice versa. Carloman's plan was for church and state to reinforce one another. Moreover, Schmidt adds, the bishops were often more able to carry out the burdens of state on account of their education and maturity.[25] The collaboration between church and state – each providing the other with "practical and moral support" [*Rath und That*] – was mutually beneficial. Boniface was able to call on the secular authority for assistance, and Carloman was able to push through reforms as he wished, all the while claiming that they emanated from a higher source.[26] Schmidt concludes his section on Boniface by noting that even if he "was not able to do everything that he should have done, then the times in which he lived were more to blame than the man himself." To Boniface,

Germany owes endless gratitude: not only was he its instructor in religion as well as other branches of knowledge, he also persuaded the Germans to stop eating horsemeat, taught them how to write, and, in the end, did not hesitate to shed his blood for them.[27]

Schmidt's emphasis on Boniface's significance for the refinement of German manners can be contrasted with the brief (almost dismissive) account in Johann Lorenz Mosheim's *Institutes of Ecclesiastical History* (1754), perhaps the most influential work of Church history in the

---

[24] Ibid., 423–6.
[25] Ibid., 426.
[26] Ibid., 427.
[27] Ibid., 428.

period.[28] While, as Mosheim says, Boniface was later considered the "apostle" of Germany, his methods and attitude hardly make him worthy to a title best reserved for the genuine apostles of the early church.

> He did not oppose superstition with the weapons which the ancients apostles used, but he often coerced the minds of the people by violence and terrors, and at other times caught them by artifices and fraud. His epistles also betray here and there an ambitious and arrogant spirit, a crafty and insidious disposition, an immoderate eagerness to increase the honours and extend the prerogatives of the clergy, and a great degree of ignorance not only of many things which an *apostle* ought to know, but in particular of the true character of the Christian religion.[29]

Mosheim, who was concerned with defending the independence of the Lutheran church from the encroachments of the state, here draws a sharp division between methods and teachings. While Schmidt had conflated Boniface's role as the preceptor of Germany in both the elements of the Christian faith and in manners, Mosheim focused on the saint's deficiencies in propagating true Christianity – which for Mosheim could be the only standard of evaluation.[30]

Whereas Mosheim's emphasis was on the history of the church – and its "external" changes over the centuries – Schmidt's focus is on the cultural and political history of the Germans. It is thanks to Boniface, in Schmidt's view, that Christianity had now been established, and was constituted as an essential part of the government and culture of the German people. The history of the German church and the history of the German Empire are parts of the same story – which is not to say that Schmidt subsumes German history into a larger, Rome-centered Catholic history. Instead, the story of Germany is told as part of the progress of European society, not unlike in the narratives of his eighteenth-century counterparts. Only for Schmidt, the German connection to the Catholic church does not represent a threat to its autonomy. On the contrary, the church provides a link with the other civilized nations of the world. The struggles between popes and emperors that Schmidt

---

[28] Mosheim (1693–1755) had helped found the University of Göttingen (perhaps the most important center of German historical studies), served as its chancellor, and is credited with creating the modern discipline of church history by separating it from the faculty of theology. See John Stroup, *The Struggle for Identity in the Clerical Estate: Northwest German Protestant Opposition to Absolutist Policy in the eighteenth Century* (Leiden: E. J. Brill, 1984), 51.

[29] Johann Lorenz Mosheim, *Institutes of Ecclesiastical History, Ancient and Modern*, trans. James Murdock, 3 vols. (New York: Harper and Brothers, 1839), vol. 2, 8f.

[30] For an account of Mosheim's efforts to secure the independence of the clergy, see especially Stroup, *The Struggle for Identity in the Clerical Estate*, 50–81.

subsequently narrates are not mobilized to depict the papacy as a persistent threat to local customs and the rights of secular powers (unlike, for example, the "civil history" of the Neapolitan Pietro Gianonne). As important to Schmidt's narrative is disunity among the Germans and the seemingly perpetual weakness of the emperors. Throughout his history, Schmidt pursues the thesis that Germany was at risk when the powerful were able to prevent the development of a strong state or monarch. This inability would ultimately render Germany susceptible to further divisions, as in the Reformation, and more tragically, in the Thirty Years' War. "There was a period," he states, at the time just before the accession of Rudolph of Habsburg in 1273 "when the nation was indeed internally strong but externally weak and without a ruler, because its strengths could never be unified toward a common goal." After Rudolph restored imperial power, German history "began to become interesting again."[31] By the time of the Reformation, however, the emperor was unable to maintain unity, and dissention tore apart the nation again.

Unlike some of his colleagues among eighteenth-century historians, Schmidt does not necessarily see the Middle Ages as a period of intellectual stagnation. "It is true," he notes:

that there is a fair amount of useless stuff in Scholasticism. But it is also certain that there are also great truths as well, and those things that people are so proud of today are to be found in Scholasticism, even if only the kernel thereof, or as something that was left on the wayside.[32]

Disputes were held over worthy as well as unworthy subjects, and this spirit of disputation could often lead one into empty wordplay. Nevertheless, the mere fact that so much argumentation and discussion was underway meant that important truths were bound to be brought to the fore.[33] For Schmidt, in other words, even the widespread employment of what many considered obscure Scholasticism could not prevent the gradual emergence of truth and understanding.

In a similar vein, Schmidt also contends that the German political system, despite weaknesses that would later prove tragic, did not hinder the development of the nation. For example, aspects of which Schmidt disapproves, namely the law of the feud (*Faustrecht*), did not prevent

---

[31] Schmidt, *Geschichte der Deutschen*, I, xiv.
[32] Ibid., III, 141.
[33] Ibid.

trade.[34] Schmidt also seeks to place the discomforts of medieval life in context:

and how bad was all that banditry when compared to the indescribable misery that is spread by war nowadays? How would it compare to the hundreds of thousands that are wiped out by the sword and by disease, and against the innocent victims who are affected?[35]

The point is that the Middle Ages were not devoid of social and economic development, and that manners continued to be refined through trade, scholasticism, and even in the crusades (because of the contact with foreigners). But while national culture and manners did not stagnate, the authority of the Emperor was always under threat.

The same forces that kept the imperial office weak – namely the ambition of the nobility – also worked upon the German church. The cathedral chapters preferred to pick the lower nobility for episcopal sees, because they did not want to have to obey a great prince.

If they were given a great prince, then they would have to fear the rod and the bridle [*Ruth und Zaum*], and therefore it happened that few great princes were elected in Germany, except for Cologne and Strasbourg, where the chapters had members of the great houses.

Schmidt comments that papal influence was always at its height when the imperial power was at its lowest.[36] If this were true, then the weakness of the papacy in the fourteenth and fifteenth centuries should have finally put to rest the struggles between church and state that had periodically erupted since the Investiture controversy. The Conciliar movement and the German Concordat should have been the happy outcome. Why did the Concordat and autonomy of German church not prevent the disaster of the Reformation? The answer can only be that the political weakness of

---

[34] Ibid., 103. For an analysis of the importance of the concept (or myth) of the feud in western legal and political thought, see Otto Brunner, *Land and Lordship. Structures of Governance in Medieval Austria*, trans. Howard Kaminsky and James Van Horn Melton, fourth revised edition (Philadelphia: University of Pennsylvania Press, 1992 [1965]). Brunner's account, which refers frequently to Carl Schmitt, raises interesting questions about the Enlightenment's understanding of medieval politics and society, especially insofar as Enlightenment thinkers saw the suppression of the fued as a key moment in the establishment of the sovereign state. Pütter, for example, saw the ending of *Faustrecht* (with the establishment of the *Allgemeine Landfriede* in 1495) as a key moment in the constitutional development of the Empire. See Johann S. Pütter, *Historische Entwicklung der heutigen Staatsverfassung des Teutschn Reichs*, 3 vols., Göttingen, 1786.

[35] Schmidt, *Geschichte der Deutschen*, 220.

[36] Ibid., IV, 653.

the German nation left it open for further disruption, only this time not by the pope but by fanatical reformers.

This theme of the refinement of manners and intellect is part of the larger story of Schmidt's history. It is a principal theme, and also puts Schmidt into a larger context of European historiography of the eighteenth century. The Catholic Schmidt and his Protestant colleagues needed to historicize European, and especially German, religious history to account for the progress of Enlightenment and for the weakness of Germany. Yet they did so in fundamentally different ways. Hume, Gibbon, and Voltaire could easily characterize Luther and Calvin as fanatics, because they were writing about the progress of civil society that had – as they believed – liberated itself from religious superstition. German Protestant historians had a peculiar problem in that Luther's break with Rome was a defining moment in the development of German independence. Yet, as we shall see, Schmidt suggests, recent Protestant theology, in its critique of orthodox Lutheranism, was coming to reject core doctrines propounded by the Reformers. Schmidt was holistic in his historical explanations, which meant that the church did not have to be written out of the process of Enlightenment, even if elements in the church had stood in its way. Indeed, Enlightenment and Christianity are concomitant (and sometimes identical) in Schmidt's conception.

Schmidt shares with some of his historian colleagues the notion that the reign of Charles V marked the emergence of a new epoch of European history. Where he differs markedly from other writers of the Enlightened narrative is that Germany's path to modernity involved the emergence of several semi-sovereign states, not a single centralized one. The Germans could still claim to be united by a single religious culture, and the Empire provided the framework in which, ideally, the German people could live in peace.[37] The "failure" of the Empire to evolve into a genuine state did not, in other words, preclude the Germans from becoming enlightened. While Schmidt candidly points to the political weaknesses in the German political system, he does not propose any unrealistic solutions that would involve a strengthening of the imperial office.

The period around Charles' accession represented a "dividing wall between the old and the new political world."[38] Luther's intervention

---

[37] On arguments for the "federal" idea in German political thought in the eighteenth century, see Maiken Umbach, *Federalism and Enlightenment in Germany, 1740–1806* (London: Hambeldon Press, 2000).
[38] Schmidt, *Geschichte der Deutschen*, V, 1.

need not have disrupted the continued progress of Enlightenment. Luther's disputed point started with the current system, which, it must be noted, was not set forth in any council or church ordinance. Hardly any one or the other of Luther's points had not already been made by another theologian, without them having been labeled heretics.[39] Yet as Schmidt contends throughout *The History of the Germans*, the slow but deliberate progress of human manners and intellect was too easily disrupted by political weakness. This is a historical argument that sat well with supporters of strong state intervention in questions of religious reform in the eighteenth century. It was a vision of history that saw the emergence of the strong state as a key factor in the continued refinement of civilization. Together, state and church (or, more broadly, Christianity) would help each other in fulfilling their respective missions.

Throughout his narrative, Schmidt indicates that civil authority is recovering its proper role, and, moreover, points to the powers of the Emperor to reform and protect the church. While many of the "Enlightened" historians were fiercely anticlerical, if not actual unbelievers, some, like William Robertson, sought to place the history of the clergy "within the history of civil society and manners."[40] This strategy was eminently suited to the general plan of the "Moderate" Presbyterian clergy in Scotland, which aimed toward assuring a continued role for the Kirk and for Christianity in modern society. They sought to do so by tempering the rigors of traditional Calvinistic theology and by encouraging presbyterian ministers to embrace contemporary literature, art, and culture.[41]

Schmidt's *History* should certainly be included in the broader family of Enlightened narrative history. It demonstrates an attempt to balance the competing demands of philosophical history (i.e., the argument about the development of German manners and culture) and learned research

---

[39] Ibid., 57.

[40] Pocock, *Barbarism and Religion, Volume II: Narratives of Civil Government*, 282.

[41] For an excellent discussion of this plan and the reasons for their success, see Sher, *Church and University in the Scottish Enlightenment*. Sher argues that while these "Moderates" did not include the greatest lights of Scotland's eighteenth century (notably Smith and Hume), their influence in the Scottish educational system largely prepared the ground for the Scottish Enlightenment. While they were a numerical minority, the Moderate party was better organized than their traditional ("Popular") opponents, and placed themselves in influential positions through important patrons, but also through their own skillful arguments at the general assembly of the Kirk. A symbol of their success can be seen in William Robertson's accession to the Principalship of the University of Edinburgh in 1762.

(especially after he was appointed director of the House and State Archives in Vienna, and had access to the Imperial Archives). Most important was his attention to a consistent narrative voice and structure, an important factor for popular literary success.[42] If we consider Schmidt as part of this family of Enlightened narrative and philosophical historians, two distinctive problems come to the fore. The first has to do with the problem of writing a national history for a politically and religiously fragmented Germany and the second centers on the difficulties of Catholic cosmopolitanism.[43]

First, in contradistinction to the other major German historians of the eighteenth century, Schmidt retained the entire Empire as the structure for his narrative.[44] To be sure, in the seventeenth century there had been significant histories of the Empire – notably by Pufendorf and Conring – but those were critical histories that provided the background for the eighteenth-century legal historians of Germany.[45] Schmidt, who in the early nineteenth century was called "the first historian of the Germans" by a Würzburg colleague, was the first to attempt a cultural history of the Germans on a national scale in the spirit of Enlightenment philosophical history.[46] It is tempting to suggest that Schmidt's Catholicism enabled

---

[42] The tension between learning and narrative style can be illustrated with reference to Friedrich Schiller. While it would be unfair to compare Schmidt to Schiller for literary genius, even Schiller's admirers in the nineteenth century pointed to his weakness as a historical scholar. This weakness was due partly to the fact the Schiller did not conduct any original research, but also is due to his insistence on certain narrative conceits and themes (e.g., Gustavus Adolphus as Protestant hero) could get in the way of balanced assessment.

[43] The strategy of writing national history in a cosmopolitan context is discussed by Karen O'Brien, *Narratives of Enlightenment*.

[44] This is not to say that several very significant works, like Justus Möser's *Osnabrückische Geschichte*, did not reach beyond their immediate or local subject. See Jonathan B. Knudsen, "Justus Möser: Local History as Cosmopolitan History," in *Auflkärung und Geschichte*, Bödecker, ed.

[45] Mention should also be made of Johann Jakob Mascov's *Geschichte der Teutschen* (1726). Berney notes that while Mascov's history remained a "Fragment," and, while an important attempt to describe all of Germany's regions and peoples, it was an "Ablauf unzähliger, aufeinander folgender Augenblicke, seine Geschichtsschreibung ein Museum meist völlig charakterlose, aber vorbildlich sauberer Reproduktionen gewesener Dinge." Berney, "Michael Ignaz Schmidt," *Historisches Jahrbuch* 44 (1924), 211–2. See also Notker Hammerstein, *Jus und Historie* (Göttingen: Vendenhoeck und Ruprecht, 1972), 284f.

[46] It must be mentioned that Schmidt also changed his plan a bit and moved toward more state-history – this largely a result of the access to archives in Vienna that presented him with the opportunity of presenting this material to the public. See Christina Sauter-Bergerhausen, "Michael Ignaz Schmidt 'Erster Geschichtsscreiber der Deutschen?'" in *Michael Ignaz Schmidt (1736–1794) in seiner Zeit.*

him to embrace the church as the other pillar (alongside the state) of German civil society and culture. He did not need to defend the church and the papacy in all their actions – certainly he did not. But because he also did not need to deny its central role in the civilizing of the German people – in the past, and, by implication, in the future – he could adopt a moderate attitude toward it. To write an Enlightened narrative of the German people that took into account its development as a whole – and distinguished it from the other great nations of Europe, one needed an institution that embraced them all politically (however, loosely), namely the Empire. And to write a narrative of the cultural and moral history of the German people, the only possible institution that could stand alongside the civil authority of the Empire was the Imperial church (*Reichskirche*).

The second problem posed by Schmidt's version of the Enlightened narrative – which considers the church an agent, not just an obstacle, to the march of civilization – gets to the core of a struggle over authority within Catholicism more broadly. Schmidt's history could not have been an ultramontane one, but it was perfectly suited to the *Aufklärung* Catholicism of ecclesiastical and state reformers. Schmidt's vision of the civilizing role of religion in German history was in part a projection of Reform Catholics' ambitions to make the church an agent not only of religious and moral education, but also of Enlightenment. At this point, the cosmopolitan aspirations of the German Catholic Enlightenment foundered, for German Catholic *Aufklärer* wanted to remake the church in their own image. However, as long as they wanted to be a part of the larger Roman Catholic communion, they were committed to a universal notion of the church of which they were only a part.

A NATION DIVIDED: THE PROBLEM OF THE REFORMATION

It is with a broken heart that Schmidt begins the sixth volume (the last he would live to write) of his *Modern History of the Germans* [*Neuere Geschichte der Deutschen*]: "Since the beginning of its political existence," he states, "Germany had never found itself in such a sorry state as it did at the time when the peace negotiations at Münster and Osnabrück were supposed to commence." For nearly 30 years, Germany had been the scene "upon which Swedes, Frenchmen, Hungarians and Croats, for a while Spaniards, even Poles and Cossacks, and, finally, Germans ... wrestled about [*herumtummelten*] with one another and drove their armies across the land in the struggle for friends and enemies."[47] Germany had been

shaken to its marrow. It was covered in all places with the rubble of collapsed or destroyed buildings, was soaked with the blood of its own citizens, and defeated itself even when victorious. It was now populated by a generation of dispirited offspring, which had replaced the numerous and happy tribe the Germans had once been. On account of the swift, uncertain, and sometimes most unexpected movements of armies, Germany hovered in an uninterrupted fear of death, and its people had become apathetic and numb, and, what was worse, dependent on the will of foreign powers, who were doubtful in their commitment to peace, and may not even have allowed it. And yet now, the parties into which Germany was divided, reconciled with each other.[48]

Despite their war-weariness, Germans could not hope for peace so long as their country was the stage upon which the great powers bid for position. Even the wisest and most insightful men "did not dare hope" that peace could be achieved without the intervention of foreign crowns, "so much had everything been torn out of joint and men's hearts filled with mistrust and bitterness."[49] So many previous attempts at peaceful resolution had failed that even those desirous of a cessation of conflict on the part of Sweden and France counted more on achieving their goals through arms than through reason and diplomacy. Moreover, those wishing peace were fearful of what they would have to give up to achieve it.[50] According to Schmidt, Germans were at the mercy of foreign powers who had only their own national and dynastic interests in mind.

How had it come to this? What were the causes of Germany's impotence and disunity? These are the questions posed by Schmidt's *History of the Germans*. To Schmidt, the roots of this situation lay in the Reformation. In itself, this was hardly a novel thesis. What is interesting in Schmidt's account is that the Reformation represents a break in what should have been Germany's normal development as an Enlightened, cultured nation. This is why the Thirty Years' War is so painful in his account. It is hardly surprising that Schmidt, a Catholic priest, would lay the blame for Germany's troubles on the Reformation. Yet if Schmidt is a critic of Luther and Calvin, he also has little good to say about the Jesuits and frequently adopts an anti-curial tone. Unlike his Protestant counterparts among German historians, Schmidt does not see the Reformation as an essential

[47] Schmidt, *Geschichte der Deutschen*, XI, 1–2.
[48] Ibid.
[49] Ibid., 2–3.
[50] Ibid.

stage in the development of German culture, customs, and government. Instead, it caused a break in the progress of manners and religion.

Schmidt's account of the Reformation holds the key to his historical enterprise. Themes of progress, civilization, and the role of religion and religious institutions in society are laid out in his depiction of the key figures and events of the Reformation era. Luther, of course, plays an important part. But as important is the political history of the German nation, as well as the customs and manners of the German people. For if the period between the Reformation and the Peace of Westphalia represented a tragic interruption of the progress of German civilization, then hints of the path not taken are to be found in the account of the history of the German people before that time.

Luther, Schmidt admits, had good qualities, and was rightly concerned with abuses in the church.[51] Yet he was also a fanatic, who merely replaced one dogma with a new one, even though clothed in an apparent "freedom of conscience":

A man who has played such a role as Luther must necessarily draw the most varied of judgments. How could it be otherwise with someone who is seen, on the one hand, to have such an undeniable reserve of honesty and selflessness, combined with a courageous love of country and religion, while, on the other, capable of such strong and unbounded passions, brazen in his assertions, irreconcilable, and given to unrestrained vehemence against all those who do not share his opinions. That he was disturbed by abuses that had crept into religion in his time; that he wanted to return this religion back to its inner core of feeling and understanding, away from the surfeit of external works that had been promoted by the monks; that he wanted to make the sources of the Christian religion commonly understood and available to anyone who had the will and aptitude required: this he had in common with people of good will.[52]

Luther, Schmidt continues, took action where others had only expressed "pious wishes." However, he "dogmatized [*dogmatisiert*],[53] replacing Aristotelian-scholastic Thomism and Scotism (which were never actually supposed to be seen as official doctrines of the church) with the Augustinianism he had absorbed in the cloister." Even if this new dogma was based on sounder psychology than Scholasticism, and even if

---

[51] See also Heinrich Lutz, "Zum Wandel der katholischen Lutherinterpretation," in *Politik, Kultur and Religion im Werdeprozeß der frühen Neuzeit. Aufsätze und Vorträge, aus Anlaß des 60. Geburtstags von Heinrich Lutz*, Moritz Csásky et al., eds. (Klagenfurt: Universitätsverlag Carinthia, 1982), 225–39.

[52] Schmidt, *Geschichte der Deutschen*, VI, 86.

[53] This term, while capable of neutral connotations in the context of Catholic theology, was wholly at odds with Schmidt's Enlightened attitude.

it had some authority in Scripture, Luther was wrong to "set it up on a throne as pure Scriptural truth."[54] With his new dogmatism, Luther

sowed the seeds for embitterment and hatred that is the shame of Christianity and dishonors humankind. He, who according to his own principle should have been the most tolerant man in the world, did not even feel that he should take into account the times and conditions in which he lived. Instead, once he was convinced of the truth of his position, he began to publish it and preach it to the world.[55]

Luther is portrayed here as a fanatic, whose teachings cannot be at the root of Enlightenment, because they cannot have been the source of tolerance and moderation.

As Schmidt had shown throughout his history, dissension had been frequent in the history of the Empire, and emperors had often been challenged by strong princes. Until the appearance of Luther, however, dissent had never reached such a level as to almost destroy the Empire. Yet this is what happened in the Schmalkaldic War. Had the Protestant League of Schmalkalden not boldly asserted its power, Schmidt writes, the Emperor would not have started the war. While acknowledging Charles's ambition and desire for conquest, Schmidt argues that he is also to be recognized as the preserver of the Empire and the current imperial system: "Without the dissolution of the over-powerful Schmalkaldic League, either the Empire itself would have dissolved, or the Catholic parts of the Empire – especially the bishoprics – would have been destroyed." Moreover, had the Protestants won, it is certain that they would have been much harder on Catholics than Charles had been with them – particularly with respect to the episcopal territories and ecclesiastical property.[56]

Schmidt dedicates a chapter to the question: "What did theoretical and practical religion gain through the Reformation?" Schmidt suggests that any gains made by the Reformers were nullified by the fervor with which they pursued their goals. "Was mind and heart so improved" as to justify the "hate, streams of blood, and misery of millions?" Moreover, the Reformation only delayed further progress:

He who has the opportunity to look at the literature from that time would need to concur that some theologians would have done what the recent reformers among the Protestants are doing a few centuries earlier, if only Luther had not intervened.[57]

---

[54] Schmidt, *Geschichte der Deutschen*, VI, 86.
[55] Ibid.
[56] Ibid., 282.
[57] Ibid., 289.

It is a sad irony for the Catholic reformer of the eighteenth century that only now could he peacefully implement his program of reform.

Schmidt implies that Luther has become a problematic figure for recent German Protestant theologians and historians. The catalyst for this new assessment of Luther is the criticism of dogma and Lutheran orthodoxy.[58]

> There is certainly some truth to the notion that Luther held back heresy, sects, and opinions (and perhaps even deism, which certainly would have been invented earlier), and thereby made a break in the progress of human ideas. Whether one should be thankful or not is a question best answered by the recent reformers among the Protestants. While it is certain that on the one side new tools were found to defend against the progress of knowledge, one must wonder that, at the same time, they claim that Luther opened the path for their efforts.[59]

Schmidt contrasts the Reformers with Erasmus, whose writings he argues more easily pave the way for the work of current Protestant "Reformers." Erasmus's "party, which was equally distanced from fanaticism, monasticism and spiritual despotism, was at first mocked by both sides, and then suppressed ... How astonished would Luther be today if he were to see what his pupils were up to!"[60]

It is in this context that Schmidt questions the Protestant assertion that Luther had enabled freedom of *thought* – an assertion, according to Karl Friedrich Stäudlin, that was novel to the eighteenth century.[61] It is true, Schmidt notes, that Protestants do not have a pope and his hierarchy to deal with nor need their theologians worry about a church that could claim the right to issue infallible statements about belief. But he suggests that Catholics were able to work within these constraints, and that even when the hierarchy was at its strongest, philosophy (even if imperfect) had had an important influence in the explication of morality and doctrine (he presumably refers to the medieval scholastics). Moreover, the Catholic understanding of dogma and morality had indeed changed, even when the same expressions and terminology were retained.[62] While he does not pursue the point in depth, Schmidt implies that while the edifice of Catholic doctrine seemed immobile, deep changes had occurred

---

[58] Karl Barth, *Protestant Theology in the Nineteenth Century. Its Background and History*, trans. Brian Cozens and John Bowden (Grand Rapids, MI: Eerdmans, 2001 [orig. 1947]), 107. See the comments of Felix Anton Blau discussed in Chapter 7.

[59] Schmidt, *Geschichte der Deutschen*, VI, 293.

[60] Ibid.

[61] See K. F. Stäudlin, *Kirchliche Geographie und Statistik*, 2 vols. (Tübingen: 1804), 320f.

[62] Wie oft hat sich diese [dogmas and morals] ganz unvermerkt geändert, wenn auch die nähmlichen Ausdrücke, und eben die Terminologie beybehalten worden.

beneath the surface. His historicism is subtle, yet undeniably present. For their part, Schmidt alleges, the Protestants are not as free as they claim. Do they not have to deal "with their own authorities [*Obrigkeiten*], with their own half- or full scholars [*Halb- oder Ganzgelehrten*], or, what is even worse, is their crowd [*Pöbel*] not more fearsome than a pope?"[63] Schmidt's language here is hardly flattering to the papacy, but it reveals his commitment to and appreciation of moderation and tact in matters of theology. Erasmus, he claims, certainly had to be wary, given that the pope – whom he acknowledged as judge in theological controversies – was surrounded by enemies of Enlightenment. Yet, Erasmus held that Christians of good will would eventually come around without needing to resort to a claim of "freedom" that would carry such costs.[64]

In Schmidt's view, the Lutheran Reformers, claiming that they wanted to bring the bible to the common people [*den Pöbel bibelgelehert ... machen*], made things worse for themselves. Indeed, they wound up with even more difficulties than the Catholics:

The more the teachers tried to refine their religion and to bring it in accord with reason at every turn, the more they sank into absurdity. That which they finally produced through much sifting and refining [*Seigern und Feilen*] the scholars either needed to keep to themselves, or they needed to take care that it did not reach the people.[65]

In its search to bring everything in line with reason, Protestant theology, Schmidt argues, could either build "foolish" systems or wind up believing nothing at all. "After the elimination of so many positives from the Christian religion so little of the original is left that these improvers are basically deists and naturalists, only that they refuse to admit it and carry bibles under their arms."[66] For Schmidt, these developments render the struggles of the Reformation absurd:

If things were supposed to have been set according to Luther's teachings and the Augsburg Confession, then there can be no greater contradiction than to have moved heaven and earth to attain freedom of conscience, that is, to have some fewer articles of faith, and then to go and swear upon a new system of belief, and thereupon to become involved in controversies that are even more absurd than those of the Scholastics.[67]

---

[63] Schmidt, *Geschichte der Deutschen*, VI, 294.
[64] Ibid., 294–5.
[65] Ibid., 295.
[66] Ibid., 295–6.
[67] Ibid., 296.

206 Enlightenment and the Creation of German Catholicism

The controversies among Lutheran theologians lead one to believe that the much-praised notion of "freedom" was "merely a play on words [*bloßes Wortspiel*]." To support this accusation, Schmidt refers to the struggles over the "so-called Book of Concord," crypto-Calvinism, the reforms that the Protestants undertook against other Protestants (in the Palatinate and partly in Brandenburg), and, especially, the question of swearing oaths to the symbolic books.[68] Matters were made worse by the doctrines of the Calvinists, Schmidt continues, which further upset the confessional balance in the Empire: "It is certain that had the Reformed [i.e. Calvinists] not intervened, there would not have been a new religious war in Germany."[69]

Schmidt – in what seems like a curious anticipation (and rejection) of Max Weber's famous thesis – denies that religious attitudes alone are responsible for economic behavior:

It is apparent that these qualities are not attributes of any particular religion, but instead are products of education, government, and the constitution of the land. Also significant are factors that help or hinder the agricultural cultivation, and especially that great educator of mankind, namely, the relationship of its physical needs to the fruitfulness or infertility of the land. In Germany, we see exceptions on both sides. It is upon the government that falls the responsibility to do away with accidental [*Zufällig*] hindrances on industry and opportunities for laziness that arise merely from external church discipline. The only difference is that had Luther and Calvin not intervened, rulers would have done a few hundred years earlier what they are doing now.[70]

In the last two sentences of this passage lies the rub of Schmidt's argument. Religion itself is not to blame for Catholic Germany's economic backwardness. Rather, it is the political and cultural effects of the Reformation and the subsequent disunity in Germany that has prevented Catholic rulers from doing away with "accidental" church policies ("accidental" in that they do not touch the essence of the faith) that prevent certain economic activity. In this passage one sees support for ecclesiastical policies like those of Maria Theresa and Joseph II in Austria and in Bavaria, which curtailed monastic institutions as superfluous relics of outworn piety and with an eye toward redirecting their resources for education and charitable works. Likewise, Schmidt here rehearses the

[68] Ibid.
[69] Ibid.
[70] Ibid., 304.

common complaint that certain traditional attitudes toward charity encouraged begging and idleness (*Mußigang*).[71]

Schmidt's support of the ecclesiastical policies favored by Josephine and Bavarian reformers points to a key theme in his history of the German people. For Schmidt, as we have seen, the Reformation retarded Germany's development. He is quite clear in indicating that the Reformers had valid criticisms of the church and of German politics and society. But the effect of their intervention was to further weaken the nation, and to prevent the emergence of a secular authority capable of fostering appropriate economic, cultural, and political progress.

Schmidt directly addresses the question of whether the Reformation promoted the Enlightenment.[72] Its effects, he believes, were negative, largely because the Reformation led to confessional polarization, as well as to a hardening of attitudes that prevented each side from acknowledging the positive aspects of the other. The Reformation, for example, enabled the continued use of Aristotle, because even Luther's followers saw Aristotelian scholasticism as necessary for "theological war [*theologischen Kriege*]."[73] If, in general, Luther's intervention slowed down enlightenment among Protestants, this was

doubly true for the adherents to the old system of religion, who were driven so much into a corner that it took more that two hundred years for them to be able to breathe more freely. For fear of being accused of heresy, they needed either to remain completely silent, defend everything as it was, or tread so lightly that one could not suspect them of heresy or innovation.[74]

Just as two parties in a dispute make sure to distance themselves from one another, so did Protestants and Catholics take pains to disassociate themselves. One thing was found to be perfect only because the other found it bad. A Protestant would not put on a choir robe because this was a Catholic practice; in the same way, many Catholics did not want to hear any thing about catechism because, Schmidt mistakenly thought, Luther was the first to introduce one. Schmidt blames Catholics as much as Protestants, even if he portrays their fears sympathetically. Because Luther has turned the pope into "the Anti-Christ, the Catholics made him

---

[71] Cf. Peter Hersche, "Intendierte Rückständigkeit: Zur Charakteristik des geisltichen Staates im Alten Reich," in *Stände und Gesellschaft im Alten Reich*, Georg Schmidt, ed. (Veröffentlichen des Instituts für europäische Geschichte, Bd. 29), (Stuttgart, 1989).

[72] "In wie weit die Aufklärung dadurch befördert worden." Schmidt, *Geschichte der Deutschen*, VI, 305.

[73] Ibid.

[74] Ibid., 309.

into a vice-God."[75] The papacy grew in reputation among Catholics as much as it declined among Protestants. No Catholic could see himself saying that which, 100 years earlier, conciliarists Jean Gerson (d. 1429) and Pierre D'Ailly (d. 1420) had preached.[76]

The effects of the confessional struggle were particularly dire for Catholic Germany. Catholic education, if not suffocated, was severely hindered. The study of classical languages was discouraged for fear of accusations of heresy.[77] Echoing other Catholic moderates and reformers, Schmidt holds the Jesuits, who came to Germany in response to the Lutheran threat, responsible for the defects in German Catholic education.[78] In the political sphere, Protestant princes initially had an advantage, though the cities could not prevent their own decline. Of great benefit to the Protestants were the episcopal foundations and ecclesiastical lands they were able to absorb. Catholic princes did not make things better for themselves by exiling dissenters by the thousand and by their general negligence in educating their subjects.[79] However, Schmidt states, the differences between Protestant and Catholic states have largely been eliminated, and Catholics may even have an advantage, in that they can start their reorganization with a blank slate:

Now that the holes are mostly being filled, it would not be too hard for a Catholic prince who knows both his rights and the welfare of his lands to not only make up on what has been neglected, but perhaps even in some ways to recuperate the capital with interest.[80]

The Reformation was nevertheless not an unmitigated disaster for German manners. Indeed, one consequence of religious disunity was that matters of religion became important topics for political discussion as well.

That religious matters were so often the topic of discussion at the German Diet was a marvelous occurrence that the grandfathers of these princes, who themselves could neither read nor write (though certainly they were no less upright, respectable, and honest), would no more have believed than they would have believed the prediction that there would come a time in Germany when a suit of armor not only was not the chief ornament of a man, but that even the body had

---

[75] Ibid. "Die stärksten Beweise davon gibt uns der Papst. Da Luther denselben zu Antichrist machte, stellten ihn manche Katholische als Vice-Gott auf."

[76] Ibid., 310.

[77] Ibid., 312.

[78] Ibid., 311.

[79] Ibid., 323–4.

[80] Ibid.

become so tender that it could not support such equipment. Now, however, body and mind had changed so much that they contrasted in the most wondrous way with those of preceding times. And what is most peculiar is that instead of training the body for conflict through riding, fencing, and tournaments (although physical activities were not entirely forgotten), one took more care to equip one's mind for intellectual bouts.[81]

The overcoming of political and economic differences among the confessions in the eighteenth century provides the general framework and impulse for Schmidt's history. He does not essentialize confessional differences, but instead employs sociological arguments to explain why manners and customs did not always unfold as they should have – that is, from barbaric customs to civilized practices. He makes a particular point about the introduction of the death penalty under Charles V. The severity of the *Peinliche Halsgerichtsordnung* (1532) is explained by the previous years of chaos and robbery as a result of religious conflict. Germany had not had the death penalty in its "barbaric childhood," but conditions were such that by the sixteenth century, "civil security" (bürgerliche Sicherheit) was in a sorry state.[82] The Reformation, therefore, was an interruption in the course of German history, one that would have tragic consequences for the unity of the German people. While Charles V managed to keep the Empire intact, the Reformation divided Germany into parties, and created a situation that would eventually allow it to become the theatre for an international war in the seventeenth century. It was not Protestantism itself that rendered Germany weak; rather it was Germany's religious disunity.

In a direct response to Schmidt's volume on the Reformation, Karl Leonhard Reinhold – better known as a popularizer of Kant's philosophy – sought to rescue the "honor" of the Reformation by asserting that Schmidt had confused Luther's work with the Reformation itself.[83] "Wherever the Reformation took effect," Reinhold claimed, "it drained the swamps, so to speak. But no matter how important and indispensable this step was, it nevertheless was only the first one, and it prepared the

---

[81] Ibid., 329–30.
[82] Ibid., 326.
[83] K. L. Reinhold, "Ehrenrettung der Reformation, gegen zwei Kapitel in des k.k. Hofraths und Archivars, Hrn. M. I. Schmidts Geschichte der Teutschen, 6. Band," in *Der Teutsche Merkur*, C. M. Wieland, ed. (Weimar, 1786), 138. On Reinhold, see Sabine Roehr, *A Primer on German Enlightenment: with a Translation of Karl Leonhard Reinhold's The Fundamental Concepts and Principles of Ethics* (Columbia: University of Missouri Press, 1995).

way for the others that must take place."[84] Reinhold was in a unique position to understand both Catholic and Protestant versions of the Enlightenment. He converted to Protestantism after having spent 10 years as a Barnabite (i.e., a Cleric Regular of St. Paul) in Vienna. In his defense of the Reformation's "honor," Reinhold laid out an evolutionary theory of the freedom of thought. While Reinhold's ideas are not entirely original – they may be found, for example, in the writings of Johann Salamo Semler – they do provide unique insight into the way in which German Protestants and Catholics recognized the new intellectual territory over which they fought.[85]

According to Reinhold, his Protestant contemporaries split into two main camps with regard to the relationship of reason to revealed religion. The first group,

which at the present is so apparently declining in numbers, believes that external limits must be set upon reason once it is freed from its obedience to the hierarchy. This group remains with the old system, which, nevertheless, has been significantly purified by the Reformation.[86]

Though not explicitly named, the Lutheran establishment is clearly intended. The other group of Protestants, however, is convinced that

Reason should not be set any limits outside of its own laws, and that Luther and his assistants do not have the exclusive privilege to improve the system. Instead, we are allowed at all times to continue farther down the path that has been opened by them. The first group of contemporary Protestants prizes the Reformation simply on account of the good that it actually accomplished. Among this group the wish quite naturally is to stand by the confessional statements of the symbolic books. . . . The second group however, in its admiration for the Reformation, goes much farther. Like the first group, it is grateful for the concrete achievements of the first Reformation, but cherishes even more that which it made possible, and sees the Reformation therefore as a step toward new and further improvements.[87]

Reinhold's statement represents a significant redefinition of "Reformation," which has gone from meaning a restoration and repair to a meaning

---

[84] Reinhold, "Ehrenrettung," 120. Reinhold's desire to defend the Reformation's "honor" can certainly be understood, given Schmidt's attack on Luther's character (though it was quite mild in comparison to the tradition of Catholic anti-Luther polemic).

[85] See Ernst Walter Zeeden, *The Legacy of the Reformation: Martin Luther and the Reformation in the Estimation of the German Lutherans from Luther's Death to the Beginning of the Age of Goethe*, trans. Ruth Mary Bethel (Westmister, MD: Newman Press, 1954).

[86] Reinhold, "Ehrenrettung der Reformation," 195.

[87] Ibid.

that implies continual improvement. Not unlike the transformations of "revolution" in the late seventeenth and eighteenth centuries, the Reformation is now oriented toward the future instead of the past.[88]

How, then, to reconcile the Luther who gave birth to a new notion of freedom with the Luther who believed that his conscience was "captive" to Scripture? Reinhold developed a notion of freedom as a process:

Freedom developed, but that does not mean that it sprung fully formed from the early days of the Reformation. The reformers had no other name than freedom for that which they won. Just like a prisoner who has exited the prison, he can only walk slowly at first once the chains are released from his legs. Freedom is therefore not a play on words [as Schmidt had alleged], but a reality, even if the early reformers were not as free as we are today.[89]

While Reinhold's expressed concern was to rescue the "honor" of the Reformation from Schmidt's attacks on Luther's character, he was offering more than a critique of Schmidt's specific points. Indeed, in placing Luther and the other early Reformers in the genealogy of Enlightened reason, Reinhold sought to secure the place of the Reformation in the evolution of modern thought – against not just the Catholic Schmidt, but also against the antireligious and anti-clerical Enlightenment of Hume and Voltaire. This strategy became a cornerstone both of liberal Protestant theology and of *Kulturprotestantismus*.[90]

The Reformation of the German Catholic reformers was one that did not want to focus on the matter of dogma, and as such, it was not an implausible source for both practical reform and – at the least – cultural union with Protestants. Yet this vision was also a product of a Holy Roman Empire in which confessional parity was more or less established, and which had witnessed a certain cooling of confessional conflict after the treaties of 1763. The sense of union, however, was fragile, and seeds of its unraveling can already be seen in Reinhold's refutation of Schmidt.

---

[88] See the article on "Revolution" in *Geschichtliche Grundbegriffe; historisches Lexikon zur politisch-sozialen Sprache in Deutschland*, Otto Brunner et al., eds., 8 vols. (Stuttgart: E. Klett, 1972–1997) 5: 653–788.

[89] Reinhold, 58.

[90] On the centrality of anti-Catholicism to the liberal imagination in Germany, see most recently Michael Gross, *The War against Catholicism: Liberal Identity and the Anti-Catholic Imagination in Nineteenth-Century Germany* (Ann Arbor: Unversity of Michigan Press, 2004).

Conclusion

ENLIGHTENMENT AND THE CREATION OF GERMAN CATHOLICISM

In the end, there was Napoleon.[1] The destruction of the *Reichskirche* removed the conditions that had allowed German Catholics to rethink the church. But this does not mean that the effort was all for naught. In rethinking the church in the eighteenth century, German Catholics entered a new century of revolution and upheaval with a greater sense of identity and cohesion than they had at the close of the seventeenth century. A lasting legacy of the *katholische Aufklärung*, therefore, was the articulation of an entity that could survive the collapse of its own legal underpinnings. Moreover, in recognizing that the church could be rethought in the eighteenth century, German Catholics were well-prepared for the intellectual task of rebuilding. As the tensions and contradictions of the *katholische Aufklärung* themselves reveal, the idea of a cohesive German Catholic church did not preclude radical differences of visions about the nature of that church.

The first task at hand, however, was reconstruction. While many were happy to see the old aristocratic German church brought to an end, the Secularization of 1803 (as drawn up in the Peace of Lunéville and for-malized with the *Reichsdeputationshauptschluss*) did not in any way solve the long-standing problems facing the German church. These included such issues as large ungovernable dioceses, inadequate training

---

[1] Thomas Nipperdey, *Deutsche Geschichte, 1800–1866. Bürgerwelt und starker Staat* (Munich: C. H. Beck, 1983), 11.

of clergy, deficiency of proper episcopal authority in areas of Catholic diaspora in Protestant territories, and the fact that territorial and ecclesiastical boundaries often did not coincide. To these older issues came the collapse of Church finance and the general disorganization brought by the wars and occupations.[2] Vacant sees remained empty for years, as they had in France before the Concordat of 1801.

In this vacuum of power, Archchancellor and Bishop of Mainz Karl Theodor von Dalberg (1744–1817) and his vicar Heinrich Ignaz Wessenberg (1744–1860) sought to establish a "national" concordat with the pope that would establish some measure of official unity for the German episcopate. But these plans were undermined at the Congress of Vienna by Pius VII's secretary of state Ercole Consalvi as well as by the greater German powers: neither side wanted a strong – that is to say, independent – German episcopate. Instead, concordats with individual German states were concluded in the early nineteenth century. In a series of (originally secret) conferences in Frankfurt from 1818 to 1828, diplomats from several German states met to deal with the future of the German church, and especially the new dioceses created in the wake of the Secularization.[3] This generation of early nineteenth century churchmen were later criticized from various angles: Dalberg, for example, for "collaborating" with Napoleon, and Wessenberg for propagating "anti-papal" national German Catholicism and unreformed Febronianism. Others were held to be too willing to embrace the new German states. These criticisms were made with the intent of lionizing later stalwart bishops such as Clemens August Droste zu Vischering, who famously resisted the pressure of the Prussian state and was able to mobilize throngs of Catholic supporters at the height of the Cologne troubles in the 1830s. However, this base of support was only possible because the pragmatic reforms of the first generation of nineteenth century enabled the general improvement in the quality of bishops.[4]

Efforts such as those of Wessenberg and Dalberg to create some type of institutional unity for the German church ultimately failed, a result that

---

[2] Dominik Burkard, *Staatskirche, Papstkirche, Bischofskirche. Die "Frankfurter Konferenzen" und die Neuordnung der Kirche in Deutschland nach der Säkularisation* (Rome, Freiburg and Vienna: Herder, 2000), 111–7.

[3] These meetings are painstakingly reconstructed by Dominik Burkard in *Staatskirche, Papstkirche, Bischofskirche*.

[4] Hubert Wolf, "Pfründenjäger, Dunkelmänner, Lichtgestalten," in *Säkularisation der Reichskirche 1803: Aspekte kirchlichen Umbruchs*, Rolf Decot, ed., *Veröffentlichungen des Instituts für europäische Geschichte Mainz, Abteilung für abendländische Religionsgeschichte* (Mainz: Philipp von Zabern, 2001).

was widely seen as the final chapter of Febronian ideas in Germany.[5] Yet the *katholische Aufklärung* did not evaporate with its institutional aspirations. The German church was recast by its Enlightenment. This process was not unlike the creation of a "national" German literary culture by a relatively restricted circle of writers and the reading public in the age of Goethe and Schiller. And just as this cultural form was elevated and exaggerated by its subsequent mobilization in the process of state and nation building, so too is it possible to see the ways in which the specific social and political conditions that shaped the *katholische Aufklärung* also helped define the church for the next century.[6]

There was, in other words, alongside the famous "German idea of freedom" a German idea of the church as well.[7] In the eighteenth century, German Catholics rethought the church in a series of efforts at practical reform. Their efforts were made possible by a confluence of crisis and opportunity. By the middle of the eighteenth century, the papacy seemed to be at a political low point. The easing of confessional tensions in Germany – as well as the perception that Catholics and Protestants could make common cause against freethinking as well as superstition – rendered the need for defensive postures less acute. The rethinking of the church, therefore, proceeded in a pragmatic and detailed fashion, but it could not anticipate the total collapse of the Empire.

What is the connection, then, between the church imagined by eighteenth-century intellectuals and the German Catholic church of the nineteenth century? Given that the nineteenth-century church was by some measure more ultramontane, populist, and even superstitious (by the standards of the *katholishe Aufklärung*) than it had been at the close of the eighteenth century, it would seem that the break with the Catholic Enlightenment was total. This image of German Catholicism, however, reflects the situation in the latter third of the century, after the declaration of papal infallibility and in the wake of the *Kulturkampf*. These events favored

---

[5] Heribert Raab, *Die Concordata Nationis Germanicae in der kanonischen Diskussion des 17. bis 19. Jahrhunderts. Ein Beitrag zur Geschichte der episkopalischen Theorie in Deutschland* (Wiesbaden: Franz Steiner, 1956), 177f.

[6] James J. Sheehan, "What is German History? Reflections on the Role of *Nation* in German History and Historiography," *Journal of Modern History* 53, no. 1 (1981): 9–10. Sheehan's admonition not to "confuse aspirations with accomplishments" of German national thinkers must be applied inversely to the idea of the German Catholic church. While the legal program of Hontheim and the Febronians failed, a powerful idea was created that served German Catholic thinkers in many ways in subsequent centuries.

[7] Leonard Krieger, *The German Idea of Freedom. History of a Political Tradition* (Chicago: University of Chicago Press, 1957).

tendencies toward increased outward devotion, popular religious practices, and the centralization of religious authority, although it must be recalled that official pronouncements of authority from Rome were met with trepidation even by loyal bishops who feared a backlash. Despite the heavy blows to the institutional church and its educational system wrought by the Secularization of 1803, German Catholicism in the first half of the nineteenth century was characterized by a bewildering plurality of religious ideas and movements.[8] Although opponents of the Catholic Enlightenment gained the upper hand in the seminaries – for example by pushing aside proponents of Hermesianism or in sidelining Wessenberg, the legacy of the Catholic Enlightenment in Germany was still felt in two important ways.[9]

First, even with the renewed attention to dogmatic differences – most notably with Möhler's *Symbolik* – there was nonetheless an important irenic strain embodied in the type of practical pastoral theology propagated by Johann Michael Sailer. Irenecism was of course difficult to maintain in the midst of the rising confessional-political tension that characterized nineteenth-century Germany, but it drew from the Catholic Enlightenment the sense that unbelief posed a greater threat to the faith than did Protestantism.

A less obvious, but longer lasting legacy of the Catholic rethinking of the church was the deep impression that there existed a specifically *German* Catholicism. This Catholicism was not as far from Rome as Hontheim and his supporters would have liked. But even when German Catholics could enthusiastically embrace Roman supremacy, they could at the same time resist the coupling of Protestantism and the nation. This sense was not merely a reaction to the times – it had deeper roots in the

---

[8] Franz Schnabel discusses the "deep contradiction within the Catholic revival," and how eventually the drive toward centralization gained the upper hand after mid-century in Franz Schnabel, *Deutsche Geschichte im Neuenzehnten Jahrhundert. Volume 4: Die Religiösen Kräfte* (Freiburg: Herder, 1951), 261. In Schnabel's view, Catholic culture moved from plurality to increasing centralization, whereas Protestantism in Germany tended toward fragmentation. For a recent discussion of the effects of the revival on Catholic intellectual life see Richard Schaefer, "Program for a New Catholic Wissenschaft: Devotional Activism and Catholic Modernity in the Nineteenth-Century," *Modern Intellectual History* 4, no. 3 (2007). Along similar lines, it is also useful to recall that ideas about the nature of German identity in the first half of the century were quite open. See, for example, Brian E. Vick, *Defining Germany. The 1848 Frankfurt Parliamentarians and National Identity* (Cambridge: Harvard University Press, 2002).

[9] Georg Hermes (1775–1831) was a philosopher and theologian who sought to secure Catholic doctrine on rational grounds in light of Kantian philosophy. On the campaign against Hermesianiam, see Christoph Weber, *Aufklärung und Orthodoxie am Mittelrhein, 1829–1859* (Munich, Paderborn and Vienna: Ferdinand Schöningh, 1973).

creation of confessional identity in the eighteenth century. This confessional identity was formed within the confines of the legally secure *Reichskirche*, but was strong enough to survive in the wake of the Secularization. And, most importantly, this German Catholic confessional identity was formed at the same time that Protestants were forging a powerful narrative that placed Protestant culture at the core of the German nation. In so doing, Protestants made strong claims to the German language in particular, and, more contentiously, to German history itself.

What shifted over the course of the nineteenth century is that bourgeois German Catholics who enacted this initial rethinking of the church were increasingly left behind by mass politics and Ultramontantism. But they were not entirely gone, and what remained of the *katholische Aufklärung* trickled into Catholic liberalism, leaving the German Catholic *Mittelstand*, in Thomas Mergel's words "between class and confession."[10] That sense of betweenness, rather than representing a "peculiarity" of German Catholicism, was indeed its defining feature, a situation that fundamentally changed only after 1945. Although the nineteenth century witnessed a hierarchical church that grew increasingly hostile to liberalism ("progress, liberalism, and modern civilization" itself, in the language of the *Syllabus of Errors*), it is important to realize that nineteenth-century Catholicism was not predetermined by its past. The official and also populist wing of the church was indeed very hostile to liberalism (the favor was returned), putting liberal Catholic heirs of the Enlightenment in a difficult spot. The failure of their argument to carry the day has been marked up as a failure of the Catholic Enlightenment itself. However, what the bourgeois Catholic *Aufklärer* did create was an idea. This book has shown how and why that idea was created. But this does not mean that the idea of German Catholicism was their exclusive property. Much like the early fusion of liberalism and German nationalism, German Catholicism and Catholic liberalism could eventually become uncoupled. But the legacy was there, always ready to be reclaimed, and, throughout the nineteenth century, something to be fought over.

Moreover, it gave Catholics a powerful tool in their arsenal, strengthening them at least inwardly against the assumption of the dominant Protestant culture that Catholicism itself was inimical to the German nation. "In Protestant and liberal Germany," Franz Schnabel

---

[10] Thomas Mergel, *Zwischen Klasse und Konfession. Katholisches Bürgertum in Rheinland 1794–1814 Göttingen* (Göttingen: Vandenhoek & Ruprecht, 1994).

wrote, "hardly ever was a sincere effort made to distinguish between 'German' and 'Roman' Catholics. Whoever went beyond Wessenberg and Classicism was called 'ultramontane.'"[11] This attitude was not merely the political fallout of the *Kulturkampf*, but, as Michael Gross has argued, lay at the heart of German liberal culture.[12] The roots of the typically German Protestant amalgamation of nation, the Reformation, and the progress of civilization – *Kulturprotestantismus*, in short – lay in the eighteenth century. And so too did the German Catholic capacity to resist it.

BETWEEN GERMANY AND ROME

What happens when the church is treated as a human society, and thereby is placed on the same level as states and empires? This question, too, emerged as part of the post-Westphalian landscape. As discussed previously, the struggle over the source of canon law in the eighteenth century was part of the larger problem of translating the law of the church from its status as a universal law into one of being the particular law of a society within the state. The Josephine canonists insisted the there was a "natural church" that preceded (i.e., logically and philosophically) the revealed church. This church was simply a "society of human beings" who gathered for the purpose of worship. Such a society, once abstracted from its sacral connotations, could more easily be treated as any other human institution. Protestant church historians in the eighteenth century, as John Stroup has noted, treated "ecclesiastical societies as objects of pragmatic history" and thereby "prepared the way for a 'melting down' of *historia sacra* into world history."[13] Pietist influence had drawn attention to the fact that Protestant

---

[11] Schnabel, *Deutsche Geschichte im Neuenzehnten Jahrhundert. Volume 4: Die Religiösen Kräfte*, 269.

[12] Michael Gross, *The War Against Catholicism: Liberal Identity and the Anti-Catholic Imagination in Nineteenth-Century Germany* (Ann Arbor: University of Michigan Press, 2004).

[13] John Stroup, "Protestant Church Historians in the German Enlightenment," in *Aufklärung und Geschichte. Studien zur deutschen Geschichtewissenschaft im 18. Jahrhundert*, Hans Erich Bödeker, ed. (Göttingen: Vandenhoeck & Ruprecht, 1986), 171. On the importance of the concept of "pragmatic history" to eighteenth-century historians, see Peter Hanns Reill, *The German Enlightenment and the Rise of Historicism* (Berkeley and Los Angeles: University of California Press, 1975), 41–4. Reill emphasizes that the *Aufklärer* did not use "pragmatic" in the classical sense that history would teach universal values by example. Instead, as Gatterer defined it

the chief concern of the pragmatic historian is the search for immediate inciting circumstances and causes of important events and to develop as well as possible the whole

dogma could no longer be shown to reflect the practices of the early church. Eighteenth-century Protestant church historians embraced rather than rejected this argument, and sought to assert the harmony of Christianity and the ideals of Enlightenment.[14]

Not all such historical treatments of the church – even those that treated it as a human society – carried such significant overtones, nor did they necessarily imply a metaphysical challenge to ecclesiastical authority. After all, the natural law definition of a church used by the Josephine canonists bore similarities to those of Cardinal Bellarmine and the scholastics of Salamanca. "Pragmatic" church histories sought to understand the human element in the church, but did not necessarily imply that the church was a purely human creation. While Schmidt's treatment of the historical matter of the church was written on a grand scale, there was also a strong sense of history prevalent in the multitude of workaday treatments of the German church.

In a 1772 treatise on "the union of ecclesiastical jurisprudence with statistics," Ulrich Mayr, a Cistercian, applied the teachings of the influential Göttingen professor Gottfried Achenwall on "statistics" to the history of the church.[15] Following Achenwall, Mayr defined "statistics" as the integrated study of the influence of history, climate, geography, economy, and political constitution on the condition of a state. "There exists in the church almost innumerable peculiarities ... [and if] one brought them together into a proper system, then one would have church statistics, that is, an ecclesiastical-political science [*Kirchenstatistik, Kirchenstaatslehre*]."[16] Mayr continued by noting that

> system of causes and effects, of means and intentions, no matter how confused at first they may seem.

Quoted in Reill, 42.

[14] Stroup, "Protestant Church Historians in the German Enlightenment," 170. See also Dirk Fleischer, "Der Strukturwandel der evangelischen Kirchengeschichtsschreibung im 18. Jahrhundert," in *Aufklärung und Historik*, Horst Walter Blanke and Dirk Fleischer, eds. (Waltrop: Spenner, 1991), 141–59. For the influence of Protestant church history in Catholic Universities, especially Vienna, see Emil Clemens Scherer, *Geschichte und Kirchengeschichte an den deutschen Universitäten. Ihre Anfänge im Zeitalter des Humanismus und ihre Ausbildung zu selbständigen Disziplinen* (Freiburg: Herder, 1927; reprint, Olms, 1975).

[15] While Achenwall did not invent the discipline, he is credited with popularizing it throughout Germany. See Reill, 152–4.

[16] Mayr, Statistik, 74f. Mayr's treatise was published in Latin as Udalrici Mayr, *Dissertatio Historico-Politica Inauguralis de Nexu Statisticae cum Jurisprudentia Ecclesiastica, Quam una cum Selectis ex Univ. Jure Corollariis annuente inclyto senatu Juridico Ingolstadiensi,* 1772. It was translated and published in German – along with documentation about the

it is apparent that all those disciplines that are important for civil statistics [*bürgerliche Statistik*] will also be of use here. Only the principles of general public law must be applied with care, and without disadvantage to the divine creator of the church.[17]

Because the church is a society "indeed, a state," it requires laws, as in any "properly ordered state." The study of the church's law is called ecclesiastical jurisprudence, and Mayr argues that it is useful for this discipline to be linked to statistical science.[18]

While Mayr's work met with Roman disapproval – after all, his conclusions were not out of line with the positions of the German canonists and supporters of the German national council – his treatment of the church reveals a concept of embeddedness, not an attitude of disrespect. German Catholic reformers could treat the church pragmatically, because they did not see it as an institution fundamentally under threat: in their eyes, it may have needed major repairs, but it was solidly constituted in society, and could rely on the state for support. The idea that Christianity was the glue that held German society together was the common property of all confessions. This, after all, was the thrust of Schleiermacher's famous *Speeches on Religion* (1799). Perhaps because that conviction was so strongly held – and because it was under increasing attack throughout the nineteenth century – the division of the German church into competing confessions could give rise to a bitterness that did not seem to wholly subside until after the Second World War. But that bitterness was only half of the story, for there was also an awareness of a common fate and history. In 1863, Ignaz von Döllinger noted that

to us alone among nations has fate ensured that the sharp blade of ecclesiastical division would continually cut through us. We are carved into almost equal parts, but can neither separate from one another, nor really live properly together.[19]

---

controversy the work raised with Roman authorities – by Georg Wilhelm Zapf (with or without Mayr's permission I do not know), *as Über den Einfluß der Gelehrtengeschichte in das Studium der Gottesgelehrsamkeit, wie auch über die Verbindung der Statistik mit der kirchlichen Rechtsgelehrsamkeit. Mit einer Vorrede und der Geschichte von den Bewegungen des römischen Hofs wider diese Schriften* (Leipzig, 1778). I quote the German edition here. The controversy is recounted in "Nachrichten von den Bewegung des römischen Hofes wider die Schriften des P. Mayr von Kaisersheim, " in *Neueste Religionsgeschichte*, Christian Wilhelm Franz Walch, ed., 5 (Theil, Lemgo, 1775).
[17] Mayr, 74f.
[18] Mayr, 78.
[19] Quoted in Georg Schwaiger, ed., *Zwischen Polemik und Irenik. Untersuchungen zum Verhältnis der Konfessionen im späten 18. und frühen 19. Jahrhundert* (Göttingen: Vandenhoeck & Ruprecht, 1977), 5.

As an heir of the *katholische Aufklärung*, Döllinger was frustrated with the direction the Catholic church took in the nineteenth century.

I have argued throughout this book that, contrary to our received notions about German particularism and the frailty of the Holy Roman Empire, and about the supposed permanent backwardness of Catholicism, German Catholics in the eighteenth century rethought and restated the church "in a language intelligible" to their generation.[20] A generation, that is, of the Age of Enlightenment. The exceptionalism – or *Sonderweg* – of German Catholicism in the later Holy Roman Empire challenges the categories of latter-day historians. For eighteenth-century thinkers, the relevance of the church – albeit *semper reformanda* – to modern times was beyond a doubt. Certainly there were more than a few freethinkers and radical atheists to whom this new iteration of the church was so much wasted ink. But by far the majority of German Catholic thinkers felt that such an effort was not only possible, but also necessary. And in that, they partook of a broader restatement and recasting of values we have come to label Enlightenment.

As we have seen in Schmidt's history, German Catholics at the end of the eighteenth century saw church and state as equal partners in the progress of civilization. The direction they wanted the church to go – toward rational, moderate, and practical religion – assumed that they would lead, in partnership with the civil authority, as a moral minority of sorts. Consequently, the religious attitudes of the common people were seen as relics of a superstitious past. What they did not see was that the institutional (and international) Catholic church would be able to mobilize religious loyalties throughout the nineteenth century and become a powerful political force in the age of liberalism, nationalism, and mass politics. The *katholische Aufklärer*, so committed to reconciling the church's past with the present, did not recognize that they were witnessing its future as well. The church they imagined fell somewhere between Germany and Rome, and as the nineteenth century progressed German Catholics would try to reconcile these competing visions of the social – and moral – imaginary.[21]

---

[20] *Gaudium et Spes*, 1965, §4.
[21] For the phrase, see Charles Taylor, *Modern Social Imaginaries* (Durham and London: Duke University Press, 2004).

Bibliography

WORKS PUBLISHED BEFORE 1850

Amort, Eusebius. *Ethica Christiana* Augsburg, 1758.
Idea divini amoris seu expositio distincta primi ac maximi mandati. Augsburg, 1739.
Philosophia Pollingana ad normam Burgundicae. Augsburg, 1730.
Theologia moralis. 2 Volumes. Augsburg, 1758.
Andres, Bonaventura. *Magazin für Prediger zur Beförderung des practischen Christenthums und der populären Aufklärung.* Würzburg, 1789.
Arnoldi, Heinrich Aloys. *Tagebuch über die zur Ems gehaltene Zusammenkunft der vier Erzbischöflichen deutschen Herrn Deputierten, die Beschwerde der deutschen Natzion gegen den Römischen Stuhl und sonstige geistliche Gerechtsame betr.* Edited by Matthias Höhler. Mainz: Kirchheim, 1915 [1786].
Aschenbrenner, Beda. *Aufklärungs-Almanach für Äbbte und Vorsteher katholischer Klöster.* 1784.
Babenstuber, Ludwig. *Philosophia Thomistica Salisburgensis.* Augsburg, 1706.
Balthasar, Joseph Anton Felix. *De Helvetiorum Juribus Circa Sacra, das ist: kurzer historischen Entwurf der Freyheiten, und der Gerichtsbarkeit der Eidgenosen, in so genannten geistlichen Dingen.* Zurich, 1768.
Barthel, Johann Kaspar. *Dissertatio Praeliminaris historico-publico-canonica de Concordatis Germaniae.* Würzburg, 1740.
Opera Juris Publici Ecclesiastici ad Statum Germaniae Accomodata ... Editio novissima auctior et Emendatior. Bamberg and Würzburg, 1780.
Tractatus Historico-Canonico-Pragmaticus Loco Dissertationis Tertiae de Concordatis Germaniae Specialis Exhibens Commentarium Hermeneuticum ad Eorundem Textum et Literam. Würzburg, 1762.
Benedict XIV [Prospero Lambertini]. *Bullarium. Tom 1. In quo continentur constitutiones, epistolae &. c. Edita ab initio pontificatus usque ad annum MDCCXLVI.* Rome, Typis Sacrae Congregationis de Propaganda Fide, 1746.
Institutionum Ecclesiasticarum. Rome, 1750.

Blackstone, William. *Commentaries on the Laws of England. Volume One: Of the Rights of Persons*. Oxford: Clarendon Press, 1765. Facsimile reprint, edited by Stanley Katz. Chicago: University of Chicago Press, 1979.

Blau, Felix Anton. *Kritik der seit der Revolution in Frankreich gemachten Religions-verordnungen, auf reine Prinzipien des Staats- und Kirchenrechts gegründet*. Strasbourg: F. G. Levrault, 1797.

Kritische Geschichte der kirchlichen Unfehlbarkeit, zur Beförderung einer freieren Prüfung des katholizismus. Frankfurt, 1791.

Programma de Vera Notione Libertatis Humane. Mainz, 1784.

Blau, Felix Anton and Anton Dorsch. *Beyträge zur Verbesserung des äussern Gottesdienstes in der katholischen Kirche*. Frankfurt, 1789.

Blondel, David. *Pseudoisidorus et Turrianus Vapulantes*. Geneva, 1628.

Born, Ignaz von. *Monachologia, or Handbook of the Natural History of Monks, arranged according to the Linnaean System*. 1783. English translation with additions. Edinburgh: Johnstone and Hunter, 1852.

Brastenberger, Gebhard U. *Über den Ursprung und Werth der kirchlichen Gewohnheit, durch Symbolischen Schriften den Inhalt der christlichen Religion festzusetzen, mit Anwendung auf die neuesten Unionsprojecte*. Ulm, 1788.

Braun, Heinrich. *Anleitung zer geistlichen Beredsamkeit*. Munich, 1776.

Bedenken und Untersuchung der Frage: Ob man den Ordensgeistlichen die Pfarreyen und Seelsorge abnehmen soll oder nicht. Dem Projecte eines Weltgeistlichen der Regenspurgerdiöces entgegen gesetzt. Munich, 1769.

Cappellari, Mauro [Pope Gregory XVI]. *Der Triumph des heilige Stuhls und der Kirche, oder Bekämpfung und Widerlegung der Angriffe der Neuerer mit ihren eigenen Waffen*. Augsburg, 1833. German translation of the 1832 Italian edition, [First edition. 1799].

Commentario de Limitibus utriusque potestatis. Regensburg, 1781.

Conring, Hermann. *De Origine Iuris Germanici liber unus*. Helmstedt, 1720 [1649].

Contzen, Adam, S. J. *Politicorum libri decem*. Mainz, 1621.

Cusa, Nicholas of. *The Catholic Concordance*. Translated by Paul Sigmund. Cambridge: Cambridge University Press, 1991.

Danzer, Jakob. *Beyträge zur Reformation der christlichen Theologie überhaupt und der katholischen Dogmatik insbesondere*. Volume 1. Ulm, 1793.

Josephs des Grossen Toleranz. Ein theologisches Fragment. Salzburg, 1783.

Reflexionen über Teutschlands 18tes Jahrhundert, und seine Verfasser, nebst einer Betrachtung über die Lage des heutigen Mönchswesens und daraus entstehenden Folgen. Von einem Freund der Wahrheit. Päckchen 1–7. 1782–1783.

Was sind die Reichsprälaten und wie sind sie es worden? Aus der Geschichte beantwortet. [Salzburg], 1785.

De Dominis, Marc Antonio. *De republica ecclesiastica libri X*. 1617–1622.

Der Cölibat, oder der Wehestand der unbeweibten Priester, aus den hinterlassenen Papieren eines katholischen Geistlichen gezogen und an's Licht gefördert von einem Freunde der heiligen, allgemeinen, christlichen Kirche. Zurich, 1835.

Desing, Anselm. *Juris Naturae Larva Detracta compluribus libris sub titulo Juris Naturae Prodeuntibus.* Munich, 1753.

Opes Sacerdotii Num Reipublicae Noxiae? Ex Rerum Natura, Sana Politica et Communi Sensu Generis Humani Examinatum. 1753.

Staatsfrage: Sind die Güter und Einkünfte der Geistlichkeit dem Staate schädlich oder nicht? Beantwortet und Lochstein und Neubergern entgegen gesetzt. Munich, 1768.

DuHamel, Jean B. *De concsensu veteris et novae philosophiae.* 1663.

Philosophia vetus et nova. 1678.

"Einige Gedanken über die zu unserer Zeit erfolgte Verminderung der Priester, und damit in Verbindung stehende Punkte." *Theologische Quartalschrift.* 3. Quartalheft. Tübingen, 1826.

Einige vorläufige Anmerkungen zu den Weißmannischen Bermerkungen über das Resultat das Embser Kongresses. Frankfurt and Leipzig, 1787.

Espen, Zeger Bernard van. *Dissertation canonique sur la vice de la Proprieté des Religieux et des Religieuses.* Translated from the Latin. Lyon, 1693.

Jus ecclesiasticum universum antiquae et recentiori disciplinae paresertim Belgii, Galiae, Germaniae, & vicinarum Provinciarum accomodatum, e sacris scripturis, SS. canonibus. Louvain, 1700.

Fabritius, Karl Moritz. *Über den Werth und die Vorzüge geistlicher Staaten und Regierungen in Teutschland.* Frankfurt and Leipzig, 1797.

Felbiger, Johann Ignaz. *Vorlesungen über die Kunst zu katechisierung, die er seinen jungen geistlichen zu halten pflege.* Vienna, 1774.

Feller, François. *Coup d'oeil sur le Congres d'Ems, Tenu en 1786 par Quatre Députés des quatre Métropolitains d'Allemagne.* Dusseldorff: Kauffmann, 1787.

Fenelon, Francois de Salignac. *Explication des Maximes des Saints sur la vie Interieur.* Paris, 1697

Filangieri, Kajetan. *Die Wissenschaft der Gesezgebung.* Translated by A. W. Gustermann. Vienna, 1784.

Fingerlos, Matthäus. *Über das Bedürfniß einer Reformation des Priesterstandes.* Rome, 1811.

Wozu sind Geistliche da? 2 Volumes. Salzburg, 1800.

Fleury, Claude. *Institution au droit ecclesiastique.* 1688.

Frank, Peter Anton. *Grundbetrachtungen über Staat und Kirche nach natürlichen Grundsätzen in Anwendung auf Teutschland.* Mainz, 1784.

Friedberg, A., ed. *Corpus Iuris Canonici.* Second edition. Leipzig, 1881.

Gerbert, Martin. *De communione potestatis ecclesiasticae inter summos ecclesiae principes pontificem, & episcopos.* 1761.

De veteri liturgia Alemannica. 1770.

Geschichte des Schwarzwaldes. 2 Volumes. Translated by Adalbert Weh. Freiburg, 1993.

Historia Nigrae Silvae Ordinis Sancti Benedicti Coloniae. 2 Volumes. St. Blasien, 1783.

Monumenta veteris liturgiae alemannicae. 1777.

Vetus liturgia alemannica. 2 Volumes. St. Blasien, 1776.

Geschichte der Bettelmönche. Translated from French. Frankfurt und Leipzig, 1769.

Giftschütz, Franz. *Leitfaden für die in den k.-k. Erbländen vorgeschriebenen Vorlesung über die Pastoraltheologie.* Vienna, 1785.

Goldhagen, Hermann. *Beylagen zum Religions-Journal.* Mainz, 1777–.

Religions-Journal, oder Auszüge aus den beßten alten und neuen Schriftstellern und Vertheidigern der Christlichen Religion, mit Anmerkungen. Mainz, 1776–.

Graser, Rudolph, OSB. *Vollständige Lehrart zu predigen.* Augsburg, 1768.

Großing, Franz Rudolph von. *Papstengeschichte im Grundriß.* Göttingen und Offenbach, 1784.

Petri ab Osterwald, de Religiosis Ordinibus et euroum Reformatione liber singularis. Germania, 1781.

Grundsätze zur Feststellung der Eintracht zwischen der politischen und kirchlichen Macht in katholischen Staates. Ein Handbuch für Priester und Staatsmänner. [Augburg?], 1785.

Harzheim, Daniel [Sulzer, Johann A.] *Der Cölibat, oder der unverehlichte Stand der katholischen Geistlichkeit. Beurtheilt nach Gründen der Vernunft und Religion.* Gedruckt, nicht in Rom. 1782.

Hegel, G. F. W. *Grundlinien der Philosophie des Rechts.* Leipzig: Meiner, 1911.

Held, Willibold. *Beleuchtung der Bad-Emsischen Punktation.* Memmingen, 1787.

Jurisprudentia universalis ex iuribus canonico, civili Romano, et Germanico, tam publico, quam privato, feudali, et criminali. 5 Volumes. Memmingen 1768–1773.

Kritische Anmerkungen über die sogenannte Reformation in Deutschland zu Ende des achtzehenten Jahrhunderts. Frankfurt, 1782.

Herder, Johann Gottfried. "Warum wir noch keine Geschichte der Deutschen haben." In *Neue Deutsche Monatsschrift* 1. Berlin, 1795.

Hontheim, Niklaus. *Buch von dem Zustand der Kirche und der rechtmäßigen Gewalt des römischen Papsts die in der Religion widriggesinnten Christen zu vereinigen.* Translated from the Latin. Wardigen, 1764. Multiple editions.

Commentarius in suam retractationem, edited, with an introduction by Ulrich Lehner. Nordhausen: Bautz, 2008 [1781].

Febronius abbreviatus et emendatus, edited, with an introduction by Ulrich Lehner. Nordhausen: Bautz, 2008 [1777].

Justini Febronii JCti de Statu Ecclesiae et Legitima Potestate Romani Pontificis Liber Singularis, ad Reuniendos Dissidentes in Religione Christianos Compositus. 1763. Multiple editions.

Horix, Johann Baptist von. *Concordata nationis germanicae integra variis additamentis illustrata.* Frankfurt and Leipzig, 1771.

Huth, Philipp J. *Versuch einer Kirchengeschichte des achtzehnten Jahrhunderts.* Augsburg, 1809.

Ickstatt, Johann A. [Christian Friedrich Menschenfreund, pseud.]. *Untersuchung der Frage: Warum ist der Wohlstand der protestantischen Länder so gar viel größer als der catholishen?* Salzburg and Freising, 1772.

Journal von und für Deutchland. 1784–.

Justi, Johann Heinrich Gottlob. *Die Grundfeste zu der Macht und Glückseligkeiten der Staaten, oder ausführliche Vorstellung der gesamten Polizeiwissenschaft.* 2 Volumes. Königsberg and Leipzig, 1760. Reprint, Aalen: Scientia Verlag, 1965.

Klueting, Harm, ed. *Der Josephinismus: ausgewählte Quellen zur Geschichte der theresianisch-josphinischen Reformen.* Darmstadt: Wissenschaftliche Buchgesellschaft, 1995.

Lancelotti, Giovanni Paolo. *Institutiones iuris canonici, quibus ius Pontificum singulari methodo libris quattuor comprehenditur.* Venice, 1570.

Lang, Karl Heinrich Ritter von. *Geschichte der Jesuiten in Baiern.* Nuremberg, 1819.

Le Bret. *Magazin zum Gebrauch der Staaten- und Kirchengeschichte ... in Ansehung ihrer Geistlichkeit.* Ulm, 1771–1788.

Lessing, Gotthold Ephraim. *Theologiekritische Schriften I und II.* Volume 7 of *Werke.* Munich: Carl Hanser Verlag, 1970–.

Liguori, Alphonse. *Besuchungen des Allerheiligsten Sacraments und der allzeit unbefleckten Jungfrau Maria.* Translated from the Italian. Augsburg and Innsbruck: Joseph Wolff, 1769.

De la Communion fréquent. Translated from the Italian. Clermont-Ferrand, 1831.

Theologia Moralis, edited by Le Noir. Paris: L. Vivès, 1872.

Litteratur des katholischen Deutschlands. Continued from 1792–1798 as *Litterarisches Magazin für Katholiken und deren Freunde,* edited by Placidius Sprenger, OSB. Koburg, 1775–.

Maass, Ferdinand, ed. *Der Josephinismus, Quellen zu seiner Geschichte in Österreich 1760–1850. Amtliche Dokumente aus dem Wiener Haus-, Hof- und Staatsarchiv.* 5 volumes. Vienna: Verlag Herold, 1951–1961.

Marca, Pierre de. *De concordia sacerdotii et imperii: seu de libertatibus ecclesiae gallicanae libri octo.* Paris, 1663.

Martini, Karl Anton von. *Positiones de Iure Civitatis in ususm auditorii vindobonensis.* Vienna, 1773.

Mayr, Andreas Ulrich. *Kurzer Bemerkungen über das Resultat des Embser Kongresses nebst einigen Beylagen.* Strasbourg, 1797.

Mayr, Beda, OSB. *Der erste Schritt zur künftigen Vereinigung der katholischen und der evangelischen Kirche, gewaget von – fast wird man es nicht glauben, gewaget von einem Mönche.* 1778.

Vertheidigung der natürlichen, christlichen und katholischen Religion. Nach den Bedürfnissen unsrer Zeiten. 4 Volumes. Augsburg, 1787–1789.

Mayr, Ulrich. *Biga dissertationum de nexu historiae literariae cum studio theologiae; ac nexu statisticae cum iurisprudentia ecclesiastica.* Second edition. 1774.

Über den Einfluß der Gelehrtengeschichte in das Studium der Gottesgelehrsamkeit, wie auch über die Verbindung der Statistik mit der kirchlichen Rechtsgelehrsamkeit. Mit einer Vorrede und der Geschichte von den Bewegungen des römischen Hofs wider diese Schriften, Leipzig, 1778.

Mendelssohn, Moses. *Jerusalem: or on Religious Power and Judaism.* Translated by Allan Arkush, with introduction and commentary by Alexander Altman. Waltham, MA: Brandeis University Press, 1983.

Möhler, J. A. "Einige Gedanken über die zu unserer Zeit erfolgte Verminderung der Priester und damit in Verbindung stehende Punkte." *Theologische Quartalschrift* 8 (1826): 414–51.

Molitor, V. Anselm, OSB. *Theologische Abhandlung von der Macht der Kirche über die Kirchengüter.* Freising, 1768.

Mosheim, Johann Lorenz. *Institutes of Ecclesiastical History, Ancient and Modern.* Translated by James Murdock. 3 Volumes. New York: Harper and Brothers, 1839.

Moser, Carl Friedrich Von. *von dem Deutschen Nationalgeist.* 1766. Reprint, Notos, 1976.

Muratori, Ludovico Antonio. *Contra sublime loquentes in cathedra seu Dignitas Eloquentiae popularis.* 1757.

      Traité sur le Bonheur Public Translated from the Italian. 1772 [original edition, 1749].

Neuberger, Johann Georg, pseud. *Abhandlung von den Einkünften der Klöster und dem Amortizationsgesetze.* Second edition. 1768.

Neumayr, Francis, S. J. *Wesenheit, Kraft und Übung der Gottlichen Tugenden ....* Munich and Ingolstadt, 1757.

Oberdeutsche Allgemeine Literaturzeitung. Continued as *Neue oberdeutsche allgemeine Literaturzeitung.* 1788–1808.

Oberthür, Franz. *Michael Ignaz Schmidts des Geschichtschreibers der Deutschen Lebens-Geschichte. Ein so wichtiger als reichhaltiger Beytrag zur Kulturgeschichte der Deutschen.* Hannover, 1802.

Osterwald, Peter [Veremund von Lochstein, pseud.]. *Gründe sowohl für als wieder die Geistliche Immunität in zeitlichen Dingen.* Strasbourg, 1766.

Pacca, Bartolomeo. *Historische Denkwürdigkeiten über seinen Aufenthalt in den Jahren 1786 bis 1794, in der Eigenschaft eines Apostolischen Nuntius in den Rheinlanden, residierend zu Köln.* Translated from the Italian. Augsburg 1832.

Pehem, Josef Johann Nepomuk. *Praelectionum in Jus Ecclesiasticum Universum, Methodo Discentium Utilitati Adcommodata Congestarum.* Vienna, 1788. Translated into German as *Vorlesung über das Kirchenrecht.* 4 Volumes. Vienna, 1802–1803.

Peutinger, Ulrich. *Religion, Offenbarung und Kirche in der reinen Vernunft aufgesucht.* Salzburg, 1802.

Pey, J. *De l'Autorié des deux Puissances.* 2 Volumes. Strasbourg, 1780.

Pezzl, J. *Vertraute Briefe über Katholiken und Protestanten.* Strasbourg, 1787.

Pirhing, Enrico, S. J. *Jus canonicum in V. libros decretalium distributum, nova Methodo explicatum, ominbus capitulis titulorum ... promiscue & confuse positus, in ordinem doctrinae digestis.* 2 Volumes. Dillingen, 1722 [original, 1670].

Pitroff, Franz Christian. *Kirchenpolitik nach dem allgemeinen Verhältnissen der Kirchenstaatistik und der Pastoralklugheit, in der Anwendung auf die Seelsorgergeschäfte.* Prague, Bamberg, and Wurzburg, 1785.

Pufendorf, Samuel von. [Severinus de Monzambano, pseud.]. *Über die Verfassung des deutschen Reichs.* Translated by H. Breslau. *Klassiker der Politik* 3, edited by Friedrich Meinecke and Hermann Oncken. Berlin, 1922.

Pütter, Johann S. *Historische Entwicklung der heutigen Staatsverfassung des Teutschen Reichs.* 3 Volumes. Göttingen, 1786.

Rauttenstrauch, Stephen, OSB. *De Jure Principis praefigendi maturiorem Professione monasticae solemni aetatem Diatriba.* Prague, 1773.

Reinhold, K. L. "Ehrenrettung der Reformation, gegen zwei Kapitel in des k. k. Hofraths und Archivars, Hrn. M. I. Schmidts Geschichte der Teutschen, 6. Band." *Der Teutsche Merkur,* edited by C. M. Wieland. Weimar, 1786.

"Religion als Sitte." *Der Katholik NF* 2 (1850).

Richer, Edmund. *De ecclesiastica et civili potestate.* Paris, 1611.

Riegger, Paul Joseph. *Institutionum Iurisprudentiae Ecclesiasticae.* 4 Volumes. Second edition. Vienna, 1777–.

Robertson, William. *History of the Reign of Charles V.* 3 Volumes. Philadelphia, 1871 [1769].

Rochow, F. E. "Welches ist die beste Art, sowohl rohe als auch schon kultivierte Nationen, die sich in mancherlei Irrtümern und Aberglauben befinden, zur gesunden Vernunft zurückzuführen?" In *Sämtliche pädigogische Schriften,* edited by F. Jonas, and F. Wienecke. Berlin, 1909.

Rosolvi, F. K. *König Roderich, oder Zölibat und Regentschwäche. Historisches Schauspiel in 5 Aufzügen aus den Westgothischen Annalen des siebenten Jahrhunderts.* Hildburghausen, 1792.

Ruef, Johann K. *Beyträgen zur Beförderung des ältesten Christenthums und der neusten Philosophie.* 1788–1793.

Repertorium der neuesen philosophischen und theologischen Litteratur des katholischen Deutschlands. 1790.

Sätze aus allen Theilen der Jurisprudenz und aus der politischen Wissenschaften. 1785.

Sarpi, Paolo. *Histoire du Concile de Trente.* Translated by Pierre-François Le Courayer, 1736 [original, 1619].

Sartori, Joseph von. *Geistliches und weltliches Staatsrecht der deutschen, catholischgeistlichen Erz- Hoch- und Ritterstifter.* Nürnburg, 1788.

Staatistische Abhandlung über die Mängel in der Regierungsverfassung der geistlichen Wahlstaaten, und von den Mitteln, solchen abzuhelfen. Augsburg, 1787.

Sautier, Heinrich [Erich Servati]. *Über die Folgen des geistlichen Cölibats auf das Wohl katholischen Staaten.* 1786.

Schannat, Johann Friedrich and Joseph Hartzheim, S. J. *Concilia Germaniae.* 6 Volumes. Cologne, 1759-.

Schelle, Augustin, OSB. *Praktische Philosophie zum gebrauche akademischer Vorlesungen.* 2 Volumes. Second edition. Salzburg, 1792.

Ueber den Cölibat der Geistlichen und die Bevölkerung in katholischen Staaten, aus Gründen der politischen Rechenkunst. Voran gehen Geburts- Trauungs- und Sterbelisten von der Reischstadt Augsburg und Betrachtungen darüber. Salzburg, 1784.

Schilter, Johann. *De Libertate Ecclesiarum Germaniae, libri septem.* Jena, 1683.

Schmidt, Michael Ignaz. *Der Katechist nach seinen Eigenschaften und Pflichten, oder die rechte Weise die ersten Gründe der Religion zu lehren.* Translated from the Latin, with a preface by Johann Ignaz von Felbiger. Bamberg and Würzburg, 1772.

Die Geschichte des Selbstgefühls. Würzburg, 1772.

Geschichte der Deutschen. Ulm, 1778–1793.

Geschichte des Selbstgefühls. Frankfurt and Leipzig, 1772.

Schmidt, Philipp Anton. *Institutiones Juris Ecclesiastici Germaniae accomadatae.* 2 Volumes. Heidelberg, 1771, 1778.

Schmidt, Philipp Anton., ed. *Thesaurus iuris ecclesiastici.* ... 7 Volumes. Heidelberg, 1772–1779.

Schwarzhuber, Simpert, OSB. *Praktisch katholisches Religionshandbuch für nachdenkende Christen. Auf höchsten Befehl des Hochwürdigsten R. Fürsten und Erzbischofs zu Salzburg.* 1784/1785.

Seckendorf, Veit Ludwig von. *Deutscher Fürstenstaat: samt d. Autors* Zugabe sonderbarer u. wichtiger Materien. 7th ed., Verbessert, *mit Anm., Summarien u. Reg. vers. von Andres Simson von Biechling.* Jena, 1737 (1656). Reprint, Aalen: Scientia Verlag, 1972.

Sleidan, Johann. *The General History of the Reformation of the Church. English translation of De statu religionis et reipublicae Carlo V Ceasare.* Translated by Edmund Bohun. London, 1689.

Stattler, Benedikt. *Wahre und allein hinreichende Reformationsart des katholischen gesammten Priesterstandes, nach der ursprünglichen Idee seines göttlichen Stifters.* Ulm, 1791.

Süssmilch, Johann P. *Die göttliche Ordnung in den Veränderung des menschlichen Geschlechts ... erwiesen.* Berlin, 1741.

Spittler, Ludwig T. *Geschichte des kanonischen Rechts, bis auf die Zeiten des falschen Isodorus.* Halle, 1778.

[Spittler, Ludwig?] *Untersuchung der Frage: In wie ferne streitigkeiten in der Teutschkatholischen Kiche zur Reichstaglichen berathschlagung geeignet seien?*

Stäudlin, K. F. *Kirchliche Geographie und Statistik.* 2 Volumes. Tübingen, 1804.

Thomassin, Louis. *Ancienne et Nouvelle Discipline de l'Eglise, Touchant les Benefices et les Beneficiers.* New Edition, edited by M. André. Bar-le-Duc: L. Guérin & Co., 1864.

Verbesserungs = Vorschläge die Catholische Religion und Geistlichkeit betreffend; von einem Catholischen Professor auf einer kaiserlichen Universität. Freyburg, 1782.

Vrais Principes de la Constitution de l'Eglise Catholique, opposés aux Spéculations modernes destructives de la Hiérarchie & de la Jurisprudence canonique. 1787.

Walch, Christian Wilhelm Franz. *Neueste Religionsgeschichte,* 1771–1783.

Werkmeister, Benedikt Maria. *Freykirch Thomas, oder freymüthige Untersuchungen über die Unfehlbarkeit der katholischen Kirche von einem Gottesgelehrten.* Volume 1. Frankfurt und Leipzig, 1792.

Unmaßgeblicher Vorschlag zur Reformation des niedriegen katholischen Klerus. Nebst Materialien zur Reformation des höheren. Munich, 1782.

Wessenberg, Ignaz Heinrich Freiherr von. *Die Folgen der Säkularisation. Germanien, 1801. Excerpted in Die Säkularisation,* by Rudolfine Freiin

Von Oer. Historische Texte der Neuzeit II, 9. Göttingen: Vandenhoek und Ruprecht, 1970.

Widmann, Meinrad. *Wer sind die Aufklärer? Beantwortet nach dam ganzen Alphabet.* 1786.

Winkopp, Peter Adolf. *Uber die bürgerlich und geistliche Verbesserung des Mönchwesens.* Gera, 1783.

Winkopp, Peter Adolf and Höck. *Magazin für Geschichte, Statistik, Litteratur und Topographie der sämtlichen deutschen geistlichen Staaten.* Zürich, 1790.

Wittola, Marx Anton. *Schreiben eines österreichischen Pfarrers über die Tolerance nach der Grundsätzen der katholischen Kirche.* 1781

Wolf, Peter Philipp. *Allgemeine Geschichte der Jesuiten. von dem Ursprung ihres Ordens bis auf gegenwärtige Zeiten.* 4 Volumes. Zürich: Orell, Geßner, Füßli und Compag. 1789–.

Geschichte der römischkatholischen Kirche unter der Regierung Pius des Sechsten. 4 Volumes. Zürich, 1793–1802.

Vorschlag zu einer Reformation der katholischen Kirche. Leipzig und Luzern, 1800.

Zesch, Ambrosius, C. S. R. *Kanzelrede ... an dem Dankfest ... für die von Ihrer Röm. Kaiserl. und Apost. Königl. Majest. Marien Theresien in der Zeit der Hungersnoth empfangenen Getraidhülf. ...* 1771.

Zeuner, Karl, ed. *Quellensammlung zur Geschichte der deutschen Reichsverfassung in Mittelalter und Neuzeit.* Tübingen: Mohr, 1913.

Zinsmeister, Johann F. *Was ist der Kaiser?* 1783.

WORKS PUBLISHED AFTER 1850

Ahnert, Thomas. *Religion and the Origins of the German Enlightenment: Faith and the Reform of Learning in the Thought of Christian Thomasius.* Rochester: University of Rochester Press, 2006.

Altgeld, Wolfgang. *Katholizismus, Protestantismus, Judentum: über religiös begründete Gegensätze und nationalreligiöse Ideen in der Geschichte des deutschen Nationalismus.* Mainz: Mathias-Grünewald Verlag, 1992.

Aretin, Karl Otmar Von. *Das Alte Reich 1648–1806.* 4 Volumes. Stuttgart: Klett-Cotta, 1993–2000.

Das Reich: Friedensgarantie und europaisches Gleichgewicht, 1648–1806. Stuttgart: Klett-Cotta, 1986.

Arnold, F. X. *Die Staatslehre des Kardinals Bellarmine.* Munich, 1934.

Barth, Karl. *Protestant Theology in the Nineteenth Century. Its Background and History.* Translated by Brian Cozens and John Bowden. Grand Rapids, MI: Eerdmans, 2001 [original, 1947].

Bauer, Richard. *Der kurfürstliche gesitliche Rat und die bayerische Kirchenpolitik, 1768–1802.* Munich, 1972.

Baumgart, Peter. "Michael Ignaz Schmidt (1736–1794), Leben und Werk." In *Michael Ignaz Schmidt (1736–1794) in seiner Zeit. Der aufgeklärte Theologe, Bildungsreformer und "Historiker der Deutschen" aus Franken in neuer Sicht,* edited by Peter Baumgart. Neustadt/a.d. Aisch, 1996.

Beales, Derek. *Joseph II: In the Shadow of Maria Theresa, 1741–1780.* Cambridge: Cambridge University Press, 1987.

Prosperity and Plunder: European Catholic Monasteries in the Age of Revolution, 1650–1815. Cambridge: Cambridge University Press, 2003.

Bell, David Avrom. *The Cult of the Nation in France: Inventing Nationalism, 1680–1800.* Cambridge: Harvard University Press, 2001.

Bergerhausen, Hans-Wolfgang. "Michael Ignaz Schmidt in der historiographischen Tradition der aufklärung." In *Michael Ignaz Schmidt (1736–1794) in seiner Zeit. Der aufgeklärte Theologe, Bildungsreformer und "Historiker der Deutschen" aus Franken in neuer Sicht*, edited by Peter Baumgart. Neustadt/a.d. Aisch, 1996.

Bergin, Joseph. "Between Estate and Profession: The Catholic Parish Clergy of Early Modern Western Europe." In *Social Orders and Social Classes in Europe since 1500: Studies in Social Stratification*, edited by M. L. Bush. New York: Longman, 1992.

The Making of the French Episcopate 1589–1661. New Haven: Yale University Press, 1996.

Bireley, Robert. *The Counter-Reformation Prince. Anti-Machiavellianism or Catholic Statecraft in Early Modern Europe.* Chapel Hill: University of North Carolina Press, 1990.

The Jesuits and the Thirty Years War: Kings, Courts, and Confessors. New York: Cambridge University Press, 2003.

Blackall, *Emergence of German as a Literary Language, 1700–1775.* New York: Cambridge University Press, 1959.

Blackbourn, David and Geoff Ely. *The Peculiarities of German History. Bourgeois Politics and Society in Nineteenth-Century Germany.* Oxford, New York: Oxford University Press, 1984.

Blanning, T. C. W. *Reform and Revolution in Mainz, 1743–1803.* Cambridge: Cambridge University Press, 1974.

Blaschke, Olaf. "Das 19. Jahrhundert: Ein Zweites Konfessionelles Zeitalter?" *Geschichte und Gesellschaft* 26 (2000): 38–75.

Blitz, Hans-Martin. *Aus Liebe zum Vaterland. Die deutsche Nation im 18. Jahrhundert.* Hamburg: Humburger Edition, 2000.

Bouuaert, F. Claeys. "Un canoniste d'ancien régime: Z. B. van Espen." *Ephermerides theologicae Louvanienses* 38 (1962).

Bouwsma, William. *Venice and the Defense of Republican Liberty: Renaissance Values in the Age of the Counter-Reformation.* Berkeley and Los Angeles: University of California Press, 1968.

Bowman, William. *Priest and Parish in Vienna, 1780–1880.* Boston: Humanities Press, 1999.

Boyle, Nicholas. *Goethe: The Poet and the Age. Vol. 1: The Poetry of Desire (1749–1790).* Oxford: Oxford University Press, 1992.

Who Are We Now?: Christian Humanism and the Global Market from Hegel to Heaney. Notre Dame: University of Notre Dame Press, 1998.

Brady, Thomas A., Jr. *German Histories in the Age of Reformations, 1400–1650.* Cambridge: Cambridge University Press, 2009.

The Politics of the Reformation in Germany. Jacob Sturm (1489–1553) of Strasbourg. Atlantic Highlands, New Jersey: Humanities Press, 1997.

Braubach, Max. "Die kirchliche Aufklärung im katholischen Deutschland im Spiegel des 'Journal von und für Deutschland' 1784–92." *Historisches Jahrbuch* 54, no. 1 (1934).

Brewer, John. *The Sinews of Power: War, Money, and the English State, 1688–1783.* New York: Alfred A. Knopf, 1989.

Brückner, Wolfgang. "Zum Wandel der religiösen Kultur im 18. Jahrhundert. Einkreisversuche des 'Barockfrommen' zwischen Mittelalter und Massenmissionierung." In *Sozialer und kultureller Wandel in der ländlichen Welt des 18. Jahrhunderts,* edited by Ernst Hinrichs and GüNter Wiegelmann. Wolfenbüttel: Herzog August Bibliothek, 1982.

Brundage, James A. *Medieval Canon Law.* New York: Longman, 1995.

Brunner, Otto. *Land and Lordship. Structures of Governance in Medieval Austria.* Translated by Howard Kaminsky and James Van Horn Melton. Fourth revised edition. Philadelphia: University of Pennsylvania Press, 1992 [1965].

Burgdorf, Wolfgang. *Reichskonstitution und Nation. Verfassungsreformprojekte für das Heilige Römische Reich Deutscher Nation im Politischen Schrifttum von 1648 bis 1806.* Mainz: Philipp von Zabern, 1998.

Burkard, Dominik. *Staatskirche, Papstkirche, Bischofskirche. Die "Frankfurter Konferenzen" und die Neuordnung der Kirche in Deutschland nach der Säkularisation.* Rome, Freiburg and Vienna: Herder, 2000.

Burkarth, Klaus-Peter. *"Raisonable" Katholiken. Volksaufklärung im katholischen Deutschland um 1800.* Unpublished Ph.D. dissertation, University of Essen, 1994.

Büttner, Frank. "Abschied von Pracht und Rhetorik. Überlegungen zu den geistesgeschichtlichen Voraussetzungen des Stilwandels in der Sakraldekoration des ausgehenden 18. Jahrhunderts in Süddeutschland." In *Herbst des Barock. Studien zum Stilwandel,* edited by Andreas Tacke. Munich and Berlin: Deutscher Kunstverlag, 1998.

Châtellier, Louis. *The Europe of the Devout: The Catholic Reformation and the Formation of a New Society.* Translated by Jean Birrell. New York: Cambridge University Press, 1989.

The Religion of the Poor. Rural Missions in Europe and the Formation of Modern Catholicism, c.1500–c. 1800. Translated by Brian Pearce. New York: Cambridge University Press, 1997.

Cooman, G., M. Van Stiphout, and B. Wauters, eds. *Zeger-Bernard van Espen at the Crossroads of Canon Law, History, Theology, and Church–State Relations.* Volume 170, Bibliotheca Ephemeridum Theologicarum Lovaniensium. Leuven: Leuven University Press, 2003.

Cunningham, Richard G. *The Tridentine Concept of Sacerdotal Celibacy.* Rome: Pontifical Lateran University, 1972.

Dann, Otto. "Das historische Interesse in der deutschen Gesellschaft des 18. Jahrhunderts. Geschichte und historische Forschung in den zeitgenössichen Zeitschriften." In *Historische Forschung im 18. Jahrhundert. Organisation-*

Zielsetzung-Ergebnisse, edited by Karl Hammer and Jürgen Voss. Bonn, 1976.

Darnton, Robert. *The Great Cat Massacre, and Other Episodes in French Cultural History*. New York: Vintage, 1984.

Dickson, P. G. M. *Finance and Government under Maria Theresia, 1740–1780*. 2 Volumes. Oxford: Clarendon Press, 1987.

Dixon, C. Scott and Luise Schorn-Schütte, eds. *The Protestant Clergy in Early Modern Europe*. London: Palgrave, 2003.

Duggan, Lawrence G. "The Church as an Institution of the Reich." In *The Old Reich. Essays on German Political Institutions 1495–1806*, edited by James A. Vann and Steven Rowan. Brussels, 1974.

Duhr, Bernhard. *Geschichte der Jesuiten in den Ländern deutscher Zunge*. 4 Volumes. Freiburg: Herder, 1907–1913.

Fälschungen im Mittelalter: internationaler Kongress der Monumenta Germaniae Historica, München, 16–19 September 1986. 6 Volumes, Schriften der Monumenta Germaniae Historica, 33. Hannover: Hahn, 1988–1990.

Fasolt, Constantin. *The Limits of History*. Chicago: University of Chicago Press, 2004.

Feine, Hans Erich. *Die Besetzung der Reichsbistümer vom Westphälischen Frieden bis zur Säkularisation, 1648–1803*. Stuttgart: Ferdniand Enke, 1921. Reprint, 1964.

Figgis, John Neville. *From Gerson to Grotius: 1414–1625*. Cambridge: Cambridge University Press, 1907.

Fischer, Norbert, ed. *Kant und der Katholizismus. Stationen einer wechselhaften Geschichte*. Freiburg: Herder, 2005.

Fleischer, Dirk. "Der Strukturwandel der evangelischen Kirchengeschichtss-chreibung im 18. Jahrhundert." In *Aufklärung und Historik*, edited by Horst Walter Blanke and Dirk Fleischer. Waltrop: Spenner, 1991.

Forster, Marc. *Catholic Germany from the Reformation to the Enlightenment*. Palgrave Macmillan, 2008.

Catholic Revival in the Age of the Baroque: Religious Identity in Southwest Germany, 1550–1750. New York: Cambridge University Press, 2001.

The Counter-Reformation in the Villages: Religion and Reform in the Bishopric of Speyer, 1560–1720. Ithaca: Cornell University Press, 1992.

Forster, Wilhelm. "Die kirchliche Aufklärung bei den Benediktinern der Abtei Banz." *Studien und Mitteilungen zur Geschichte des Benediktinerordens und seiner Zweige* 63 (1951): 172–233 and 64 (1952): 110–233.

Fuhrmann, Horst. *Einfluß und Verbreitung der pseudoisidorischen Fälschungen*. 3 Volumes, Schriften der Monumenta Germaniae Historica, Volume 24. Stuttgart: Anton Hiersemann, 1972–1974.

"The Pseudo-Isidorian Forgeries." In *Papal Letters in the Early Middle Ages*, edited by Detlev Jasper and Horst Fuhrmann. Washington, D.C.: Catholic University of America Press, 2001.

Gagliardo, John. *Reich and Nation: The Holy Roman Empire as Idea and Reality, 1763–1806*. Bloomington: Indiana University Press, 1980.

Gall, Lothar. *Von der ständischen zur bürgerlichen Gesellschaft*, Enzyklopädie deutscher Geschichte 25. Munich: Oldenbourg, 1993.

Gatz, Erwin, ed. *Geschichte des kirchlichen Lebens in den deutschprachigen Ländern seit dem Ende des 18. Jahrhunderts. Die katholische Kirche.* Volume 1, Die *Bisthümer und ihre Pfarreien.* Freiburg: Herder, 1991.

ed. *Geschichte des kirchlichen Lebens in den deutschprachigen Ländern* seit dem Ende des 18. Jahrhunderts. Die katholische Kirche. Volume 4, *Der Diözesanklerus.* Freiburg: Herder, 1995.

Gaudemet, Jean. *Les Sources du Droit Canonique, VIIIe – XXe siècle.* Paris: Cerf, 1993.

Groethuysen, Bernhard. *Die Entstehung der bürgerlichen Welt- und Lebensanschaung in Frankreich.* Halle: Max Niemeyer, 1927.

Gross, Hans. *Empire and Sovereignty. A History of the Public Law Literature in the Holy Roman Empire, 1599–1804.* Chicago: University of Chicago Press, 1973.

Gross, Michael. *The War against Catholicism: Liberal Identity and the Anti-Catholic Imagination in Nineteenth-Century Germany.* Ann Arbor: University of Michigan Press, 2004.

Hagen, August. *Die kirchliche Aufklärung in der Diözese Rottenburg.* Stuttgart, 1953.

Hammerstein, Notker. *Aufklärung und katholisches Reich. Untersuchungen zur Universtitätsreform und Politik katholischer Territorien des Heiligen Römischen Reichs deutscher Nation im 18. Jahrhundert.* Berlin: Dunker & Humblot, 1977.

Res publica litteraria. Ausgewählte Aufsätze zur frühneuzeitlichen Bildungs-, Wissenschafts- und Universitätsgeschichte. Berlin: Dunker & Humblot, 2000.

Harrington, Joel F. and Helmut Walser Smith. "Confessionalization, Community, and State Building in Germany, 1555–1870." *The Journal of Modern History* 69, no. 1 (1997): 77–101.

Hartmann, Peter. *Kulturgescichte des Heiligen Römischen Reiches 1648–1806.* Vienna: Böhlau, 2001.

Heckel, Johannes. "Cura religionis, ius in sacra, ius circa sacra." In *Festschrift Ulrich Stutz.* Stuttgart: F. Enke, 1938.

"Kirchengut und Staatsgewalt." In *Das blinde, undeutliche Wort "Kirche." Gesammelte Aufsätze,* edited by Siegfried Grundmann. Cologne: Böhlau, 1964.

Heckel, Martin. *Staat und Kirche nach den Lehren der evangelischen Juristen Deutschlands in der ersten Hälfte des 17. Jahrhunderts.* Volume 6, Jus ecclesiasticum. Munich: Claudius-Verlag, 1968.

Hempton, David. *Methodism: Empire of the Spirit.* New Haven: Yale University Press, 2005.

Hengst, Karl. *Jesuiten an Universitäten und Jesuitenuniversitäten. Zur Geschichte der Universitäten in der Oberdeutschen und Rheinischen Provinz der Gesellschaft Jesu im Zeitalter der konfessionellen Auseinandersetzung.* Paderborn: F. Schöningh, 1981.

Hersche, Peter. "Adel Gegen Bürgertum? Zur Frage der Refeudalisierung der Reichskirche." In *Weihbischöfe und Stifte. Beiträge zu reichskirchlichen Funktionsträgern der Frühen Neuzeit,* edited by Friedhelm Jürgensmeier. Frankfurt, 1995.

Der Spätjansenismus in Österreich. Vienna: Verlag der Österreichischen Akademie der Wissenschaften, 1977.

Die deutsche Domkapital. 3 Volumes. Bern, 1984.

Hoffmann, Anton. *Beda Aschenbrenner (1756–1817). Lezter Abte von Oberalteich: Leben und Werk*. Passau, 1964.

Hughes, Michael. *Law and Politics in Eighteenth-Century Germany: The Imperial Aulic Council in the Reign of Charles VI*. Woodbridge, Suffolk: Royal Historical Society, 1988.

Hull, Isabel V. *Sexuality, State, and Civil Society in Germany, 1700–1815*. Ithaca: Cornell University Press, 1996.

Hunter, Ian. *Rival Enlightenments: Civil and Metaphysical Philosophy in Early Modern Germany*. Cambridge: Cambridge University Press, 2001.

Ihalainen, Pasi. *Protestant Nations Redefined. Changing Perceptions of National Identity in the Rhetoric of the English, Dutch and Swedish Public Churches, 1685–1772*. Leiden: Brill, 2005.

Israel, Jonathan Irvine. *Radical Enlightenment: Philosophy and the Making of Modernity, 1650–1750*. Oxford, New York: Oxford University Press, 2001.

Jedin, Huburt. *Kardinal Caesar Baronius: der Anfang der katholischen Kirchengeschichtsschreibung im 16. Jahrhundert*. Münster: Aschendorff, 1978.

Karant-Nunn, Susan C. "The Emergence of the Pastoral Family in the German Reformation: The Parsonage as a Site of Socio-Religious Change." In *The Protestant Clergy in Early Modern Europe*, edited by C. Scott Dixon and Luise Schorn-Schütte. London: Palgrave, 2003.

Kaufmann, Thomas DaCosta. *Court, Cloister, and City: The Art and Culture of Central Europe, 1450–1800*. Chicago: University of Chicago Press, 1995.

Kelley, Donald. *Foundations of Modern Historical Scholarship: Language, Law, and History in the French Renaissance*. New York: Columbia University Press, 1970.

Kirchner, Joachim. *Das Deutsche Zeitschriftenwesen. Seine Geschichte und seine Probleme. Teil 1. Von den Anfängen bis zum Zeitalter der Romantik*. Second edition. Wisbaden, 1958.

Klueting, Harm, Norbert Hinske, and Karl Hengst. *Katholische Aufklärung: Aufklärung im katholischen Deutschland*, Studien zum achtzehnten Jahrhundert, Volume 15. Hamburg: Meiner, 1993.

Knedlik, Manfred, and George Schrott, eds. *Anselm Desing (1699–1772). Ein benediktinischer Universalgelehrter im Zeitalter der Aufklärung*. Kallmünz: Michael Laßleben, 1999.

Koselleck, Reinhart. *Critique and Crisis: Enlightenment and the Pathogenesis of Modern Society*. Cambridge: MIT Press, 1988.

Kovács, Elisabeth. *Der Pabst in Teutschland: die Reise Pius VI. im Jahre 1782*. Vienna: Verlag für Geschichte und Politik, 1983.

Kreh, Fritz. *Leben und Werk des Reichsfreiherrn Johann Adam von Ickstatt: 1702–1776. Ein Beitrag zur Staatslehre der Aufklärungszeit*. Paderborn: Schöningh, 1974.

Kremer, Stephen. *Herkunft und Werdegang geistlicher Führungsschichten*. Freiburg: Herder, 1992.

Krieger, Leonard. *The German Idea of Freedom. History of a Political Tradition.* Chicago: University of Chicago Press, 1957.

The Politics of Discretion: Pufendorf and the Acceptance of Natural Law. Chicago: University of Chicago Press, 1965.

Landau, Peter. "Benedikt XIV." In *Juristen. Ein biographisches Lexikon,* edited by Michael Stolleis. Munich: C. H. Beck, 1995.

"Böhmer, Justus Henning." In *Juristen. Ein biographisches Lexikon,* edited by Michael Stolleis. Munich: C. H. Beck, 1995.

"Vom mitteralterlichen Recht zur neuzeitlichen Rechtswissenschaft." *Rechts- und staatswissenschaftliche Veröffentlichung d. Görresgesellschaft,* neue Folge, 72 (1994): 317–33.

Larkin, Emmet. "The Devotional Revolution in Ireland." *American Historical Review* 77, no. 3 (June, 1972): 625–52.

Leclerc, Gustave. *Zeger-Bernard van Espen (1646–1728) et l'autorité ecclésiastique. Contribution à l'histoire des théories gallicanes et du jansénisme,* Studia et Textus Iuris Canonici, 2. Zurich: Pas Verlag, 1964.

Lefebvre, Charles, Marcel Pacaut, and Laurent Chevailler. *L'époque moderne (1563–1789): les sources du droit et la seconde centralisation romaine.* Paris: Éditions Cujas, 1976.

Leinweber, Winfried. *Der Streit um den Zölibat im 19. Jahrhundert.* Münster: Aschendorff, 1978.

Lutz, Heinrich. "Zum Wandel der katholischen Lutherinterpretation." In *Politik, Kultur and Religion im Werdeprozeß der frühen Neuzeit. Aufsätze und Vorträge, aus Anlaß des 60. Geburtstags von Heinrich Lutz,* edited by Moritz Csásky, et al. Klagenfurt: Universitätsverlag Carinthia, 1982.

Marri, Fabio, Maria Lieber, and Christian Weyers. *Lodovico Antonio Muratori und Deutschland: Studien zur Kultur- und Geistesgeschichte der Frühaufklärung,* Italien in Geschichte und Gegenwart Bd. 8. Frankfurt am Main, New York: Peter Lang, 1997.

Maurer, Michael. *Die Biographie des Bürgers. Lebensformen und Denkweisen in der formativen Phase des deutschen Bürgertums (1680–1815).* Göttingen, 1996.

"Die konfessionelle Identität des Bürgertums um 1800." In *Die Säkularisation im Prozess der Säkularisierung Europas,* edited by Peter Blickle and Rudolf Schlögl. Ependorf: Bibliotheca Academica, 2005.

Maza, Sara. *The Myth of the French Bourgeoisie.* Cambridge: Harvard University Press, 2003.

McClelland, Charles E. *State, Society, and University in Germany, 1700–1914.* Cambridge: Cambridge University Press, 1980.

McMahon, Darrin. *Enemies of Enlightenment: The French Counter-Enlightenment and the Making of Modernity.* New York: Oxford University Press, 2001.

McManners, John. *Church and Society in Eighteenth-Century France.* 2 Volumes. Oxford: Oxford University Press, 1998.

Meinecke, Friedrich. *Weltbürgertum und Nationalstaat: Studien zur Genesis des deutschen Nationalstaates.* Munich: R. Oldenbourg, 1908.

Melton, James Van Horn. *Absolutism and the Eighteenth-Century Origins of Compulsory Schooling in Prussia and Austria.* Cambridge, New York: Cambridge University Press, 1988.

The Rise of the Public in Enlightenment Europe. New York: Cambridge University Press, 2001.

Mergel, Thomas. *Zwischen Klasse und Konfession. Katholisches Bürgertum in Rheinland 1794–1814. Göttingen.* Göttingen: Vandenhoek & Ruprecht, 1994.

Merkle, Sebastian. "Würzburg im Zeitalter der Aufklärung." In *Ausgewählte Reden und Aufsätze*, edited by Theobald Freudenberger, 421–41. Würzburg: Ferdinand Schöningh, 1965 [1912].

Midelfort, H. C. Erik. *Exorcism and Enlightenment. Johann Joseph Gassner and the Demons of Eighteenth-Century Germany.* New Haven: Yale University Press, 2005.

Möller, Horst. *Aufklärung in Preussen: der Verleger, Publizist und Geschichtsschreiber Friedrich Nicolai.* Berlin: Colloquium Verlag, 1974.

Müller, Hans. *Ursprung und Geschichte des Wortes "Sozialismus."* Hannover: J. H. W. Nietz Nachfolger, 1967.

Müller, Winfried. *Im Vorfeld der Säkularisation. Briefe aus bayerischen Klöstern 1794–1803.* Cologne: Böhlau, 1989.

Universität und Orden. Die bayerische Landesuniversität Ingolstad zwischen der Aufhebung des Jesuitenordens und der Säkularisation, 1773–1803. Berlin: Duncker & Humblot, 1986.

Nipperdey, Thomas. *Deutsche Geschichte, 1800–1866. Bürgerwelt und starker Staat.* Munich: C. H. Beck, 1983.

Nuttinck, M. *La vie et l'oeuvre de Zeger-Bernard van Espen.* Louvain: Bureaux du Recueil, Bibliothèque de l'Université, 1969.

O'Malley, John. *The First Jesuits.* Cambridge: Harvard University Press, 1993.

Oakley, Francis. *The Western Church in the Later Middle Ages.* Ithaca: Cornell University Press, 1979.

Ocker, Christopher. *Church Robbers and Reformers in Germany, 1525–1547: Confiscation and Religious Purpose in the Holy Roman Empire.* Leiden and Boston: Brill, 2006.

Oer, Rudolfine Freiin von. "Der Eigentumsbegriff in der Säkularisationsdiskussion am Ende des Alten Reichs." In *Eigentum und Verfassung. Zur Eigentumsdiskussion im ausgehenden 18. Jahrhundert*, edited by Rudolf Vierhaus. Göttingen: Vandenhoeck & Ruprecht, 1972.

Oestreich, Gerhard. *Neostoicism and the Early Modern State.* Translated by David McLintock. Cambridge: Cambridge University Press, 1982.

Pagden, Anthony. *The Fall of Natural Man. The American Indian and the Origins of Comparative Ethnology.* Cambridge: Cambridge University Press, 1982.

Picard, Paul. *Zölibatsdiskussion im katholischen Deutschland der Aufklärungszeit.* Düsseldorf, 1975.

Pillich, Walter. "Staatskanzler Kaunitz und die Archivforschung (1762–1794)." In *Festschrift zur Feier des Zweihundertjährigen Bestandes des Haus-, Hof- und Staatsarchivs*, edited by Leo Santifaller. Vienna: Druck- und Kommissions-Verlag der österreichischen Staatsdruckerei, 1949.

Pitzer, Volker. "Febronius/Febronianismus." In *Theologisches Realenzyklopädie*, 67–9, 1983.

Justinus Febronius. Das Ringen eines katholichen Irenikers um die Einheit der Kirche im Zeitalter der Aufklärung. Volume 20, Kirche und Konfession. Göttingen: Vandenhoek und Ruprecht, 1976.

Plöchel, Willibald M. *Geschichte des Kirchenrechts. Band V: Das katholische Kirchenrecht in der Neuzeit. Dritter Teil.* Munich and Vienna: Velag Herold, 1969.

Pocock, J. G. A. *Barbarism and Religion, Volume I: The Enlightenments of Edward Gibbon.* Cambridge: Cambridge University Press, 1999.

Barbarism and Religion, Volume II: Narratives of Civil Government. Cambridge: Cambridge University Press, 1999.

The Ancient Constitution and the Feudal Law. A Study of English Historical Thought in the Seventeenth Century. A Reissue with a Retrospect. Cambridge: Cambridge University Press, 1987 (1957).

Printy, Michael. "The Intellectual Origins of Popular Catholicism: Catholic Moral Theology in the Age of Enlightenment." *Catholic Historical Review* 91, no. 3 (2005): 438–61.

"The Reformation of the Enlightenment: German Histories in the eighteenth century." In *Politics and Reformations: Histories and Reformations. Studies in Honor of Thomas A. Brady, Jr.*, edited by Christopher Ocker, Michael Printy, Peter Wallace, and Peter Starenko. Leiden: Brill, 2007.

Pullapilly, Cyriac K. *Caesar Baronius, Counter-Reformation Historian.* Notre Dame: University of Notre Dame Press, 1975.

Raab, Heribert. *Die Concordata Nationis Germanicae in der kanonischen Diskussion des 17. bis 19. Jahrhunderts. Ein Beitrag zur Geschichte der episkopalischen Theorie in Deutschland.* Wiesbaden: Franz Steiner, 1956.

Reill, Peter Hanns. *The German Enlightenment and the Rise of Historicism.* Berkeley: University of California Press, 1975.

Reinalter, Helmut. *Der Josephinismus: Bedeutung, Einflüsse und Wirkungen.* Frankfurt am Main, New York: Peter Lang, 1993.

Repgen, Konrad. "Der päpstlicher Protest gegen den Westfälischen Frieden und die Friedenspolitik Urbans VIII." *Historisches Jahrbuch* 75 (1956): 94–122.

Die Römische Kurie und der Westfälische Friede. Idee und Wirklichkeit des Papsttums im 16. und 17. Jahrhundert. 2 Volumes. Tübingen, 1962–.

Robertson, Ritchie. "Religion and the Enlightenment: A Review Essay." *German History* 25, no. 3 (2007): 422–31.

Roeck, Bernd. *Reichssystem und Reichsherkommen: die Diskussion über die Staatlichkeit des Reiches in der politischen Publizistik des 17. und 18. Jahrhunderts.* Stuttgart: F. Steiner, 1984.

Rudersdorf, Manfred. "Die Generation der lutherischen Landesväter im Reich. Bausteine zu einer Typologie des deutschen Reformationsfürsten." In *Die Territorien des Reichs im Zeitalter der Reformation und Konfessionalisierung: Land und Konfession 1500–1650. Band 7: Bilanz, Forschungsperspektiven, Register*, edited by Walter Ziegler and Anton Schindling. Münster: Aschendorff, 1997.

Sauter-Bergerhausen, Christina. "Michael Ignaz Schmidt 'Erster Geschichts-schreiber der Deutschen?'" In *Michael Ignaz Schmidt (1736–1794) in seiner Zeit. Der aufgeklärte Theologe, Bildungsreformer und "Historiker der Deutschen" aus Franken in neuer Sicht*, edited by Peter Baumgart. Neustadt/a.d. Aisch, 1996.

Schaefer, Richard. "Program for a New Catholic Wissenschaft: Devotional Activism and Catholic Modernity in the Nineteenth-Century." *Modern Intellectual History* 4, no. 3 (2007): 433–62.

Schaich, Michael. "'Religionis defensor acerrimus.' Joseph Anton Weissenbach und der Kreis der Augsburger Exjesuiten." In *Von "Obscuranten" und Eudämonisten: Gegenaufklärische, konservative und antirevolutionäre Publizisten im späten 18. Jahrhundert*, edited by Christoph Weiß. St. Ingelbert: Röhrig Universitäts Verlag, 1997.

Scherer, Emil Clemens. *Geschichte und Kirchengeschichte an den deutschen Universitäten. Ihre Anfänge im Zeitalter des Humanismus und ihre Ausbildung zu selbständigen Disziplinen*. Freiburg: Herder, 1927. Reprint, Olms, 1975.

Schindling, Anton, and Walter Ziegler. *Die Territorien des Reichs im Zeitalter der Reformation und Konfessionalisierung: Land und Konfession 1500–1650*. 7 Volumes. Münster: Aschendorff, 1989–.

Schlaich, Klaus. *Kollegialtheorie. Kirche, Recht und Staat in der Aufklärung. Jus Ecclesiasticum*, Volume 8. Munich, 1969.

Schleunes, Karl A. *Schooling and Society: the Politics of Education in Prussia and Bavaria 1750–1900*. Oxford: Oxford University Press, 1989.

Schlögl, Rudolf. *Glaube und Religion in der Säkularisierung: Die Katholische Stadt – Köln, Aachen, Münster – 1700–1840*. Munich: Oldenbourg, 1995.

Schmidt, James, ed. *What is Enlightenment. Eighteenth-Century Answers and Twentieth-Century Questions*. Berkeley and Los Angeles: University of California Press, 1996.

Schmidt, Peter. *Das Collegium Germanicum in Rom und die Germaniker. Zur Funktion eines römischen Ausländerseminars (1552–1914)*. Tubingen: Max Niemeyer, 1984.

Schnabel, Franz. *Deutsche Geschichte im Neuenzehnten Jahrhundert*. Volume 4, *Die Religiösen Kräfte*. Freiburg: Herder, 1951.

Schneyer, Johann Baptist. *Die Rechtsphilosophie Anselm Desings O. S. B. (1699–1772)*. Kallmünz: Michael Lassleben, 1932.

Schorn-Schütte, Luise. "Priest, Preacher, Pastor: Research on Clerical Office in Early Modern Europe." *Central European History* (2000): 1–39.

Schwaiger, Georg, ed. *Zwischen Polemik und Irenik. Untersuchungen zum Verhältnis der Konfessionen im späten 18. und frühen 19. Jahrhundert*. Göttingen: Vandenhoeck & Ruprecht, 1977.

Schwennicke, Andreas. *"Ohne Steuer kein Staat." Zur Entwicklung und politischen Funktion des Steuerrechts in den Territorien des Heiligen Römischen Reichs (1500–1800)*. Frankfurt: Vittorio Klostermann, 1996.

Seils, Ernst-Albert. *Die Staatslehre des Jesuiten Adam Contzen, Beichtvater Kurfurst Maximilian I. von Bayern*. Lübeck:Matthiesen, 1968.

Selwyn, Pamela Eve. *Everyday Life in the German Book Trade: Friedrich Nicolai as Bookseller and Publisher in the Age of Enlightenment, 1750–1810.* University Park: Pennsylvania State University Press, 2000.

Sheehan, James J. *German History, 1770–1866.* Oxford, New York: Oxford University Press, 1989.

"What is German History? Reflections on the Role of Nation in German History and Historiography." *Journal of Modern History* 53, no. 1 (1981): 1–23.

Sheehan, Jonathan. "Enlightenment, Religion, and the Enigma of Secularization: A Review Essay." *American Historical Review* 108, no. 4 (2003): 1061–80.

Sher, Richard B. *Church and University in the Scottish Enlightenment: The Moderate Literati of Edinburgh.* Princeton: Princeton University Press, 1985.

Sieben, Herman-Josef. "Die Schannat-Hartzheimische Sammlung der deutschen Konzilien (1759–1790)." *Theologie und Philosophie* 76 (2001): 1–30.

Sigmund, Paul. *Nicolas of Cusa and Medieval Political Thought.* Cambridge: Harvard University Press, 1963.

Skinner, Quentin. *The Foundations of Modern Political Thought.* 2 Volumes. Cambridge: Cambridge University Press, 1978.

Smith, Helmut Walser. *German Nationalism and Religious Conflict: Culture, Ideology, Politics, 1870–1914.* Princeton, NJ: Princeton University Press, 1995.

ed. *Protestants, Catholics and Jews in Germany, 1800–1914.* Oxford and New York: Berg, 2001.

Smith, Jeffrey Chipps. *Sensuous Worship: Jesuits and the Art of the Early Catholic Reformation in Germany.* Princeton: Princeton University Press, 2002.

Sorkin, David. *The Berlin Haskalah and German Religious Thought: Orphans of Knowledge.* London: Vallentine Mitchell, 2000.

Stolleis, Michael. "Conring, Hermann." In *Juristen. Ein biographisches Lexikon,* edited by Michael Stolleis. Munich: C. H. Beck, 1995.

Geschichte des öffentlichen Rechts in Deutschland. 1: Reichspublizistik und Policeywissenschaft 1600–1800. Munich: Beck, 1988.

ed. *Hermann Conring (1606–1681): Beiträge zu Leben und Werk.* Berlin: Duncker & Humblot, 1983.

Staatsdenker im 17. und 18. Jahrhundert: Reichspublizistik, Politik, Naturrecht. Second edition. Frankfurt am Main: A. Metzner, 1987.

Stroup, John. "Protestant Church Historians in the German Enlightenment." In *Aufklärung und Geschichte. Studien zur deutschen Geschichtewissenschaft im 18. Jahrhundert,* edited by Hans Erich Bödeker. Göttingen: Vandenhoeck & Ruprecht, 1986.

The Struggle for Identity in the Clerical Estate: Northwest German Protestant Opposition to Absolutist Policy in the Eighteenth Century. Leiden: E. J. Brill, 1984.

Taylor, Charles. *A Secular Age.* Cambridge: Harvard University Press, 2007.

Modern Social Imaginaries. Durham and London: Duke University Press, 2004.

Thompson, W. D. J. Cargill. *Political Thought of Martin Luther*. Brighton, Sussex: Harvester Press, 1984.

Tocqueville, Alexis de. *The Old Regime and the French Revolution*. translated by Stuart Gilbert. New York: Anchor, 1955.

Tournyol de Clos, Jean. *Les amortissements de la propriété ecclésiastique sous Louis XIII, 1639–1640*. Paris: M. Giard & E. Briere, 1912.

Tribe, Keith. *Governing Economy. The Reformation of German Economic Discourse 1750–1840*. Cambridge: Cambridge University Press, 1988.

Troeltsch, Ernst. *Religion in History*. Essays translated by James Luther Adams and Walter E. Bense, with an introduction by James Luther Adams. Minneapolis: Fortress Press, 1991.

Umbach, Maiken. *Federalism and Enlightenment in Germany, 1740–1806*. London: Hambeldon Press, 2000.

Van Dülmen, Richard. Antijesuitismus und katholische Aufklärung in Deutschland." *Historisches Jahrbuch* 89 no.1 (1969): 52–80.

Propst Franziskus Töpsl (1711–1796) und das Augustiner-Chorherrenstift Polling. Kallmünz: Michael Lassleben, 1967.

Van Kley, Dale K. "Catholic Conciliar Reform in an Age of Anti-Catholic Revolution. France, Italy, and the Netherlands, 1758–180." In *Religion and Politics in Enlightenment Europe*, edited by James Bradley and Dale K. Van Kley, 46–118. Notre Dame, IN: University of Notre Dame Press, 2001.

The Jansenists and the Expulsion of the Jesuits from France, 1757–1765. New Haven: Yale University Press, 1975.

The Religious Origins of the French Revolution: From Calvin to the Civil Constitution, 1560–1791. New Haven: Yale University Press, 1996.

Vazsonyi, Nicholas. "Montesquieu, Friedrich Carl von Moser, and the 'National Spirit Debate' in Germany, 1765–67." *German Studies Review* 22, no. 2 (1999): 225–46.

Venturi, Franco. *Utopia and Reform in the Enlightenment*. Cambridge: Cambridge University Press, 1971.

Vick, Brian E. *Defining Germany. The 1848 Frankfurt Parliamentarians and National Identity*. Cambridge, MA: Harvard University Press, 2002.

Walker, Mack. *German Home Towns: Community, State, and General Estate, 1648–1871*. Ithaca: Cornell University Press, 1998.

Ward, Albert. *Book Production, Fiction, and the German Reading Public, 1740–1800*. Oxford: Clarendon Press, 1974.

Ward, W. R. *Christianity under the Ancien Régime, 1648–1789*. Cambridge and New York: Cambridge University Press, 1999.

Weber, Christoph. *Aufklärung und Orthodoxie am Mittelrhein, 1829–1859*. Munich, Paderborn and Vienna: Ferdinand Schöningh, 1973.

Weber, Wolfgang. *Prudentia gubernatoria: Studien zur Herrschaftslehre in der deutschen politischen Wissenschaft des 17. Jahrhunderts*. Tübingen: Max Niemeyer, 1992.

Weiß, Christoph, ed. *von "Obscuranten" und Eudämonisten: Gegenaufklärische, konservative und antirevolutionäre Publizisten im späten 18. Jahrhundert*. St. Ingelbert: Röhrig Universitäts Verlag, 1997.

Wesel-Roth, Ruth. *Thomas Erastus. Ein Beitrag zur Geschichte der reformierten Kirche und zur Lehre von der Staatssouveränität.* Veröffentlichungen des Vereins für Kirchengeschichte in der evangelischen Landeskirche Badens XV. Lahr/Baden: Moritz Schauenburg, 1954.

Wiel, Constant van de. *History of Canon Law*, Louvain Theological and Pastoral Monographs, 5. Louvain, 1991.

Wilczek, Gerhard. " Johann Adam Freiherr von Ickstatt und die Hohe Schule zu Ingolstadt. *Ingolstädter Heimatblätter* 32, no. 1 (1969).

Williams, Charles E. *The French Oratorians and Absolutism, 1611–1641.* New York: Peter Lang, 1989.

Willoweit, Dietmar. *Rechtsgrundlagen der Territorialgewalt: Landesobrigkeit, Herrschaftsrechte und Territorium in der Rechtswissenschaft der Neuzeit.* Köln: Böhlau, 1975.

Wilson, Peter H. *From Reich to Revolution: German history, 1558–1806.* New York: Palgrave Macmillan, 2004.

War, State and Society in Württemberg, 1677–1793. Cambridge: Cambridge University Press, 1995.

Winroth, Anders. *The Making of Gratian's Decretum.* New York: Cambridge University Press, 2000.

Wolf, Hubert. "Pfründenjäger, Dunkelmänner, Lichtgestalten." In *Säkularisation der Reichskirche 1803: Aspekte kirchlichen Umbruchs*, edited by Rolf Decot. Mainz: Philipp von Zabern, 2001.

Zeeden, Ernst Walter. *Die Entstehung der Konfessionen: Grundlagen und Formen der Konfessionsbildung im Zeitalter der Glaubenskämpfe.* München: R. Oldenbourg, 1965.

The Legacy of the Reformation: Martin Luther and the Reformation in the Estimation of the German Lutherans from Luther's Death to the Beginning of the Age of Goethe. Translated by Ruth Mary, Bethel. Westmister, MD: Newman Press, 1954.

Ziegler, Walter. "Altgläubige Territorien im Konfessionalisierungsprozess." In *Die Territorien des Reichs im Zeitalter der Reformation und Konfessionalisierung: Land und Konfession 1500–1650. Band 7: Bilans, Forschungsperspektiven, Register.* Münster: Aschendorf, 1997.

"Bayern." In *Die Territorien des Reichs im Zeitalter der Reformation und Konfessionalisierung: Land und Konfession 1500–1650. Band 1: Der Südosten*, edited by Walter Ziegler and Anton Schindling, 57–70. Münster: Aschendorff, 1989.

Index